THE CHURCH
—AS—
THEOLOGICAL
COMMUNITY

THE CHURCH
——AS——
THEOLOGICAL COMMUNITY

Essays in Honour of
David Schroeder

edited by
Harry Huebner

CMBC Publications
600 Shaftesbury Blvd
Winnipeg, Manitoba
R3P OM4

Cover: Gerald Loewen

Canadian Cataloguing in Publication Data

Main entry under title:

The church as theological community

Based on essays presented June 14-17, 1989 at a symposium held at the Canadian Mennonite Bible College, Winnipeg, Man.
Includes bibliographical references.
ISBN 0-920718-31-0

l. Church - Congresses. 2. Theology - Congresses. 3. Sociology, Christian (Mennonite) - Congresses. 4. Mennonite Church - Doctrines - Congresses.
I. Schroeder, David.   II. Huebner, Harry John, 1943-
III. Canadian Mennonite Bible College.

BX8105.C48 1990   289.7   C90-097061-8

Printed in Canada by
Friesen Printers
Altona, Manitoba
R0G 0B0

DEDICATION

To David Schroeder, teacher and friend

CONTENTS

ACKNOWLEDGEMENTS

This book had its beginning in 1986 when the Canadian Mennonite Bible College (CMBC) faculty started planning for the David Schroeder Symposium which was held on July 14-17, 1989. The intention to publish the papers presented at the Symposium was part of the process all along. A committee, consisting of Waldemar Janzen, Peter Fast, John Friesen and Harry Huebner, planned the Symposium. The CMBC faculty appointed Harry Huebner as editor of this book.

Appreciation must be expressed to the twelve contributors who took time to write substantive essays for this occasion. We also thank the respondents for their thoughtful responses to earlier drafts of these essays. In deference to the hermeneutical community process their impact comes via the helpful criticisms given at the Symposium, and now incorporated into the essays.

Margaret Franz, staff member for CMBC Publications and copy editor for this project, worked tirelessly at the task of helping authors say correctly what they wanted to say. Not only did she work through the manuscripts several times and coordinate the production of the project, she was also an invaluable assistant to the editor as together they worked through the process of "desk top" publishing for the first time.

We thank Linda Winter Dueck for sorting through the files of David Schroeder and compiling a representative sample of his work.

A generous publication subsidy was provided by the descendants of Henry H. Schroeder, Dave's father. This symbolic endorsement of Dave's work is greatly appreciated.

And finally, we thank Dave for his unceasing inspiration to us all throughout his lifetime. That is what made this project seem just a little more like a celebration than the tedious work it actually was.

CONTRIBUTORS

(listed in order of appearance)

Rodney Sawatsky is President of Conrad Grebel College, Waterloo, Ontario.

David Schroeder is Professor of New Testament and Philosophy at Canadian Mennonite Bible College, Winnipeg, Manitoba. The Symposium and this book are in his honour.

Adolf Ens is Associate Professor of History and Theology, Canadian Mennonite Bible College, Winnipeg, Manitoba.

Waldemar Janzen is Professor of Old Testament at Canadian Mennonite Bible College, Winnipeg, Manitoba.

Mary H. Schertz is Assistant Professor of New Testament at Associated Mennonite Biblical Seminaries, Elkhart, Indiana.

William Klassen is Principal of St. Pauls United College, Waterloo, Ontario.

A. James Reimer is Associate Professor of Religious Studies and Theology at Conrad Grebel College in Waterloo, Ontario.

Lydia Harder is a doctoral student in theology at the Toronto School of Theology, Toronto, Ontario.

Duane K. Friesen is Professor of Bible and Religion at Bethel College, North Newton, Kansas.

Harry Huebner is Associate Professor of Philosophy and Theology at Canadian Mennonite Bible College, Winnipeg, Manitoba.

Peter C. Erb is Professor of Religion and Culture at Wilfrid Laurier University in Waterloo, Ontario.

James N. Pankratz is President of Mennonite Brethren Bible College, Winnipeg, Manitoba.

INTRODUCTION

Dietrich Bonhoeffer has said that "the more theologians have considered the significance of the sociological category for theology, the more clearly the social intention of all the basic Christian concepts has emerged."[1] This is an apt reminder that theologians are servants of the church, hence that the church is a theological community. Christian theology cannot appropriately segregate itself from that social reality, the church, which endeavours to embody the convictions it seeks to articulate. Nor can the theologian simply be a mouthpiece for the common beliefs held by the community which calls itself church. The tension between the theologian and the church member (and this may well be a tension within one person) can never be fully resolved on either side. It is deeply imbedded in the very essence of the *Sanctorum Communio* (Community of Saints).

This book is dedicated to David Schroeder, our respected teacher and friend. Yet it is not primarily an analysis of his theology. Nor is it simply an immortalized gift acknowledging his contribution at the time of his retirement. This project is the tangible manifestation of the very convictions he has expressed as a scholar and churchman, namely, that the test of the truthfulness of our basic convictions lies not only in their careful and consistent articulation, but in their expression within a community of Christians. This heuristic principle underlies Dave's approach as a Christian scholar. Its scrutiny and application to several key theological and ecclesial issues inspired this project and brought together Mennonite scholars who are united in their commitment to both scholarship and the church.

Earlier drafts of these essays were presented and discussed on June 14-17, 1989, at a symposium held at Canadian Men-

---

[1]Dietrich Bonhoeffer, *Sanctorum Communio: A Dogmatic Inquiry into the Sociology of the Church,* trans. R. Gregor Smith (London: Collins Press, 1963), 13.

nonite Bible College, Winnipeg, Manitoba. The essays in this book were revised in light of the input by the respondents and the discussion at the Symposium.

The first section of this book focuses on David Schroeder as theologian and churchman. Rodney Sawatsky's banquet presentation provides a biographical sketch of Dave's life. Sawatsky maintains that it is in the integration of Dave's sociological roots and his best theological insights that we are able to understand his dual yet unified emphasis on: suffering and salvation, structures and freedom, the church today and the Bible of history, philosophy and theology, charisma and solemnity. How is Dave's charisma to be explained? People have perceived him to articulate the truthfulness of the gospel on their behalf in his inclusive embrace of these dualities.

Included in this volume is a selection from Dave's writings and presentations over the years on an assortment of topics and to a variety of groups. Although he is not noted for his many publications—somehow the incessant calls to address church matters prevented him from giving the sustained attention necessary for major publishing—this list of sermons, lectures and treatment of issues offers an interesting study of the agenda of the Mennonite church spanning five decades and of his influence in dealing with its programme. This selection is not exhaustive but includes a representative sample of his many lectures and sermons.

Dave's essay "Once You Were No People . . ." is an especially good example of how he integrates theology and church. His underlying presupposition is that the central task of biblical and contemporary theology is the formation of a people through whom the glory of God might be revealed. Dave's pioneering work on the *Haustafeln* is significant (and controversial for some mainline theologians) precisely because he interprets them as having the power to shape a people which wills to be faithful to Jesus. Their ethical significance lies not in their truth as isolated moral principles which are capable of effecting the good life for individuals who embrace them, but rather in their truth as power to create a people which may be called holy because it embodies the character of the one sent from God.

The rest of the book, divided into five main areas, roughly

parallels the structure of the academic programme of Canadian Mennonite Bible College, the institution in which Dave has taught for thirty years. Each section contains two essays on selected topics.

In the first section, "Historical Theology," Adolf Ens reminds us of the historical-theological roots of the "hermeneutical community." In applying this concept to the contemporary church he appeals to his readers to consider the congregation as the locus for testing theological findings. This, he says, has implications for how we understand schisms, biblical interpretation and the church's pursuit of truth. Mennonite scholarly meetings, such as the Symposium, should "take themselves more seriously as Christian congregations" (89) by modelling a process of truth-seeking which emanates as much from the inspired unity of those present as from the scholar's insights.

Waldemar Janzen addresses the much debated, and misunderstood, issue of the relationship of the two Testaments in the biblical canon. Does the New Testament supersede the Old? Does it correct, fulfill, complete? In rethinking the New Testament orientation of Anabaptist-Mennonite theology he builds on the model provided by the school of "canonical criticism" made popular by two contemporary Old Testament scholars, James Sanders and Brevard Childs. This model provides him with the basis for advocating the "re-enfranchisement of the Old Testament" (100) so that the Bible, embracing both Testaments, can be seen as the Word of God.

In the "Biblical Theology" section, Mary Schertz takes a specific text, Luke 24, as a basis for formulating a believers' church theology of discipleship. Employing a specific type of literary analysis, advocated by Susan Snaider Lanser, *inter alia*, which is especially designed to highlight the different narrative voices within a text, she argues that interpretation itself should be seen as a category of discipleship which enables the marginal to become "readers" of the text. She shows how this approach generates a different view of discipleship than perfectionism which Mennonites have often been associated with. It "demands a kind of wry anthropology—an understanding that to be human in relation to the divine is to stand in humility and to expect surprises" (139).

William Klassen examines how the "Voice of the People" has functioned among the faithful in the past, and how, by implication, it ought to function in the church today, especially in the formation of our theological imagination. He examines three specific components of the process. First, he shows how the people participated in the shaping of God-language by tracing the gradual shift from understanding God as warrior to speaking of God as peacemaker. Second, he recounts how the people took part in developing an understanding of Jesus by moving from a revolutionary Jesus to a pacifist Christ. Third, he examines how the peoples' involvement in the formation of a moral identity led to a self-understanding not in their apartness from each other but in their unity. This process historically involved the interaction between the people and the specialist, and today likewise requires both the careful skills of the theologian's "specialized investigations" as well as the faithful critical testing by members of the Christian community.

James Reimer's essay, the first in the "Contemporary Theology" section, warns of the dangers of modernity in the determination of the current theological agenda and of contemporary theology's failure to address fundamental issues properly. He relies on two theologians, Hans Jonas and Gregory Baum, to analyze what it means to be modern. On this basis he concludes that modernity, especially as impacted by the technological revolution, demands of the faithful a return to a "non-relativistic metaphysics and ontology" (196). By implication Christian theology generally and Mennonite theology specifically should reaffirm that "classical trinitarian and christological doctrinal categories are richer in potential for interpreting God, human and nonhuman nature and historical action than are other alternatives" (196). How modern should theology be? Thoroughly modern in addressing current matters at hand; not so modern regarding the theological-philosophical method of address.

In the essay "Discipleship Reexamined: Women in the Hermeneutical Community," Lydia Harder examines the role of women in the church. Embracing an approach which integrates theory and practice—one which she might have learned from Anabaptism but in fact has learned from feminist theology—she explores the basis for the ambivalence women are experiencing as they become full participants in the theological discussion. This ambivalence, she argues, is due to the way our tradition has interpreted discipleship, namely, by affirming "the status quo for women in a patriarchal society" (204). However, when she examines the biblical story, especially the Markan gospel of the Way, she discovers that the notion of discipleship is far more inclusive than our tradition has taught us. Although the gospel story ends in ambiguity, nevertheless "women are challenged to become the proclaimers of the good news of the resurrection" (215). Thus a biblical version of discipleship teaches us that we must find ways of empowering the silent ones in our communities to become full participants in giving shape to our theology.

Duane Friesen's article, which begins the section on "Theological Ethics," examines the narrative approach to ethics which, he argues, is especially helpful in illuminating the way Mennonites have understood ethics. This approach, ironically made popular by a Methodist theologian, Stanley Hauerwas, is seen as an alternative to natural law ethics and democratic liberalism. Building on the notions of narrative, community and character, narrative ethics is able to overcome the quandary approach which focuses on individual decision-making and thereby ignores the church as a moral category. Yet Friesen raises his own questions about Hauerwas' ethical language. Is there a way that narrative ethics can determine the truth of the narrative it embraces? Is it really able to overcome the charge of sectarianism? Ultimately, says Friesen, "the categories of narrative ethics do not give very precise guidance for our decisions" (240). For this we must find more specific rules and principles to guide our actions than Hauerwas provides.

In "Christian Pacifism and the Character of God," Harry Huebner deals with the larger issue of relating theology and ethics. How does our view of God, which we receive from the biblical narrative, relate to the moral imagination by which we define our being and action? Two dominant models are examined, one where history is the central category, the other where nature is the prime category. Both have misled us into accepting a moral discontinuity between the nature of God and the moral character of God's people. This is no less so in Anabaptist-Mennonite theology than it is in mainline Protestant and Catholic theologies. In order to integrate our view of God with our deepest convictions about what is good and right, we need to rethink the way we speak about God and the church with the help of forgotten traditional moral categories such as character and virtue. Then we can speak of a "moral-continuity-pacifism" rooted in the character of God made manifest in Jesus Christ, and thus avoid a dual moral-ontological base. More significantly, this model provides us with a basis for making intelligible the claim that "God wills to rule the world through the servant community" (270), because in Christ we see servanthood as the very essence of moral goodness.

Peter Erb's essay begins the "Practical Theology" section, by sorting out how traditional spirituality and Mennonite life fit together. He relies on both the classical spiritualists as well as the biblical materials, especially the *unum necessarium* (the one thing necessary) for which Christ praised Mary (Luke 10:42). Throughout, he supports a close relationship between traditional spirituality and Mennonite life, relying especially on "the trinitarian structure of the spiritual life as consistently developed by the spiritual masters of the West" (286). He ends his essay with a statement on the implications this view of spirituality has for adult baptism and for integrating an active and contemplative way of life.

In the final essay, "Mennonite Identity and Religious Pluralism," James Pankratz addresses the much discussed issue of how one religious group, the Mennonites, ought to understand itself vis-a-vis other religious and cultural groups. He argues "that Mennonite religious self-definition assumes and even defends a pluralistic context, and that the Mennonite religious tradition has developed a theological and ethical framework which is well suited for pluralism" (301). The Mennonite commitment to voluntarism, religious toleration, evangelism, the separated church and an ethic of love is intelligible for Mennonites because these concepts are expressions of a Mennonite commitment to confessing Jesus as Lord in a pluralistic world. These theological tenets are shaped by and also give shape to our view of religious pluralism.

These essays do not form an integrated theological system, yet they share a common conviction that the church is central to the theological enterprise. The reader must now judge whether this conviction has been substantiated. In the process the reader will have entered into the very dynamic which characterizes the church as theological community: where truth-seeking is paramount, faithfulness is the precondition and honest criticism the servant of both.

Harry Huebner
Ash Wednesday
February 28, 1990
Winnipeg, Manitoba

I. David Schroeder:
Theologian and Churchman

BANQUET SPEECH

Rodney Sawatsky[*]

WORDS BECOMING FLESH: THE LIFE AND THOUGHT OF DAVID SCHROEDER[**]

How is Dave Schroeder's charisma to be explained? This is one of the questions deserving our attention tonight. Lynette (one of Dave's two daughters) assures us that the answer is not to be found in his dynamic preaching. Rather, in her unbiased opinion, his preaching might better be described as boring. If Lynette is right—and she may well be—why do so many churches keep inviting Dave back to preach?

I took homiletics from Dave to learn his secret. Yes, he taught homiletics. In fact, I suspect that at one time or other he has taught every course offered by Canadian Mennonite Bible College (CMBC) except conducting. He probably would have given conducting a crack as well (that is, while George Wiebe was away on sabbatical!) had it not been for a mysterious intervention of providence which kept him from waving his arms in the air. And although he plays a pretty good game of volleyball with his head and manages to comb the few wisps of hair left on the playing field, using one arm to prop up the other, conducting is out of the question. That there is a relationship between his bout with polio and his charisma is definitely not out of the question.

Back to homiletics. Dave did not advocate that we tell jokes when we preached. Preaching is serious business. We were not being trained as stand-up comics! Subtle humour is fine! Indeed a good joke readily reduces Dave to stammering as tears stream down his cheeks. Humour has its place but only rarely and in

---

[*]Rodney Sawatsky is President of Conrad Grebel College, Waterloo, Ontario.

[**]This is the text of the speech given at the Symposium banquet, July 17, 1989.

moderation in the pulpit. I am not sure his position on humour has served us well. Given the immense influence of Dave Schroeder in the Canadian Mennonite churches—which is, by the way, another subject for our reflection tonight—I think Dave will need to take some of the blame for the sobriety and seriousness of those of us who walk in his shadow. An after dinner speech like this one should be full of wit and humour. Unfortunately I cannot deliver because of the influence of my homiletics teacher. Dave is to blame! Dave Schroeder is thus not only the subject matter of what I have to say; he has also determined the style of my speech. (Lynette, if this is boring, do not come to me with your complaints. Talk to your Dad!)

Excuses for taking my assignment seriously aside, I do want to say how very honoured I am to be invited to speak about Dave on behalf of all of you at this significant event. Dave has played a very important role in my life even as he has in the lives of most of you here tonight. Although I am some 20 years younger than Dave, our worlds have overlapped in interesting ways. We are both children of the most culturally, socially and intellectually conservative Mennonites to come to North America from Russia in the 1870s—those who came to Manitoba rather than to the United States. We both grew up in the environs of Altona and graduated from the Altona Collegiate, *not* from the Mennonite Collegiate Institute in Gretna and this for reasons of Mennonite and community politics.

In his late teens, Dave became very active in the southern Manitoba co-operative movement. Here he and his young colleagues, including his brother Jake, found social expression for their Christian faith. J.J. Siemens, the guru of southern Manitoba co-operatives, influenced Dave profoundly. My experience of Siemens and his associates was more removed, that is, through my parents who were very much involved in the same movement. But Dave tells me that my Dad encouraged him to continue his studies rather than immediately becoming pre-occupied with co-operative endeavors. Dave accepted such counsel and became one of the first of the 1870s' people in Canada to both earn a doctorate and remain active in the Mennonite Church.

All his studies did not, however, turn Dave from that early

concern for practical Christianity nurtured by the likes of J.J. Siemens. Economics, social organization, politics—these are never far from Dave's thought. Yet Dave managed to combine his social agenda with a warm personal piety and Christian orthodoxy—a feat not attained by nearly all in his home community.

At this time in Altona a rivalry developed between J.J. Siemens of the co-operatives and David Schulz, bishop of the Bergthaler Church in Manitoba. These two men had been playmates in the small village of Weidenfeld but came to understand the essence of the Mennonite tradition in almost diametrically opposite ways. Siemens championed a more social-type gospel, Schulz a more pietistically-oriented gospel. The community chose sides and the church became seriously divided. Siemens, a man alienated from the church in which he was baptized, was buried from a Unitarian church. Dave Schroeder, a younger man, but also from Weidenfeld, bridged the chasm between Siemens and Schulz in both his teaching and in his person. He found a way of saying "yes" to both Schulz *and* Siemens, not "either/or."

This both/and approach, I believe, is central to the genius of Dave Schroeder's ministry. He combines seemingly alien currents and insights by insisting that one cannot do without the other. This model is of course not foreign to Mennonites. Walter Klaassen has been emphasizing recently that the Anabaptists were both Roman Catholic and Protestant (and now need also to learn from the Eastern Othrodox). Others have recognized that Mennonites share a social consciousness with more liberal Christians, and a personal piety and biblicism with the more evangelical. This both/and approach has characterized Canadian Mennonite Bible College as well as the Conference of Mennonites in Canada. And a major force, perhaps *the* major force, in shaping the both/and orientation of this College and this Conference is Dave Schroeder. Hence, when a doctoral student at the Toronto School of Theology asked me for a representative and formative figure of post-World War II Canadian Mennonites, I did not hesitate to identify Dave Schroeder as that person. And that is why it is so appropriate to have a David Schroeder Symposium.

But we are getting ahead of ourselves. Dave and I both graduated from Bible Colleges in Winnipeg—he from Mennonite Brethren Bible College (MBBC) and I from CMBC. Here we also met our wives—both from Drake, Saskatchewan. And here our stories part: he was and is my teacher; the opposite does not hold true. For all of us who were his students at CMBC he was a most revered teacher, friend and counsellor. We all called him Doc Schroeder, a label of affection uniquely reserved for Dave. With many other students I remember him as much for his personal counsel as for his classes in exegesis and apologetics. Even when I returned to CMBC to teach he remained my mentor, although now he was also a colleague. This is why I am so honoured that my CMBC colleagues invited me to give this address about our brother Dave.

I have obviously said too much about myself and perhaps also too much about Dave. True, we are here to honour Dave, but not him alone. Dave is not Dave without Mildred—indeed where would he be today without Mildred? Nor is Dave Dave without Dorothy and Lynette and Alan—and now also their spouses and the grandchildren. And Grandpa Bartel, he too was and is a part of Dave. Dave's parents and siblings, aunts and uncles, who with him were nurtured in the close ethno-religious community in the environs of Altona and some of whom, like Dave, moved away both geographically and psychologically—these too are a part of Dave. Yet however far he moved, even to Hamburg, Germany, the ancient saying still holds: you can get Dave out of his southern Manitoba, Sommerfelder roots but you cannot get those southern Manitoba, Sommerfelder roots out of Dave!

Just look at Dave's three- and even four-generation household. It is a little Weidenfeld in Charleswood. He remains a communalist, uncomfortable with modern individualism and even the nuclear family. And his handshake retains its traditional symbolism. Words are easy, words are cheap, according to this perspective. Honesty, integrity and true friendship are known only in action, not in many words. A genuine handshake—Sommerfelder style—communicates all. Sure, Dave has also learned the full embrace Drake-style. And he has also learned the words of affection and caring characteristic of more emotive and less reserved cultures. But when he is invited by his own folk to preach in Paraguay, he still knows the meaning of the handshake, when to speak and when to be silent, and the integrity of a communalist ethic.

Dave is, however, not simply a Sommerfelder preacher in a sheepskin hood. After all, instead of allowing the bishop to speak for him before the judge on the matter of his conscientious objector status (CO), he went to Winnipeg to face the judge himself. While serving as a CO in Winnipeg, he became an active associate of Benjamin Ewert and I.I. Friesen at Bethel Mission Church, the first English General Conference Mennonite church in Winnipeg. Here he was baptized by Ewert. I.I. Friesen's background was very similar to Dave's (and by the way, his wife was also from Drake). Both Friesen and Schroeder were from rural and conservative roots, yet both knew that, given Mennonite urbanization and professionalization, merely transplanting the rural church into the urban setting would not do. Changing circumstances required a different religious style. Attending MBBC surely helped shape that new style for Dave.

Probably his greatest struggle with his Sommerfelder roots and perhaps also with what he experienced at MBBC—albeit quite differently—came with his refusal to accept a simple legalism. Dave has been a consistent proponent of church discipline, particularly under the rubrics of binding and loosing. Yet the purpose of such discipline is to genuinely free the individual, not to purify the church. In 1958 he said this about church discipline ". . . legalism is not the answer. There is too much biblical evidence that legalism is not in favor of but counter to the essence and the spirit of the Christian gospel."[1] With reference to his work at the College, a colleague of his wrote: "For many years, Dave was very active . . . in fighting with all his might for placing the individual's interests over those of the community and institution. He combatted tirelessly any trend towards a legalistic form of discipline. The institution (and often also the community) should cope with the faults of individuals by

---

[1]David Schroeder and Esko W. Loewen, "Loyalty and Lodges," in *Studies in Church Discipline: A Source Book for Study*, ed. Maynard Shelly (Newton, KS: Mennonite Publication Office, 1958), 179.

'suffering them,' as modelled by Christ."[2] Yet his opposition to legalism did not mean a rejection of his Sommerfelder heritage nor of the community in favour of the individual. Not at all! Rather he was struggling for a both/and, not an either/or.

Indeed Dave has been a champion of individuality but an opponent of individualism. He has great appreciation and respect for those individuals who have developed their gifts and achieved acclaim, for example, as soloists on a concert stage or as published poets or novelists. And he is not so humble that he is reticent to air his own views. On the contrary, Dave is quite ready to speak his mind on almost any and every subject. Such assertions of individuality, which may sometimes include, particularly for our authors and artists, standing on the fringes of the community, does not necessarily mean individualism. Dave rejects that contemporary school of psychology which maintains that the individual is essentially good and simply needs to be freed from all limiting relationships and other external con-straints to realize full potential. Relationships and community on this model are seen to deter rather than to determine individual identity. But for Dave we become who we are in relationships and in community—as we make covenants, to use his preferred theological language.[3] He is who he is, Dave would be the first to insist, because of his tradition and community, because of those near and dear to him, not in spite of them.

Dave would not dispute his colleagues' evaluation that Mildred deserves much of the credit for who he is today. Especially after being handicapped by polio, Mildred became more than his right hand. Listen to Mildred's account of those days when polio struck:

> Dave was a very young pastor of a large church and worked hard. The night before coming down with his first symptoms of infantile paralysis, he had spent the night on a railway track, trying to persuade a desperate fellow not to commit suicide. This was a Saturday in September, 1953. On the following day, he spoke at three services. That evening he complained of a

[2]Letter from Waldemar Janzen to the author, February 2, 1989.

[3]See David Schroeder, *Invited to Faith* (Newton, KS: Faith and Life Press, 1981), especially chapter 5.

severe headache and queer back pains. Since the polio epidemic was rampant in Winnipeg, and we had several nurses and interns living with us in our boarding house, we naturally feared the worst. I phoned two good friends, Sue Martens and Mary Peters. Both were on duty at Misericordia Hospital just a block away. They promised to come right after their shift at 11:30 pm. Since I had my hands full with 6-week old Lynette and 20-month old Dorothy, Sue and Mary decided to stay and treat the dreadful pain with applications of hot compresses through the night.

The following days were filled with tireless support from the congregation, friends, Doctor Isaac, and nurses. By Monday evening Dave's breathing was becoming shallower and his colour was ashen. As the ambulance took him to the Municipal Hospital, I clutched my girls in my arms and prayed for a miracle that we would soon be brought together as a family again.

Bethel Mission church stood by us faithfully. They had an all-night vigil of prayer and intercession. Dave's lung capacity became less and less and by Tuesday night they suggested putting him into an iron lung. However, Dr. Rubin, one of the roomers in our home on 70 Maryland, offered to stay with him through the night and watch for more symptoms. Dave, as you know, is very determined and did not want to be put into the Lung. Since his chest muscles were giving out he resorted to consciously forcing air in and out of his lungs with his diaphragm. This necessitated his staying awake for most of the night and day until his breathing gradually came automatically and he could sleep short stretches.

I remember coming to his beside and he said, "You will need to do the talking, as I have a full-time job just breathing." The two hours spent with him every evening were frustrating, yet very special. Sixteen patients, from various walks of life (all with polio) shared his room. I remember the fellow in the next bed being surprised that a minister would be struck down with the dreaded disease.

From Dave's window we could see the emergency entrance. Day after day more polio victims were admitted. Also the hearse was a daily visitor. Every new sensation in muscles of his body was a cause for celebration, and we were thankful. By December he was able to keep his balance and to begin walking. His arms hung limp, and the absence of shoulder muscles made him look undernourished. Unlike many of his buddies in the hospital, he was able to come home for Christmas, and everyone rejoiced.

Even with the help of physiotherapy and aquatherapy, the doctors informed us that Dave would not be able to hold down a job for at least 5 years. This was quite a blow. In retrospect we realize that God had plans that would lead Dave into the direction of teaching rather than the ministry. After resigning from the church, the General Conference offered some financial help to attend Bethany Seminary in Chicago, in exchange for service after graduation. During the next two and a half years Dave covered three years of study. He also exercised his remaining healthy muscles in his arms by pushing a large brush under church pews as janitor of the Woodlawn Mennonite Church. This was a family project which provided us with $10 a week (with which we bought our groceries). During these five years of study in Chicago and Hamburg, Germany, our family became a unit which has continued to flourish through the years.

And we must also hear Lynette's reflections:

Dad has never made polio a handicap for himself or for others. He continues to do as much and more than we often think is possible. As a young man he loved sports and continues to do so now, although he doesn't play soccer and volleyball as much any more. Perhaps the smack on the bald head when the volleyball hits it is getting to be too much. It certainly is not for lack of enthusiasm. Anyone who watches hockey or football on TV with him knows they better have x-ray vision because he helps every player with every play by standing in front of the set and pushing them along. As a family we have never felt that polio affected us in any way except that we couldn't arm wrestle with him. (And I always preferred his spankings to Mom's. There was more energy, but less effect!)[4]

Polio, Mildred tells us, sent Dave to Mennonite Biblical Seminary[5] and to the University of Hamburg. Polio surely also influenced his theology and his approach to life. Polio did not only limit Dave's options, it also seems to have given him a new sense of calling and urgency—a sense that his life was spared for a purpose. Is this why he can never say "no" to an invitation from a church even when the problem of logistics alone would provide more than ample reason to respond negatively?

Perhaps here is one more clue to Dave's charisma. Not only is he always ready to go to whichever church he is invited, no

---

[4]Letters from Mildred Schroeder and Lynette Wiebe to author, March 16, 1989.

[5]The Mennonite Biblical Seminary was then still in Chicago and its students were granted degrees from Bethany Theological Seminary.

matter how busy he is, but he also exudes a certain strength in weakness. He looks somewhat fragile, as if he needs to be helped more than he can help. Perhaps his slight physique and his voice, which periodically grows foggy, evoke our sympathy. We look at him and we listen to him not as we do to a tall, dark, handsome evangelist exuding self-confidence, nimbly tossing off scripture verses and dropping names with a rapid-fire, powerful voice. Dave is not made for TV. He should not sell in this generation and the TV generation may yet find Dave less compelling. But it may be precisely Dave's appearance, his voice, his apparent weakness, which draw us to him. His smile, his warmth, his unusual handshake—we know they are not contrived; they are genuine. The symbolism is powerful. "The meek shall inherit the earth, the humble shall be exalted, the last shall be first." Is this not the essence of Jesus? Is this not the basis of Mennonite self-perception? Is this not the spirit Dave embodies?

Repeatedly Dave's theology returns to the theme of suffering. In his excellent little summary of biblical theology entitled *Invited to Faith*, Dave wrote, "We cannot do without a theology of suffering if we want to be Christian in the world."[6] Because Christians live within structures which are frequently at variance with the way of Christ, suffering results. Dave points to Jesus' suffering and death and to martyrs who, throughout the ages, have followed the example of Jesus. So also today, Christians are called to respond to evil and injustice, as Jesus did, with suffering.

Jesus is, however, not only a model in the Suffering Servant tradition of Isaiah for us to emulate, says Dave. He is also the completion of the Jewish sacrificial system. As such, he was sacrificed so that we may live. Dave thus works comfortably with both the ransom theory of the atonement as well as other theories such as those championed by liberation theologies.[7] Salvation is both personal and social; it is past, present and future.

Although Jesus uniquely suffered and died for our sins,

---

[6]*Invited to Faith*, 76.
[7]Ibid., 55. See also "Once You Were No People . . .," infra, 43 and 54.

according to Dave's understanding we are called to follow the
way of Jesus in suffering and service. This is now a response of
freedom on the part of those who are redeemed. Dave's extensive work on the household codes (*Haustafeln*) emphasizes that
the Christian freely chooses to serve and to suffer, even to be
subject rather than to rebel or resort to violence. For liberation-
ists this surely is too conservative an ethic. Yet for Dave this
emphasis represents nonconformity to the world. It is the basis
for Christian pacifism and service. It is the scandal of the cross.[8]

The suffering theme recurs in Dave's theologizing under a
number of other rubrics which are more or less synonymous.
Hearing the Word,[9] covenanting with God,[10] obedience to
Christ, discipleship of Christ—these motifs, as Dave develops
them, emphasize the nature and character of God especially as
revealed in Jesus Christ and our rightful response if we would be
followers of Christ.

We could hardly argue that suffering is so central to Dave's
theology primarily because of his own suffering. To do so would
be illegitimately reductionist. It would overlook his term as a
CO and his three years of service with the Mennonite Central
Committee, both prior to his contracting polio. Furthermore, it
would fail to recognize the continuity of his reading of scripture
with the long tradition of Mennonite biblical interpretation in
which he shares. Nevertheless, his own experience undoubtedly
has influenced his perspective on the Christian faith and the
degree to which he, in comparison to other Mennonite theologians, emphasizes suffering.

Dave pursued his graduate studies during the height of the
post-World War II Mennonite renewal movement. These were
the recovery-of-the-Anabaptist-vision days, the days when the
Mennonite Central Committee was pursuing ever new directions
of service, the days when new Mennonite institutions were being
established and the days when a coterie of young Mennonite

---

[8]"Once You Were No People . . .," infra, 58f.

[9]David Schroeder, "Command and Obedience," in *Call to Faithfulness: Essays
in Canadian Mennonite Studies*, ed. Henry Poettcker and Rudy Regehr (Winnipeg,
MB: Canadian Mennonite Bible College, 1972).

[10]A central theme in *Invited to Faith*.

graduate students gathered in Europe as the Concern Group to challenge the church to even greater Anabaptist faithfulness. Dave shared in this renewal movement in many ways. He participated in the General Conference study conferences designed to renew that community, including especially the Believers' Church Conference in Chicago in 1955. A few years thereafter he accepted an appointment to teach New Testament at the recently founded Canadian Mennonite Bible College, the centre of this renewal movement for the Conference of Mennonites in Canada. A renewed and revitalized Mennonite church was as dear to Dave's heart as it was to any of the other proponents of Anabaptist recovery in his generation.

Yet those of us who studied with Dave, even in his first years at CMBC, heard very little about the Anabaptist vision. Why not? Perhaps because he studied at the Seminary in Chicago, not at Goshen and before the days of Elkhart, or because he was from the General Conference and not the (Old) Mennonite Church. Possibly because he was a Canadian with a less separatist orientation to society than that which characterized particularly the (Old) Mennonite Church in the United States. Whatever the reasons, he did not, at least to my knowledge, become involved in the Concern Group movement while he lived in Germany, nor did he write his dissertation on the Anabaptists as did so many of his peers. Although he did not closely identify himself with Anabaptist-recovery language or politics, his theological emphases shared much with his fellow Mennonite scholars who worked more directly with Anabaptism and used its categories more deliberately. We cannot attend to all these commonalities but the more original elements of his thought warrant our attention. I will try to ferret out a few other distinct Schroederisms and place them into some kind of schema.

Dave's thinking remains dynamic. On the topic of peace, for example, he now attends much more to the concept of justice than when I was his student. On God, he now speaks more about the character of God, and in ethics, on the role of the character of the moral agent. Various topics and concerns were of greater importance to him at one point in his career than in others. It was this development of Mennonite doctrine, particularly with reference to peace, that Joe Mihevic wrote about in his doctoral dissertation when he considered Dave's work as prototypical of Canadian Mennonites.[11] And these same developments and changes make the systematizing of Dave's thought difficult. Nevertheless there are, I believe, a series of constants that anchor much of his work.

Professor of New Testament and Philosophy is Dave's title. But which do we consider first? We could go either way but logically his philosophical concerns come first. Even before, but especially after, Dave spent a sabbatical leave pursuing a graduate degree in philosophy at the University of Western Ontario, he paid close attention to presuppositions. All disciplines and all world views are premised upon presuppositions, says Dave. These presuppositions are grounded in faith. This faith may be thoroughly logical and rational and substantiated by warrants, but it cannot ultimately be proven. We cannot prove the resurrection but neither can we prove the opposite. Both positions assume faith. All people live by faith presuppositions. Faith is not unique to religious folk.

This perspective has many implications. For me it has been particularly helpful in developing a Christian apologetic. The supposed conflict between science and Christian faith can be readily addressed when presuppositions are compared and contrasted. So too the attempt to ground the authority of scripture in an inerrantist scholasticism is seen from this perspective to be little more than circular logic. Biblical authority cannot be proven. The faith presuppositions which we bring to our reading of scripture determine if the Bible is authoritative for us or not. Our presuppositions also influence our interpretation of scripture. In Dave's own words: "We must be willing always to look at our own presuppositions that we bring to the interpretation of scripture. This is where the greatest difficulties are encountered in interpretation."[12]

Dave's philosophical sensitivities require of him that he also be particularly concerned about methodological issues, most notably in biblical studies. One only needs to read his booklet

---

[11]Joe Mihevic, "The Politicization of the Mennonite Peace Witness in the Twentieth Century" (Ph.D. dissertation, University of St. Michael's College, 1988).

[12]*Learning to Know the Bible* (Newton, KS: Faith and Life Press, 1966), 90.

Learning to Know the Bible to recognize his detailed attention to methodology. Yet when addressing methodology, his writing lacks the obtuseness which is popularly assumed to characterize the philosopher's craft. We might be tempted to argue that Dave writes too simply; that he is too concerned with being understood by the layperson to be a good philosopher. I would argue the opposite! Philosophical precision in the hands of the likes of Dave contributes to clarity of thought and expression.

Even if logically Dave's philosophical agenda comes first, the Bible is absolutely central to his thought. Philosophy only provides Dave with the tools of his trade. The Bible is the source of his message.

Dave has a very high view of scripture. It is the authoritative word of God to and for the church. It becomes authoritative for us when God ". . . works in us the miracle of accepting the Scriptures as God's Word. . . . It is not [human] arguments, not the number of quotations that [we] can cite, that convince [us] of the authority of God's Word; it is rather the revelation of God in our own hearts, to which we respond in faith, that makes us accept the Bible as God's Word and that makes us yield our lives in obedience to that Word under the guidance of the Spirit of Christ."[13]

(By the way, in this quote which dates back to the 1960s, I neutralized the gender specific language because that is precisely what Dave would do today. He has become a strong champion of women's equality in the church. For our family this became particularly real when Dave, in his sermon at my mother's funeral, spoke of her in terms of being an early feminist.)

Dave's orientation to the Scriptures is clearly not readily identified as Liberal nor Fundamentalist. Indeed, even when writing for the layperson, Dave employs all critical methodologies that might assist in gaining the true meaning of the text. He argues for the documentary theory of the Pentateuch, and he urges that the Bible not be read as a science text that necessarily contradicts evolution. Yet for Dave the very text remains the Word of God, because "the Spirit of God . . . guarded the text

---

[13]Ibid., 15.

of Scripture over all these centuries."[14]

In his studies at Hamburg with Leonhard Goppelt and Helmut Thielicke, Dave came under the influence of a relatively conservative neo-orthodoxy, or more accurately, a parallel Lutheran renaissance. He developed strong affinities with the biblical theology school which essentially translated neo-orthodoxy into biblical studies. Here Dave, like Henry Poettcker and their younger colleagues at CMBC, as well as most of the Bible teachers at Associated Mennonite Biblical Seminaries (AMBS), found a way beyond the Fundamentalist-Liberal controversy which haunted so much of Protestantism as well as parts of the Mennonite church. It was essentially this same orientation that nurtured the recovery-of-the-Anabaptist-vision school. When I was studying at CMBC we heard little about Fundamentalism or Liberalism, and from the 1960s on this polarization only rarely invaded the Conference of Mennonites in Canada. Thanks to Dave Schroeder and his like-minded colleagues who also accepted the both/and approach, both the liberal and the fundamentalist perspectives were accepted; simultaneously the weaknesses of both were rejected. In this way they adapted and contributed to the formation of an approach to the Bible appropriate to their day.

Dave is absolutely convinced that the Bible holds profound relevance for the modern situation. It is a living Word. Not only has he spent most of his career teaching in a Bible college but he also remains a strong apologist for retaining biblical studies at the core of the CMBC curriculum. When Dave teaches the Bible he first does careful exegesis, then he does not hesitate to jump from the first generation to the present to indicate how the Bible speaks to current situations. He describes his approach thus:

> The promise-fulfillment way of thinking about our relationship to God reminds us that we are responsible for discerning the will of God for our time. Such discernment takes into account both the Scriptures and the situation in which we live. We must seek a further and deeper understanding of the Word of God—what its message was in its own time, how that message applied to life then, and what it says to our own time.

---

[14]Ibid., 59.

> We must also seek deeper understandings of the context in which we live our lives—understandings of our culture, of the immediate situation and our weaknesses, of the principalities and powers that operate in our time, and the pressures that cause us to lean in one direction or another. All of these need to be considered when we seek to discern God's promises for us."[15]

For Dave the Bible is God's Word to God's church. The Bible is interpreted by the church for the church. Indeed, Dave's career could be summarized as a response to two questions: What does the Bible say? What must the church then do? The answer to these questions is found when, through the work of the Holy Spirit, the church becomes the "discerning community" or the "hermeneutical community" in determining the will of God.[16] Earlier he frequently spoke of this as a matter of mutual exhortation. In recent years he has increasingly described this process in terms of binding and loosing. In baptism the Christian is bound to God and to the people of God, and is simultaneously freed from the principalities and powers of this world. Says Dave:

> Whenever we, as a church, seek the will of God in some matter, and come to a decision which we feel to be the promise of God to us, then it is a binding word and we should hold each other to it. The decision becomes normative for a group. However, how often do we work through issues deeply enough that this binding normative quality is reached? Much sacrifice and hard work is needed to become a loosing (liberating, saving) and binding fellowship.[17]

To so discern God's will and to live accordingly in obedience models a new way of living—the kingdom way. The church thus is the creator of alternative models for humanity.

For Dave the church is of central importance, yet he does not envision a church without spot and wrinkle within history. He is too close to the reality of the church to become a perfec-

---

[15]*Invited to Faith*, 42.
[16]*Learning to Know the Bible*, 89.
[17]*Invited to Faith*, 69.

tionist. He is too much a pastor and remains that for numerous
individuals, couples and families all over central and western
Canada. He is repeatedly called on to mediate conflicts in
congregations across the country and has experienced such
conflict in his own congregation. But he does not become
pessimistic nor cynical. He remains optimistic, even idealistic,
about the church—his own congregation, the Mennonite churches
generally and the larger ecumenical community. So he continues
to teach and to preach, calling the church to be the church.

Is Dave too optimistic? He believes that the individual is
free to make choices. When the individual responds to God in
faith, she or he, in turn, ought to live a life of obedience. Yet
he sees that repeatedly we do not. Couples who covenant before
God and the church to be faithful, renege on that covenant. I
have heard Dave wonder aloud how this could be. Yet he does
not abandon those who thus break covenant and urges the
church to respond similarly. I do not know where Dave finally
draws the line when individuals freely choose to negate their
Christian vows and yet want to be accepted by the Christian
community. Perhaps never! He seems to say, "Surely some day
they will know the truth and the truth will set them free."

True freedom entails freely choosing obedience to Christ.
This is the essence of rebirth, the new being in Christ. For Dave,
acting on such freedom is what Christian ethics is all about. His
ethics, in turn, assume a sociology relatively unique among
Mennonite theologians. In his paper at the Symposium, he
summarized this sociology in terms of the way the *Haustafeln*
speak to "how Christians are to live in the structures of society;
how they are to live in their given stations of life."[18] These
structures are human constructs which order society, and hence
they "have dominion." They include the political, social, economic, cultural aspects of society, and even the church. To some
extent these structures overlap with the New Testament understanding of principalities and powers.

In Dave's view these structures are essential to human
community. They are a necessary extension of creation. Hence,

---

[18]"Once You Were No People . . .," infra, 37.

Christians not only can be, but ought to be, co-creators in all these areas. These structures cannot simply be dismissed as part of the world. Nevertheless, as orders of creation, they are not simply pronounced good. Discernment is always necessary. "There are no perfect structures, because it is not the structures in themselves that are good or bad as a rule."[19] "As long as people have freedom of choice, no structure is free from misuse, free from sin. The more a structure is misused, the more chaos is created; and this calls for a new ordering, a new structuring that will be just and equitable."[20] Here again, the church needs to give leadership in modelling such new structures.

Dave's Lutheran teachers probably were the ones from whom he developed an appreciation for the concept of calling, vocations and stations of life. Yet he has filled this category with his own Mennonite understandings. Thus we are called "to be Christian in our vocations and be willing to suffer for it." The businessman, for example, "must in all things be Christian regardless whether he can compete with the world or not (he may have to suffer for it)."[21] For direction in our stations as sons, daughters, wives, husbands and church leaders, Dave turns to the *Haustafeln*. The "mutual subordination" outlined in these household codes is not a conservative subjugation to unjust structures in society but an act of radical freedom. The power of the structures is broken when the Christian freely chooses to live in those structures according to the model of Christ—if need be even to the point of suffering.

Again Dave returns to the theme of suffering, even as he returned at this Symposium to the *Haustafeln*, the topic he addressed already in his Hamburg dissertation in 1959.[22] The misunderstanding and misrepresentation of these household codes remain matters of grave concern to Dave. The problem, he says, is that readers of these texts do not recognize that the codes are written to a people, a new people of God, who,

---

[19]*Invited to Faith*, 77.

[20]Ibid., 76.

[21]*Learning to Know the Bible*, 99.

[22]"Die Haustafeln des Neuen Testaments: Ihre Herkunft und ihr theologisher Sinn" (Th.D. dissertation, University of Hamburg, 1959).

because they are born anew, view all of life with new eyes and live their lives on the basis of this new being. The result may well be suffering but that is not the essence. The essence is that they are a new people who live in the world but not of the world. They are of Christ; they are in Christ. Dave's theology is thus fundamentally incarnational. The church is the very body of Christ.

What makes his theology so important to us in the Mennonite church is that his is a theology of the church for the church. Dave is a doctor of the church, much more than a doctor of the academy. He has written almost exclusively for the church, only rarely for the academy. He teaches in the churches, rather than presenting papers to learned societies. Perhaps he feels more at home in church contexts. Perhaps rather mundane reasons have kept him from ever getting his *Haustafeln* study to the publisher. Yet I believe in terms of agenda and priorities there is something more profound here to which we as Mennonite academics must give very serious attention.

Dave's life and work are characterized by an unusual integrity. He has sought to live a life—in his person, in his family, in the church—in keeping with his incarnational theology. His theology is directed fundamentally to a new people, to the church. Hence, he has invested his whole life teaching in a church college and teaching in the congregations. If the Mennonite church is to maintain its identity—an identity based in an ecclesiology premised upon the incarnation—then it must have teachers who themselves are not only committed to this theology intellectually but who also incarnate this theology personally.

What makes Dave Schroeder such a charismatic figure? Dave is heard by the churches because of who he is, not only because of what he says. He is heard because he does not so much negate or scold or imply his intellectual or spiritual superiority but rather he adds to, builds bridges, surprises, encourages and assures. He breathes new life, new faith, new hope and new love. His master teacher is Jesus the Christ, the Word made flesh. We honour Dave best when we too, as teachers of the church, look to Jesus as our master teacher, when our words too become flesh in and through us. Then and only then will we have been true students of Dave Schroeder.

Then and only then will we be servants of the church as Dave has modelled so powerfully for us!

———

A SELECTION FROM DAVID SCHROEDER'S PRESENTATIONS AND WRITINGS*

1959

"Die Haustafeln des Neuen Testaments: Ihre Herkunft und ihr theologischer Sinn." Th.D. dissertation, University of Hamburg, 1959.

1962

"Development in Mennonite Theological Studies." Paper presented at Seventh Mennonite World Conference, St. Catharines, Ontario, July 1962.

1963

"Revelation and Christian Education." Paper presented at Christian Education Seminar, North Newton, Kansas, 22-26 July 1963.

1964

"Our Witness for Peace: 1 Peter 2:18-25." Sermon series on peace witness at Elmwood Mennonite Brethren Church, Winnipeg, Manitoba, 8 November 1964.

1965

"A Survey of Development toward Higher Education." Paper presented at an exploratory meeting to consider the possibility of establishing a Christian liberal arts college. Also presented as "Residential College in Manitoba" at Bethel Mennonite Church, Winnipeg, Manitoba, 23 April 1965.

1966

Learning to Know the Bible. Newton, Kansas: Faith and Life Press, 1966.

"The Mennonite Theology of Ecumenical Involvement." Paper presented at symposium on "The Ecumenical Situation of the Church in Canada" at the 42nd annual meeting of the Conference of Manitoba, The United Church of Canada, Winnipeg, Manitoba, 8 June 1966.

1967

"The Ministry of the Deacon in our Time." Presentation at Saskatchewan Ministers' and Deacons' Conference, Saskatoon, Saskatchewan, 7 March, 1967.

"Theology and Philosophy." Paper presented at conference on "The Christian in Philosophy" at Camp Friedenswald, Cassopolis, Michigan, 28-30 September 1967.

---

*This list was prepared by Linda Winter Dueck, Winnipeg, Manitoba.

1968

"Personal Relations in the New Life: The Christian in the Structures of Society, Colossians 3:18-4:1." Paper presented at Inter-Mennonite Ministers' Meeting, Wabash YMCA Hotel, Chicago, Illinois, 14-16 May 1968.

1969

"The So-Called 'New Morality.'" Paper presented at Conference on Sexuality, Camp Arnes, Manitoba, 7-8 February 1969.

1970

"The Origin of the New Testament Ethical Codes." In *Annual Proceedings of the Canadian Society for the Study of Religion,* June 1970, 73-88.

1972

"Command and Obedience." In *Call to Faithfulness,* ed. Henry Poettcker and Rudy Regehr. Winnipeg, Manitoba: CMBC Publications, 1972, 13-22.

"New Testament Ethics and War." Paper presented at a peace seminar at Canadian Mennonite Bible College, Winnipeg, Manitoba, 1972-73.

"Evangelism in Education." Paper presented at "Probe '72," an inter-Mennonite consultation on evangelism, Minneapolis, Minnesota, 13-16 April 1972.

"The Mennonite Theology of Ecumenical Involvement." Paper presented at a Baptist-Mennonite meeting, Toronto, Ontario, 22-23 June 1972.

"Education-Evangelism." *Gospel Herald,* 12 September 1972, 709-711.

1973

"Accent on Values." Commencement address at Freeman Junior College and Academy, Freeman, South Dakota, 20 May 1973.

1974

"Remember, Respond, Reach Out." Sermon preached at "Key 73," Grace Mennonite Church, Steinbach, Manitoba, 27 January 1974.

"The Visible Church: Freedom or Bondage." Presentation at Manitoba Ministers' and Deacons' Conference, Winnipeg, Manitoba, 22 February 1974. Later published in *Mennonite Reporter,* 15 April 1974, 10-12.

"Ye have heard that it has been said . . . Matthew 5." Baccalaureate address at Canadian Mennonite Bible College graduation, Winnipeg, Manitoba, 28 April 1974.

"Nationalism and Internationalism: Ground Rules for a Discussion." *The Mennonite,* 9 July 1974, 426-427. Also published in *Citizens and Disciples: Christian Essays on Nationalism.* Akron, Pennsylvania; MCC Peace Section, 1974.

"The Commitment of Thanksgiving." Sermon preached at Manitoba Mennonite Centennial Celebration, Winnipeg, Manitoba, 28 July 1974.

"Issues of the '70s." Paper presented at seminar of Mennonite-Brethren in Christ Editors and Associates, Cabrini Contact Centre, Des Plaines, Illinois, 18-20 September 1974.

1975

"Hermeneutics." Class lectures used at Associated Mennonite Biblical Seminaries, Elkhart, Indiana, 1975.

"Communication," "The Task of the Scholar in Communication." Presentations to Graduate Seminar of Associated Mennonite Biblical Seminaries, Elkhart, Indiana, 1975.

"Ethics." Ethics lectures presented at Associated Mennonite Biblical Seminaries, Elkhart, Indiana, 1975.

"Women in Church and Society." Class notes presented at Associated Mennonite Biblical Seminaries, Elkhart, Indiana, 1975.

"New Testament Ethics and Preaching," "Relativism in Preaching," "Biblical Ethics and Preaching." Presented at Inter-term course at Associated Mennonite Biblical Seminaries, Elkhart, Indiana, January 1975.

"Jesus relates to sinners; to people; to tradition; to women; to structures." Messages given at General Conference triennium, St. Catharines, Ontario, 1974. Later published in *The Mennonite*, 7 January-4 February 1975.

"The Nature of Civil Religion." Presentation at symposium on Civil Religion sponsored by Mennonite Central Committee, Fort Wayne, Indiana, 17-18 January 1975.

"Jubilee Means Release of Slaves." Sermon preached at Hively Mennonite Church, Elkhart, Indiana, 2 February 1975.

"The Heritage of the People of God," "Returning to Your Heritage," "Jesus and Tradition." Sermons preached at Flanagan Mennonite Church, Flanagan, Illinois, 4-6 April 1975.

"Issues in the General Conference." Sunday School presentation at Eighth Street Mennonite Church, Goshen, Indiana, 13 April 1975.

"Human Sexuality." Class notes at Associated Mennonite Biblical Seminaries, Elkhart, Indiana, 17 April 1975.

"Discrimination." Lecture given at Associated Mennonite Biblical Seminaries, Elkhart, Indiana, May 1975.

"Christian Belief: Baptism and Church Membership." Sermon preached at Floradale Mennonite Church, Floradale, Ontario, 4 May 1975.

"Freedom from Bondage: Freedom through Covenant." Sermon preached at First Mennonite Church, Bluffton, Ohio, 18 May 1975.

"Understanding the Grace of God in Truth: Colossians 1:3-14 and Mark 10:32-45." Graduation address at Associated Mennonite Biblical Seminaries, Elkhart, Indiana, 23 May 1975.

"Discipleship as Found in Mark." Class presentations for Summer Course at Associated Mennonite Biblical Seminaries, Elkhart, Indiana, 7-18 July 1975.

"The Orders of Creation: The Chain of Command," "The Single State." Papers presented at Conference on Singleness, British Columbia, August 1975.

"New Family Patterns." *The Mennonite*, 16 September 1975, 506-507. Also published in *Gospel Herald*, 16 September 1975, 645-646.

"Called to Proclaim the Gospel." Paper presented at Conference on Evangelism and Church Growth, Calgary, Alberta, 20-22 November 1975.

1976

"Exhortation in the New Testament," "Haustafel," "Lists, Ethical," "Parenesis." Articles in *The Interpreter's Dictionary of the Bible*. Supplementary Volume. Nashville, Tennessee: Abingdon, 1976.

"The Father Works and I Must Work," "The Revelation of God in History," "Understanding the Word of God," "The Revelation of God in Christ," "The Manifestation of God's Salvation in Our Day." Sermons preached at Inter-Mennonite Bible Conference, Phoenix, Arizona, 22-26 February 1976.

"He Comes to His People," "He Cleanses the Temple," "Judged Worthy of Death," "Jesus Accepts Suffering and Death," "He Calls Us to Remember." Sermons preached during Passion Week at First Mennonite Church, Berne, Indiana, 11-15 April 1976.

"By What Authority . . .?" Presentation given at Peace Theology Colloquium I on "Theology and *The Politics of Jesus*." Kansas City, Missouri, 7 October 1976.

"Biblical Perspectives," "The God Who Comes to Save," "Called to Proclaim the Gospel," "Ministering through the Body." Meditations given at Consultation on Church Growth, Bluffton College, Bluffton, Ohio, 8-10 November 1976.

1977

"Called to be Servants." Main address at Conference of Mennonites in Manitoba, Steinbach, Manitoba, 25-26 February 1977.

"A Theology of Mission." Presentations at Native Ministries study conference at Canadian Mennonite Bible College, Winnipeg, Manitoba, 5 March 1977.

"Enter: the King," "Who Speaks for God?" "Who Judges the Son?" "The Last Supper," "Father Forgive Them." Sermons preached at Pre-Easter services at Bethesda Mennonite Church, Henderson, Nebraska, 3-8 April 1977.

"God's Revelation to Mankind," "God's Revelation of Himself in History and Its Implications for Biblical Interpretation," "God Calls to Himself a People." Presentations at Commission on Overseas Mission retreat at Canadian Mennonite Bible College, Winnipeg, Manitoba, 22-29 June 1977.

"Missions and Service: Service and Missions." Paper presented at Voluntary Service orientation, Mennonite Central Committee, Winnipeg, Manitoba, 2-11 August 1977.

"Love to the Neighbour." Paper presented at Manitoba Ministers' and Deacons' Conference, North Kildonan Mennonite Church, Winnipeg, Manitoba, 29 October 1977.

1978

"God at Work in the World." Presentations at missionary conference held in Kikwit, Zaire, 1978.

"How to Study the Bible." Four presentations at Pandora, Ohio, March 1978.

"Ethical Norms that Govern Male/Female Relations before and after Marriage." Sermon presented at Stirling Avenue Mennonite Church, Kitchener, Ontario, 16 April 1978.

"Is There a Biblical Case for Civil Disobedience? Is Civil Disobedience Called For in the Specific Case of War Taxes?" Paper presented at Consultation on Civil Responsibility, Elkhart, Indiana, 1-4 June 1978.

1979

"The Church Representing the Kingdom." In *The Kingdom of God in a Changing World.* Lombard, Illinois: Mennonite World Conference, 1979, 40-55. First presented at Mennonite World Conference, 10th Assembly, Wichita, Kansas, August 1978.

"Biblical Authority and Denominational Traditions." In *The Believers Church in Canada*, ed. J. Zeman and W. Klaassen. Waterloo, Ontario: Waterloo Printing Company, 1979, 93-107.

"Revelation: An Historicist Perspective." Paper on Gordon Kaufman's, *Systematic Theology*, presented at Graduate Seminar at Canadian Mennonite Bible College, Winnipeg, Manitoba, January 1979. (Originally given to Associated Mennonite Biblical Seminaries Faculty and used as base for missionary retreat in Zaire and also at orientation for China Educational Exchange in 1982.)

"Working with Tension in our Families." Sermon preached at Whitewater Mennonite Church, Boissevain, Manitoba, 14 January 1979.

"Interpreting the Scriptures," "Jewish Interpretation," "Discerning the Truth in Ethics." Presentations at study conference on "Our Theology in Theory and Practice" at Ebenezer Mennonite Church, Abbotsford, British Columbia, 10 June 1979.

"Women in the New Testament." Presented at symposium on "Questions on Sexuality" at Conference on New Men/New Roles, British Columbia, 15-16 June 1979.

"Justice and the Family." Presentations at Family Camp, Conference of Mennonites in Alberta, Camp Valaqua, Alberta, 12-24 July 1979.

"Capital Punishment." Presentation at Evangelical Covenant Church, Winnipeg, Manitoba, 12-13 October 1979.

"Tasks in Education." Inauguration address at "Service of Inauguration: Ralph A. Lebold, President," Conrad Grebel College, University of Waterloo, Waterloo, Ontario, 14 October 1979.

"The Call to Follow," "The Call to Mission," "The Call to Discipleship." Sermons preached in Elbing, Kansas, 16-18 November 1979.

"Gospel of John." Five radio messages recorded by Faith and Life Communications, Winnipeg, Manitoba, 10 December 1979.

"Response to Revelation." Sermon preached at North Star Mennonite Church, Drake, Saskatchewan, 30 December 1979.

1980

"Comments on Aspects of the Hearings Related to the Socioeconomic Community Impact of the Proposed Refinery at Warman." Presentation made to a panel and representatives of the Eldorado Nuclear Company at hearings held in Warman, Saskatchewan, 23 January 1980.

"About Whom Does the Prophet Say This? Acts 7:34." Sermon preached at Charleswood Mennonite Church, Winnipeg, Manitoba, 10 February 1980.

"Facing the Inevitable: John 11:45-57." Sermon preached on Good Friday at Lendrum Mennonite Brethren Church, Edmonton, Alberta, 2 March 1980.

"Interpreting the Bible." *The Mennonite*, 4 March 1980, 152-153.

"Marriage, Divorce, Remarriage, and Related Themes." Three lectures presented in Drake, Saskatchewan, 29-30 March 1980 (Tapes are also available).

"What Ought We to Do?" Paper presented at symposium on "Christian Ethics in Health Care" at Canadian Mennonite Health Assembly, Winnipeg, Manitoba, 7-9 May 1980.

"Covenanting Together." Sermon preached at baptismal service at Charleswood Mennonite Church, Winnipeg, Manitoba, 1 June 1980.

"The Healing of the Inner Person." Paper presented at conference of Mennonite Medical Association, Snow Mountain Ranch, Colorado, 9-12 July 1980.

"Anabaptist Theology and Community Action and the Handicapped." Paper presented at Handicapped Awareness conference sponsored by Mennonite Central Committee, Winnipeg, Manitoba, 16 August 1980.

"Moral Issues and Nursing Ethics." Paper presented at conference on "Dilemmas of Nursing Practice" at Manitoba Association of Nursing Students and Manitoba Association of Registered Nurses Conference, Winnipeg, Manitoba, 14 November 1980.

"Called to be a People." Sermon preached at St. Catharines United Mennonite Church, St. Catharines, Ontario, 30 November 1980.

1981

Invited to Faith. Newton, Kansas: Faith and Life Press, 1981.

"Rudolph Bultmann." In *A Cloud of Witnesses: Profiles of Church Leaders*, ed. J. C. Wenger. Harrisonburg, Virginia: Eastern Mennonite Seminary,

1981, 237-240.

"De Sabbat es fe de Mensche jemoakt worde, nich de Mensche fe den Sabbat." Four Low German messages based on Mark, recorded for "Wort des Lebens" by Faith and Life Communications, Winnipeg, Manitoba, 1981.

"Interpreting the Scriptures: A Dialogue with the Scribes, Jesus and Paul," "A Dialogue with Jesus," "Sacred Tradition," "The Interpreting of the Word." Presentations given at symposium on "Study of God and His People at Work" at Keystone Bible Institute, Christopher Dock School, 12-16 January 1981.

"Owe No One Anything, Except to Love One Another, Romans 13:8." Sermon preached at Fort Garry Mennonite Brethren Church, Winnipeg, Manitoba, 25 January 1981.

"The Collapse of the Mind." Paper presented at a workshop at Peace-It-Together Conference, Canadian Mennonite Bible College, Winnipeg, Manitoba, 6-8 March 1981.

"The Will of God: Which Direction? Matthew 23." Sermon preached at joint sessions of the Illinois Mennonite Conference/Central District Conference, Illinois State University, Normal, Illinois, 5 April 1981.

"Hitherto." Sermon preached at 25th anniversary of Grace Mennonite Church, St. Catharines, Ontario, 26 April 1981.

"Co-creators with God," "God is liberating." Presentations at "Great Trek I," a Conference of Mennonites in Canada youth gathering, Lakehead University, Thunder Bay, Ontario, August 1981.

"Thus Says the Lord." Paper presented at conference on "Rediscovering the Place of the Church in Health Issues" at annual meeting of Canadian Mennonite Health Assembly, Morrow Gospel Church, Winnipeg, Manitoba, 16 October 1981.

1982

"Biblical Foundations for Service Ministries of the Church." Paper presented at Consultation on Theology and Service, North Webster, Indiana, 1 April 1982.

"Biblical Perspectives: The Christian as a Victim." Paper presented at conference on "The Christian as Victim," Kansas City, Kansas, 1-3 April 1982.

"Stewards of God's Varied Grace." Graduation address at Columbia Bible Institute, Clearbrook, British Columbia, 2 May 1982.

"A Tentative, Exploratory Statement on Education: Canadian Mennonite Bible College in Relation to Other Educational Institutions." Presentation given to Faculty, Canadian Mennonite Bible College, Winnipeg, Manitoba, 4 June 1982.

"Sailing into the Future." Graduation address at Garden Valley Collegiate, Winkler, Manitoba, 25 June 1982.

"Systemic Evil," "Salvation and the Structures of Society," "Being in the World, Not of the World." Chapel messages at Canadian Mennonite Bible College, Winnipeg, Manitoba, September 1982.

"Divorce: Mark 10:2-12." Presentation at Altona Bergthaler Mennonite Church, Altona, Manitoba, 12 September 1982.

"Giving Meaning to Old Age." Workshop at Ministers' and Deacons' Conference, Fort Garry Mennonite Brethren Church, Winnipeg, Manitoba, 23 October 1982.

"Philosophie oder Kreuz? Colossians 2:8." Sermon preached at North Kildonan Mennonite Church, Winnipeg, Manitoba, 24 October 1982.

1983

"Faith-Full Living," "Creating New Worlds," "Living in the Structures," "Exercising the Power of Powerlessness," "Liberating the Oppressed." Presentations at annual Religion and Life Week Lectures, University of Winnipeg, Winnipeg, Manitoba, 24-28 January 1983.

"Teaching-Evaluation of Students." Presentation to the School of Nursing, Grace General Hospital, Winnipeg, Manitoba, February 1983.

"Neugeboren (Hoffnung)," "Neues Leben (Heiligung)," "Das Christsein in den Ständen," "Leiden als Zeugnis" (1 Petri 1:13-4:19)." Sermons preached for Bible week at Springfield Heights Mennonite Church, Winnipeg, Manitoba, 27 February 1983.

"Abortion." Presentation at Bethel Mennonite Church, Winnipeg, Manitoba, 26 April 1983.

"The Catholic Bishops Concern for the Economy." In *Seeds* 2 (June 1983): 21.

"Who is Jesus?" "Jesus: The Stone That Crushes," "Christ: The Stone We Accept." Presentations at "Bethlehem '83," the North American youth gathering, Bethlehem, Pennsylvania, 1-4 August 1983.

"Biblical Perspectives on Stress," "Rest and Renewal." Presentations at MCC (Akron) Committee of Personnel Services meetings, Camp Assiniboia, Headingly, Manitoba, 5-7 October 1983.

"Shalom: Peace and Wholeness," "The Way of the Cross." Presentations at MCC meetings, Edmonton, Alberta, 28-30 October 1983.

"Relief-Insurance." Presentation at annual Mennonite Mutual Relief Insurance Corporation meetings, Edmonton, Alberta, 28-30 October 1983.

1984

"In the Image of God." In *Celebrating Differences*, ed. Aldred H. Neufeldt. Newton, Kansas: Faith and Life Press, 1984, 1-14.

Response to "Contemporary Biotechnology in the Context of Conflicting Theological Perspectives" by Donald Demarco, and "Abortion: A Christian Response" by Stanley Grenz. In *The Conrad Grebel Review* 2 (Spring 1984): 155-158.

"Should the Emphasis be on Converting Individuals or on Converting Social Structures?" Paper presented at special board meeting of MCC (Manitoba), Winnipeg, Manitoba, 14 January 1984.

"Biblical Perspectives on Authority." Paper presented at study conference on "Authority in the Church," Winnipeg, Manitoba, 30 January 1984.

"Binding and Loosing: The Way of Communal Ethics." In *Seeds* 3 (June 1984): 5-8.

1985

First Peter: Faith Refined by Fire. Faith and Life Bible Studies. Newton, Kansas: Faith and Life Press, 1985.

Review of *God of the Lowly: Socio-Historical Interpretations of the Bible,* ed. Willy Schottroff and Wolfgang Stegemannn. In *Mission Focus* 13 (September 1985): 44 and *Journal of Beliefs and Values* 5 (1984): 15-18.

Review of *In Memory of Her: A Feminist Theological Reconstruction of Christian Origins,* by Elizabeth Schüssler Fiorenza. In *Journal of Beliefs and Values* 6 (1985): 15-18.

"People in the Image of God," "To Be in the Image of God Is to Be Called to Participate in God's Ongoing Work in the World." Presentations for the course "Development Issues," sponsored by Canadian Mennonite Bible College and Mennonite Brethren Bible College, Winnipeg, Manitoba, 1985.

"Interpretation: Gemeinde als hermeneutische Gruppe," "Die Auslegung Pauli," "Normen und Kriterion: Was bedeutet es Mensch zu sein," "Kanadische Konferenz." Presentations made at "Theologiestudenten-seminar" at Haus Concordia, Herdorf-Dermbach, Germany, 25-28 February 1985.

"Resistance and Non-Resistance in Christian Discipleship." Paper presented at Church and Peace Study Conference and General Assembly, Liebfrauenberg (Woerth), Alsace, France, 28 February-3 March 1985.

"Liberation: Presuppositions." Six lectures given to a Quaker group, Woodbrook, Birmingham, England, 7-19 March 1985.

"Anders leben: Wie ist das möglich?" Paper presented at Gemeindetag deutscher Mennoniten, Neuwied, Germany, 16-19 May 1985.

"Fragen an Markus." Five sermons preached in Neuwied, Germany, 28 June-2 July 1985.

"Wie interpretieren wir die Offenbarung?" Five sermons on Revelation preached at Backnang, Germany, 3-7 July 1985.

"Glaube." Sermon preached in Bechterdissen, Germany, 19 July 1985.

"Die Offenbarung des Willens Gottes," "Die Auslegung der Schriftgelehr-ten," "Die Auslegung Jesu," "Die Anwendung Pauli," "Den Willen Gottes erkennen (Die hermeneutische Gemeinde)." Five presentations at the Prediger- und Diakonenrüste, Bechterdissen, Germany, 20-21 July 1985.

"Der Sieg Christi." Four chapel messages on Revelation at Bienenberg Bible School, Liestal, Switzerland, July 1985.

"Shalom und das kommende Reich." Ten presentations on the Gospel of Mark at Bienenberg Bible School, Liestal, Switzerland, July 1985.

"Das Hören und Nichthören des Evangeliums," "Die Offenbarung Jesu Christi," "Der Leidensweg Jesu." Three sermons preached in Bielefeld, Germany, July 1985.

"Das Leben in der Welt," "Wer sind die Mennoniten." Two sermons preached in Wolfsburg, Germany, July 1985.

"Das Vorbild Jesu," "1 Korinther 11: Einige Feststellungen." Two sermons preached in Hannover, Germany, July 1985.

"The Gospel of Peace." Paper presented at Moderators' and Secretaries' Consultation, Winnipeg, Manitoba, 31 August, 1985.

"Thanks Be to God Who Gives Us the Victory through Our Lord Jesus Christ, 1 Corinthians 15:57." Sermon preached at memorial service for Rev. David D. Klassen, Bergthaler Mennonite Church, Morden, Manitoba, 4 September 1985.

"How Faith Grows within Community." Sermon preached at Charleswood Mennonite Church, Winnipeg, Manitoba, 6 October 1985.

1986

Review of *Slavery, Sabbath, War and Women,* by Willard Swartley. In *The Conrad Grebel Review* 4 (Fall 1986): 262-264.

"Pornography and Sexual Violence: An Exploration of the Issues." A seminar presented to MCC Manitoba, Peace and Social Concerns Committee, Fort Garry Mennonite Brethren Church, Winnipeg, Manitoba, 25 January 1986.

"Biblical Perspectives on Anabaptist Principles: Discipleship, Relation to the State." Presentations at Evangelical Mennonite Church Youth Conference, Aberdeen Mennonite Church, Winnipeg, Manitoba, 7-9 February 1986.

"Binding and Loosing." Presentations as part of Portable CMBC series at Emmanuel Mennonite Church, Clearbrook, British Columbia, 14-16 March 1986.

"Women in the Church," "Women and the Early Church," "Jesus and Women." Lectures held at First Mennonite Church, Vancouver, British Columbia, 4-8 May 1986.

"Salvation and Wholeness," "Salvation and Ministry." Papers presented to Pastoral Care Institute, Winkler, Manitoba, 15 May 1986.

"Liberation from the Law." Presentation at "Inter-Church Training Event" of Native Ministries, Oblate Sisters Retreat Centre, Winnipeg, Manitoba, 11 September 1986.

"More about Word and Deed." Paper presented to MCC Consultation, Winnipeg, Manitoba, 12 September 1986.

"On Worshipping God." Sermon preached at Charleswood Mennonite Church, Winnipeg, Manitoba, 28 September 1986.

"Meeting the Educational Needs of the Church." Message at the opening program of Elim Bible Institute, Altona Bergthaler Mennonite Church, Altona, Manitoba, 28 September 1986.

1987

"The New Testament Haustafel: Egalitarian or Status Quo?" In *Perspectives on Feminist Hermeneutics*, Occasional Papers No. 10, ed. Gayle Gerber Koontz and Willard Swartley. Elkhart, Indiana: Institute of Mennonite Studies, 1987, 56-65.

Review of *Shalom: The Bible's Word for Salvation, Justice and Peace*, by Perry B. Yoder. In *The Mennonite*, 9 June 1987, 262.

"Jonathan, Big Business and the Law: A Tale about Galilee." In *The Marketplace* 17 (January/February 1987): 16-18.

"The Bible and Homosexuality." Sunday school lesson at Altona Mennonite Church, Altona, Manitoba, 8 February 1987.

"The Family Redeemed," "Aufgaben des höheren Alters." Presentations at annual Ministers' and Deacons' Conference, Sherbrooke Mennonite Church, Vancouver, British Columbia, 18-19 February 1987.

"Discerning the Gifts of the Spirit," "Using the Spiritual Gifts." Presentations at Ministers' and Deacons' Conference, First Mennonite Church, Greendale, British Columbia, 20 February 1987.

"To Be Subject." Sermon preached at Charleswood Mennonite Church, Winnipeg, Manitoba, 28 June 1987.

"Women in Biblical Perspective." Paper presented at special meeting of MCC Canada, Winnipeg, Manitoba, 11 September 1987.

"God Cares." Sermon preached at Charleswood Mennonite Church, Winnipeg, Manitoba, 4 October 1987.

"Still in the Image." Sermon preached at St. Vital United Church, Winnipeg, Manitoba, 11 October 1987.

"Parakaleo (Exhortation)." Sermon preached at Charleswood Mennonite Church, Winnipeg, Manitoba, 25 October 1987.

"The Day of Visitation." Sermon preached at Charleswood Mennonite Church, Winnipeg, Manitoba, 15 November 1987.

"Isaiah the Prophet: Holiness and Righteousness." Sermon preached at Charleswood Mennonite Church, Winnipeg, Manitoba, December 1987.

"Servant(s) of God." Sermon preached at Charleswood Mennonite Church, Winnipeg, Manitoba, 6 December 1987.

1988

"Discerning What Is Bound in Heaven." In *The Bible and the Church: Essays in Honour of Dr. David Ewert*, ed. A.J. Dueck, H.J. Giesbrecht, V.G. Shillington. Winnipeg, Manitoba: Kindred Press, 1988, 63-74.

"Life and Death: Biblical-Theological Perspectives." In *Medical Ethics, Human Choices: A Christian Perspective*, ed. John Rogers. Kitchener, Ontario: Herald Press, 1988, 63-72.

"A Christian and Biblical Base for Decision-making." Presentation at a forum on farming, Winnipeg Bible Institute, Winkler, Manitoba, 26 January 1988.

"Moral Literacy: Should It Be Taught?" Presentation to Divisional Conference of the River East Teachers' Association, Winnipeg, Manitoba, 28 January 1988.

"The Basis for a Christian Ethic." Paper presented at Special Courses for Ministers and Layworkers, Canadian Mennonite Bible College, Winnipeg, Manitoba, 8-11 February 1988.

"Church Growth: Anabaptist Perspective," "Jesus: Author of the New Covenant," "The Prophetic Call: Our Prophetic Ministry." Presentations at School for Ministers, Conrad Grebel College, Waterloo, Ontario, 19 February 1988.

"The Character of God," "Jesus, Saviour and Lord," "The Character of God: Implications for the Church." Presentations at Rockway Mennonite Church, Kitchener, Ontario, 21 February 1988.

"Telling the Story," "Clues for Gracious Living I," "Clues for Gracious Living II," "Telling the Story." Sermons preached at annual sessions of Conference of Mennonites of Saskatchewan, Swift Current, Saskatchewan, 24-25 February 1988.

"Christian Responsibility in the Care of the Elderly." Presentation to the Supervised Pastoral Education program, Municipal Hospitals, Winnipeg, Manitoba, 5 April 1988.

"God's Story/Our Story," "The Story/Our Resource," "The Word Addresses Us All." Sermons preached at Hillcrest Annual Spring Renewal Meetings and CHETA School of Christian Education on "Making Bible Study Come Alive for Me" at Hillcrest, Ontario, 15-17 April 1988.

"Binding Relationships: A Matter of Commitment and Trust." Sermon preached at Charleswood Mennonite Church, Winnipeg, Manitoba, 24 April 1988.

"The Reign of God," "God Is a Covenanting God," "Human Sexuality: The Temple of God," "Loosing and Binding." Sermons preached at Yarrow Mennonite Church, Yarrow, British Columbia, 6-8 May 1988.

"New Creation Families." Sermon preached at Charleswood Mennonite Church, Winnipeg, Manitoba, 8 May 1988.

"How the Years Have Gifted Us." Sermon preached at the 25th anniversary, Charleswood Mennonite Church, Winnipeg, Manitoba, 5 June 1988.

"Reconciliation, Commitment and Celebration." Sermon preached at 50th anniversary celebration. Bethel Mennonite Church, Winnipeg, Manitoba, 26 June 1988.

"Our Response to People in Need." Paper presented at symposium on AIDS at MCC Canada meeting, Winnipeg, Manitoba, 16-17 August 1988.

"Theological Perspective: AIDS." Presentation at Bethel Mennonite Church, Winnipeg, Manitoba, 23 October 1988.

"Preaching and Teaching Ethics," "Healing Ministry Ethics." Presentations at Ministers', Elders' and Deacons' Meetings, Cedar Valley Mennonite Church, Mission, British Columbia, 29 October 1988.

"Who Is This Man?," "The Call to Faith," "What Obedience Looks Like." Sermons on Mark 1-8 at Nutana Park Mennonite Church, Saskatoon, Saskatchewan, 4-6 November 1988.

"Put on Love." Sermon at wedding at Charleswood Mennonite Church, Winnipeg, Manitoba, 12 November 1988.

1989

"The Prodigal Son." Sermon preached at Cornerstone Fellowship, Winnipeg, Manitoba, 5 March 1989.

"Becoming a Family." Sermon preached at Fort Garry Mennonite Fellowship, Winnipeg, Manitoba, April 1989.

"Judgement." Presentation to adult Sunday school class, Charleswood Mennonite Church, Winnipeg, Manitoba, 21 May 1989.

"God With Us." Presentation at orientation for China Educational Exchange, Canadian Mennonite Bible College, Winnipeg, Manitoba, 13-15 June 1988.

"On Being Persons," "Love God/Love Your Neighbour," "The Revelation of God," "Communicating the Faith." Meditations presented at orientation for summer staff, Camp Assiniboia, Headingly, Manitoba, 3-7 July 1989.

"As You Have Received Jesus: Colossians 2:6-7." Sermon preached at dedication weekend, Steinbach Mennonite Church, Steinbach, Manitoba, 14-15 October 1989.

"Sharing Gods' Love." Sermon preached at Charleswood Mennonite Church, Winnipeg, Manitoba, 29 October 1989.

"Divorce and Remarriage." Presentation made to a deacons' meeting at Bethel Mennonite Church, Winnipeg, Manitoba, 7 November 1989.

1990

"Jesus, Saviour and Lord," "Gott offenbarte sich unser." Sermons preached at Deeper Life services, Altona Bergthaler Mennonite Church, Altona, Manitoba, 7 January 1990.

David Schroeder[*]

ONCE YOU WERE NO PEOPLE . . .[**]

The first letter of Peter is addressed to people who once were no people.[1] It is addressed to strangers, pilgrims and resident aliens; to slaves, women and men who had no rights, no power and no voice; to persons who were now being persecuted for being Christian. The author[2] encourages these seemingly helpless people to rejoice in their newfound faith in Christ and empowers them to live in obedience to Christ in spite of all opposition.

The heart of the letter is 1 Peter 2:11-3:12, the so-called *Haustafel*.[3] It speaks of how Christians are to live in the structures of society; how they are to live in their given stations

---

[*]David Schroeder is Professor of New Testament and Philosophy at Canadian Mennonite Bible College, Winnipeg, Manitoba. The Symposium and this book are in his honour.

[**]The author would like to thank Willi Braun, a doctoral student in New Testament at the University of Toronto, Toronto, Ontario; Henry Poettcker, President, Mennonite Biblical Seminary, Elkhart, Indiana; and Dorothy Jean Weaver, Assistant Professor of New Testament, Eastern Mennonite Seminary, Harrisonburg, Virginia, for their critical responses to this essay at the Symposium.

[1]The writer refers rather deliberately to Hosea 1:10; 2:23 and the prophecy that those of whom it is said "you are not my people" will be called "sons of the living God."

[2]We will not argue the question of authorship here, but the direction taken by L. Goppelt and A. F. Walls will be followed. This would assume the writing to be Petrine even if it is not written by the Apostle Peter. See L. Goppelt, *Der Erste Petrusbrief* (Göttingen: Vandenhoeck & Ruprecht, 1978), 30-37; A. F. Walls, *1 Peter* (Grand Rapids, MI: Eerdmans Publishing Company, 1983), 15-68; E. G. Selwyn, *The First Epistle of Peter* (London: Macmillan & Co., 1949).

[3]So named by Luther in *Kleinen Katechismus*. It has received special attention since the mention of it by M. Dibelius, *An die Kolosser, Epheser, und Philemon* (Tübingen: J.C.B. Mohr, 1913) and K. Weidinger, *Die Haustafeln: Ein Stück urchristlicher Paraenese* (Leipzig: C. Heinrichs, 1928). See also David Schroeder, "Die Haustafeln des Neuen Testaments: Ihre Herkunft und ihr theologischer Sinn" (Th.D. dissertation, University of Hamburg, 1959); James Crouch, *The Origin and Intention of the Colossian Haustafel* (Göttingen: Vandenhoeck und Ruprecht, 1972); J. Paul Sampley, *And the Two Shall Be One Flesh: A Study of Tradition in Ephesians 5:21-33* (Cambridge: Cambridge University Press, 1971); Wolfgang Schrage, "Zur Ethik der neutestamentlichen Haustafeln," *New Testament Studies* 21 (October 1974): 1-22; David L. Balch, *Let Wives Be Submissive: A Domestic Code in 1 Peter* (Chico, CA: Scholars Press, 1981).

in life. Despite its centrality for Christian ethics, this section of the letter has often been misunderstood and misrepresented and has become a kind of watershed in biblical hermeneutics and interpretation.

Over the centuries the *Haustafel* has been used to support various non-biblical theological and ethical positions. It has been used to justify the institution of slavery,[4] patriarchal emphases in societal and familial structures,[5] unquestioned obedience to government[6] and subsumption of the Christian ethic to prevailing societal norms, whether in government, law or economics.[7] More recently it has been viewed as a denial of the egalitarian position of Jesus and Paul with respect to women and men[8] and as an attempt to avoid persecution by advising Christians to abide by the expected norms of society and to maintain the status quo.[9]

Both those who see the *Haustafel* as normative for Christian behaviour and those who reject it as a betrayal of the Christian ethic agree that its basic message is acceptance of and integration with societal norms and structures.[10] This interpretation needs to be challenged. The fact that the same passage can be seen in such contradictory ways already indicates that there is something drastically wrong with the way it is approached and interpreted. Needed is a new reading of the text in light of a different set of ethical assumptions. Both the new reading and the different assumptions can be addressed on the basis of the

---

[4]For a listing of material and a description of the pro-slavery case see Willard Swartley, *Slavery, Sabbath, War, and Women* (Scottdale, PA: Herald Press, 1983), 31-36.

[5]Larry Christenson, *The Christian Family* (Minneapolis, MN: Bethany Fellowship, 1970.)

[6]It is almost always assumed that to be subject to the state is to be obedient to the state. This assumption will need to be questioned.

[7]Robert G. Clouse, ed. *Four Christian Views on Economics* (Downers Grove, IL: Intervarsity Press, 1984). See also Paul Hayne, "Clerical Laissez-Faire: A Study in Theological Economics" in *Religion, Economics and Social Thought*, ed. Walter Block and Irving Hexham (Vancouver, BC: The Fraser Institute, 1986).

[8]Elizabeth Schüssler Fiorenza, *In Memory of Her: A Feminist Theological Reconstruction of Christian Origins* (London: SCM Press, 1983), 260-266.

[9]David L. Balch, *Let Wives be Submissive*.

[10]Even L. Goppelt who recognizes the *Haustafel* as a station code (*Ständetafel*) nevertheless concludes that Christians are to act in conformity to the stations they occupy in society. *Der Erste Petrusbrief*, 182f.

text itself, but have seldom, if ever, been expressly stated.[11]

A good beginning toward a new understanding of the *Haustafel* is to hear the text from the perspective of the author and of how he addresses the people. It is of utmost importance to the author that *those who once were no people are now the people of God.* This makes all the difference. They no longer act out of their former worldview but out of a new and vital faith. They have been born anew to a living hope. Their lives are now rooted in a new reality, a new relationship, a new participation in a living corporate community.[12] These Christians, whether of gentile or Jewish origin,[13] have now become participants in a new story, the story of God's people. Any exhortations in the letter must be understood in relation to this larger story.

The author is here espousing a specific way of doing ethics. This way is not an appeal to the law as in Judaism,[14] nor to the text interpreted as a new law as in much of Christendom.[15] It is also not one of reading into the text nuances from the present in order to find in the text our own pre-understandings.[16] The

---

[11]David W. Kendall suggests this in outline form. See "The Literary and Theological Function of 1 Peter 1:3-12" in Charles H. Talbert, ed. *Perspectives on First Peter* (Macon, GA: Mercer University Press, 1986), 103-120. Roger Stronstad, *The First Epistle of Peter* (Vancouver, BC: CLM Educational Society, 1983) uses the headings "Living Like God: Holiness" for 1 Peter 1:3-2:10 and "Living Like Christ: Submission and Suffering" for 1 Peter 2:11-4:19 but sees these passages emphasizing *obedience* to the state rather than *subjection* to the state.

[12]David W. Kendall, "The Literary and Theological Function of 1 Peter 1:3-12," 103-120.

[13]References to the Old Testament and words which describe the children of Israel as "a holy nation," for example, have often been used as arguments for the presence of Jewish Christians among the readers of the letter. But these positions have been overstated. Even if there were no Jewish Christians present, the author would have presented his exhortations on the basis of the Old Testament. By the very nature of the gospel the Christians of gentile origin participate in the whole story of Israel.

[14]Some helpful literature is now available on the subject, for example, Hans Huebner, *Law in Paul's Thought* (Edinburgh: T & T Clark, 1984); H. Räisänen, *Paul and the Law* (Philadelphia, PA: Fortress Press, 1983); E. P. Sanders, *Paul, the Law, and the Jewish People* (Philadelphia, PA: Fortress Press, 1983); Stephen Westerholm, *Israel's Law and the Church's Faith* (Grand Rapids, MI: Eerdmans Publishing Company, 1988).

[15]In spite of all attempts not to do so, much of the teaching of Jesus has been cast into a legal mode. It focuses on doing or keeping the Word rather than on being people of God in Christ.

[16]When sociological or psychological categories which have been developed in the present century are imposed on first-century materials, we have to ask

author is much less complicated in his approach, at the same time much more profound. He is simply saying that Christians ought to be what they are as people of God. The primary emphasis is on *being* a certain kind of people. All else flows from this foundation.

To *be* who they are as people of God requires that they hear and heed their own story and that they learn to know who God is and who they are in relation to God. They have become part of a people with a long and rich tradition. They have heard this story in the gospel that was preached to them (1:12) but now they need to be reminded of pertinent aspects of this story as they face opposition and challenges to their faith. Once they know who God is and who they are, they also will know how to walk and how to respond to those who persecute them.

The basic ethic is given in terms of God's imperative, "You shall be holy, for I am holy" (1:16). When applied specifically to how they are to live in society, they are told to "be subject" even as Jesus was subject to the structures of order in society. The focus is on God and on Jesus Christ, not on their own plight. Attention is called to the character of God and of Christ to whom they now belong. They are to manifest the character of Jesus in their response to the trials they are facing. As they come to know God and the people of God, they will come to know who they are.

The Story Remembered

What They Were, but Are Not

The author repeatedly reminds the readers of their former life. Once they were no people (2:10); they lived in ignorance (1:14); they followed futile ways inherited from their fathers (1:18). Once they were given to malice, guile, insincerity and envy (2:1); they were given to the passions of the flesh (2:11), returning evil for evil (3:9) and generally living in licentiousness, drunkenness, revelling, carousing and lawless idolatry (4:3). The

---

whether we are not doing violence to the text. Note the discussion by D. Balch, "Hellenization/Acculturation in 1 Peter," in Charles H. Talbert, ed. *Perspectives on First Peter*, and the literature referred to there, 79-101.

author reminds them in many different ways that their actions betrayed the fact that once they were no people. They had no single story that informed their lives.

The readers were able to hear these references to their former lives in a different way than we do. They knew how to see allusions to their former life in terms of the context in which they were living. The general populace in first-century Asia Minor lived with expectations which were often different than those which Christians required of themselves. The people were expected to worship the whole pantheon of gods.[17] Not to do so was a sign of irreligion.[18] They were also expected to pay proper homage to the emperor through appropriate sacrifices and worship.[19] This they could not do once Christ became Lord.

The Roman household,[20] consisting of the extended family together with servants and slaves, was considered to be the basic unit of society.[21] The family was a microcosm of the larger

---

[17]Simeon L. Guterman, *Religious Toleration and Persecution in Ancient Rome* (London: Aiglon Press, 1951), 22ff. See also, John Ferguson, *The Religions of the Roman Empire* (London: Thames and Hudson, 1982), 148.

[18]Morton Smith, "Pauline Worship as seen by Pagans," *The Harvard Theological Review* 73 (1980): 241-249. He argues that Christian beliefs and practice were often understood as magic. See also Ramsay MacMullen, *Enemies of the Roman Order* (New Haven, CT: Yale University Press, 1981), 95-127; T. G. Tucker, *Life in the Roman World* (New York, NY: Macmillan and Company, 1910), 382-383; Leon Hardy Canfield, *The Early Persecution of Christians* (New York, NY: Columbia University Press, 1913), 17-42; A. N. Sherwin-White, "The Early Persecution and Roman Law Again," *The Journal of Theological Studies*, New Series 3 (October 1952): 199-213.

[19]S. R. F. Price, "Between Man and God: Sacrifice in the Roman Imperial Cult," *Journal of Roman Studies* 70 (1980): 28-43, and *Rituals and Power: The Roman Imperial Cult in Asia Minor* (New York, NY: Columbia University Press, 1984); Louise Schotroff, "Gebet dem Kaiser, was dem Kaiser gehört, und Gott, was Gott gehört: Die theologische Antwort der christlichen Gemeinden auf ihre gesellschaftliche und politische Situation," in J. Moltmann, ed. *Annahme und Widerstand* (Munich: Christian Kaiser Verlag, 1984), 217; John Ferguson, *The Religions of the Roman Empire*, 148.

[20]For a listing of literature on *OIKOS* (trans. "house" or "household") see J. H. Elliott, *A Home for the Homeless* (London, SCM Press, 1982), see especially footnotes 1 to 17, 237-239. See also Hans-Josef Klauck, *Hausgemeinde und Hauskirche im frühen Christentum* (Stuttgart: Verlag Katholisches Bibelwerk, 1981); J. M. Petersen, "House-Churches in Rome," *Vigiliae Christianae* 23 (December 1969): 264-272; Robert Banks, *Paul's Idea of Community* (Exeter: Paternoster Press, 1980); H. J. Rose, "The Religion of the Greek Household," *Euphrosyne* 1 (January 1954): 95-116. See also Del Birkey, *The House Church* (Scottdale, PA: Herald Press, 1988).

[21]In a large household this could amount to 200 to 1000 slaves and servants.

society or state.[22] The "order" of the house had to be honoured. The house was governed by the *pater familias*, the head of the house. The head determined which religious practices would be permitted or outlawed.[23] If religious cults, including Christianity, disturbed the order of the house, they were viewed as treasonous against the state and consequently outlawed.[24] Not all the people were considered as moral agents. Slaves, for example, simply could not be held morally responsible.

Moral responsibility was determined by reference to each person's *stations* in life and *status* in society. What was appropriate for each person in his or her station was rationally deduced from the station itself.[25] The *rational* thing was to do what was natural in a particular station. The rights of persons, on the other hand, were determined by their status in society.[26] In this respect each house contained persons who differed in status; for example, wives, slaves, freedmen were defined according to their specific roles in society.

These societal assumptions were now being challenged by the Christian community. They belonged to a former life when they were no people but they do not pertain to their new life in Christ.

The Christian Story

From the very beginning the author of 1 Peter focuses on the *Christian* story. He is writing as an apostle of Jesus Christ (1:1). He knows the story of Jesus' earthly ministry and the tradition about Jesus (*paradosis*).[27] It is the proclamation of this story by the apostles which became the foundation of the church.

---

[22]David L. Balch, *Let Wives be Submissive*, 21-23, 51-61.

[23]E. A. Judge, *The Social Patterns of Social Groups in the First Century* (London: Tyndale Press, 1960), 35.

[24]Horst Möhring, "The Persecution of the Jews and the Adherents of the Isis Cult at Rome A.D. 19," *Novum Testamentum* 3 (October 1959): 293-304.

[25]Schroeder, *Haustafeln*, 32-78.

[26]An excellent treatment of the laws of status is given by J. A. Crook, *Law and Life in Rome* (London: Thames and Hudson, 1967), 36f.

[27]Harold Riesenfeld, *The Gospel Tradition and Its Beginnings: A Study in the Limits of 'Formgeschichte'* (London: A. R. Mowbray, 1957); B. Gerhardsson, *Tradition and Transmission in Early Christianity* (Lund: C.W.K. Gleerup, 1964) and *The Gospel Tradition* (Philadelphia, PA: Coronet Books, 1986).

Because he emphasizes the Christian story, he refers to God as the "God and Father of our Lord Jesus Christ" (1:3) and not as the "God of Israel" (Luke 1:68). It is God's work in and through Jesus Christ that has become all-important.

Through the grace and mercy of God those who were the "exiles of the Dispersion" (1:1) have become the people of God (2:10). They have been born anew to a living hope (1:3). They are now participants in a new reality, a new faith and a new life. Those who once were no people have now become a people in Christ. They love him and believe in him, though they have not seen him in person (1:8-9). Their hope is focused on an inheritance (1:4) and a salvation yet to be fully revealed (1:5, 9, 12).

How did this happen? The writer explains: First, God the Father elected them according to God's divine foreknowledge, God's sovereign will and purpose (1:2, 2:4, 6, 9). That is to say, it is God's doing.

Second, they were sanctified through the work of the Holy Spirit and set apart for obedience to Jesus Christ (1:2, 22). They became a holy (sanctified) people as they were delivered from conformity to the world and as they chose to do the will of God.

Third, they were "saved" from their former life through the work of Jesus Christ. They were set free or ransomed from their former life through the sacrifice (sprinkling of blood 1:2) of Christ (1:18f; see also 1 Timothy 2:5-6; 1 Corinthians 6:20; 7:23; Acts 20:28; Revelation 5:9; 14:4). No doubt he has Jesus' own statement in mind when he says ". . . The son of man . . . came not to be served but to serve, and to give his life a ransom for many" (Mark 10:45). The price of redemption was not silver or gold, but the precious blood of Christ (1:19). Jesus became the lamb that was slain for the sin of the world as was indicated in Isaiah 53. The fulfillment of Isaiah's prophecy is seen especially in 2:20-25 and in 3:18-19. They, the readers, are to know that they have been redeemed, liberated from their former captivity by the death of Christ. Through this grace of God they have been born anew to a living hope and become the elect of God.

The resurrection is also important to the author. Through the resurrection of Jesus the readers have come to know the truth and now have confidence in God (1:21). During Jesus' earthly ministry two prophetic voices arose. One claimed that Jesus was a false teacher and a blasphemer. The other claimed he was the servant of God, the Messiah no less. When Jesus was crucified, it seemed as if things were left open and undecided. But when God raised Jesus from the dead, the people who believed in him knew that he was indeed the one who was to redeem Israel (Luke 24), the Messiah. This is the good news that was preached to them (1:25b). As the writer says, "For Christ also died for sins once for all, the righteous for the unrighteous, that he might bring us to God, being put to death in the flesh but made alive in the spirit" (3:18).

The redeemed are the people of God. They have been set free to become obedient to Jesus Christ (1:2, 22). Through obedience to Jesus they are sanctified, set apart, made holy so that they might manifest the character of Jesus in their own lives.

The Larger Story

Though the writer speaks from the standpoint of the Christian story, he is mindful of the larger story to which the people of God belong and in terms of which the Christian story must be understood. He refers to scripture which encompasses the early tradition and also proclaims what has now transpired in Christ. It is almost as if he is stealing words from the history of Israel and willy-nilly using them for the church. But that is not the case. The author does not see the Christian story as annulling the story of Israel or displacing it, but as moving in continuity with and fulfilling it. It is in essence one story even though in Christ something new has been wrought.[28]

The "elect of God" is understood in terms of the chosen of God through the ages (Deuteronomy 7:6-7; Ezekiel 20:5; Isaiah 41:8f.; 51:2; Psalm 105:43),[29] including the Old Testament, Qumran (1QS 8:6; 11:16) and intertestamental Judaism.[30] The

---

[28]No doubt the author himself is Jewish. He speaks out of the full tradition of Judaism, as did Jesus. He is, however, making the claim that the prophetic word has been fulfilled in Jesus and that the church or the followers of Christ are the Israel of God. It is in this sense an inner-Jewish dialogue.

[29]L. Goppelt, *Der Erste Petrusbrief*, 81f.

[30]K. G. Kuhn, "The Concept of Holiness in Judaism," in *The Theological Dictionary of the New Testament* I, 97-100.

word "sanctification" is used because of its central place and purpose in the cult of Israel; it connotes the purifying and cleansing of a people and setting them apart for service to God.[31] The reference to "hope" and "inheritance" links the new Christians to the hope and heritage of Israel. To refer to the new Christians as "exiles of the dispersion" is to link them with the exiles of Israel and with the Jewish dispersion at the time of writing. The story of Israel is part of their story.[32]

As Christians they now also share in the sufferings of God's people. They are suffering (1:6-7) the way God's people have suffered as aliens and exiles in Egypt, in Babylon and now under Rome. It is a story of suffering but it also contains a message of liberation and hope. The suffering, as in the past, is for a season only (1:7) and is a time of testing to show forth the genuineness of the faith. The prophetic word (1:10-12) serves to remind them of the larger purpose of God's redemption and is a confirmation of the gospel proclaimed to them by the apostles (1:12).

The author's abundant use of scripture and his understanding of the new events in Christ in terms of the Old Testament indicate how strongly he regards Christians as part of the people of God. This is particularly evident in 1 Peter 2:4-10.[33] The stone that the builders rejected (Psalm 118:22) has become the chief cornerstone (Isaiah 28:16), the head of the church (Colossians 1:18).[34] The spiritual house promised to David as an ongoing reign is fulfilled in the coming into being of the church as the ongoing people of God. They are to be the people of God, the spiritual house, a holy priesthood offering spiritual sacrifices to God. They are called to be the church.

---

[31] O. Procksch, "*hagios* in the NT," in *The Theological Dictionary of the New Testament* I, 100-115.

[32] J. H. Elliott has shown how these terms describe the plight of Christians as actual aliens and exiles in the Roman Empire, *A Home for the Homeless*, 21-58, but this does not exhaust the meaning of these terms. The author of 1 Peter is using them to call to mind that the people of God have always been such strangers and exiles in the world.

[33] Whereas earlier the singular form of the exhortations was used, in 2:4-10 the plural is used. The attention has shifted from the individual to the community.

[34] A detailed study of 1 Peter 2:4-10 is given by J. H. Elliott in *The Elect and the Holy* (Leiden: E. J. Brill, 1966).

Words which described the people of God in the Old
Covenant now also encompass the people of God in Christ.[35]
They are a chosen race, a royal priesthood, a holy nation, God's
own people. They are set aside, sanctified or made holy so that
they may declare the deeds of God who called them to be God's
people (2:9-10).

Be Holy as God Is Holy

The focus in 1 Peter 1:13-2:10 is on the character of God
as a shared identity with the people. Who they are determines
how they will live. This is expressed both negatively and positively. Negatively, it is stated in terms of nonconformity to the world.
They are to "let the time that is past suffice for doing what the
Gentiles like to do . . . "(4:3); they are to leave what they once
were and now are not; they are no longer to be conformed to
the structures of the world (1:14).[36] A change has taken place.
They now live out of a totally different orientation. In their
former life they were no people. Few constraints influenced their
behaviour and no particular story informed their lives. Now that
is different because they have become the people of God and are
informed by the story of God's people and by the character of
the God they serve.

Positively, the readers are exhorted to be holy as God is
holy (1:15-16). The exhortation is taken from the Holiness Code
of Israel (Leviticus 17-26). It is clear that God is holy not only
in some characteristics but in his basic character or nature. God
alone is holy, hence set apart from all the rest of creation. The
very name of God is holy (Exodus 3:5).

At the same time, that which is set aside for God's use or
in God's service is also holy, for example, the altar and the
tabernacle (Exodus 29:37, 44). That which God sanctifies is holy
for sanctification comes from the Holy Spirit. Persons called into
the service of God, such as the priest and the king, were

---

[35]They are not called a "new" people of God in distinction from past people
of God. Rather they are seen as incorporated into the people of God.

[36]This is in harmony with Paul's exhortation in Romans 12:1. These are the
only two occurrences of the word in the New Testament.

dedicated to God. In like manner, a whole people was sanctified by God to be God's people at the time of the giving of the covenant (Exodus 19:14). They now were "separated unto God," which is the root meaning of the term holy.

God gave the law to the people so that they might know what would lead to life and what would lead to death. At the same time, God promised to be their God; God promised to be there for them and to will life for them. First he had set them free (exodus) so that they could freely choose to do God's will. The people committed themselves to do all that the Lord commanded (Exodus 19:8). As they did so, they were separated from the rest of society. They became a holy people and were no longer conformed to the world—to their former ways—but were dedicated to God. They became God's own people (Deuteronomy 7:6, 1 Peter 2:9), a people sanctified by God for himself.

It is not that the people earned this holiness through their deeds. It is rather that they were chosen and sanctified, made holy or separated unto God. Consequently, they began to manifest the character of God in their life together as a people. So it is in 1 Peter. God has elected them and sanctified them unto obedience to Jesus Christ (1:2). God has declared them holy by calling them out of their former ways to be wholly dedicated to God. They are now a different people. It is not something that they will become but something they already are in Christ. As a sanctified people they are to be holy as God is holy.

It is of course possible for these people to live contrary to their nature and to betray or contradict through their deeds who they are. This is why they must be exhorted to be in daily living what they already are. The concern is to manifest truthfully to others who they are and have become through the grace of God.

There are actually four imperatives in the 1 Peter 1:13-25 passage, all of which can be paraphrased in the admonition "be holy ones also" (1:16). The first imperative indicates that they are to set their hopes fully on the grace that is coming to them at the revelation of Jesus Christ. It is clear from 1:7 and 4:13 that this refers to the parousia, the time when the salvation given in Jesus will be fully revealed. But they are already to live this new life in Christ. They are even now to be God's people and thus to

be God-like. The first exhortation is contained in the second: to
be holy as God is holy. "As he who called you is holy, be holy
yourselves in all your conduct" (1:15).

The third imperative is similarly grounded in the being of
God. If God is one who judges impartially, they are to conduct
themselves accordingly (1:17). Their conduct is to be in harmony
with who God is and how God relates to humankind.

The fourth imperative, to love one another (1:22), is based
on their obedience to the truth of God, on their obedience to
the revealed will of God as received by them in the tradition. In
this tradition the love of God and the selfless love of Christ have
been revealed. They are now admonished to be like God and like
Christ in character. Thus all the imperatives in 1 Peter 1:13-25
go back to the basic exhortation, the basic ethic: they are to
manifest the character of God in daily living.

The exhortation to be holy as God is holy is applied by the
author to persons individually, each in his or her own life (1:13-
2:3) but also, and especially, corporately (2:4-10). The corporate
Christian community is the author's ultimate concern. They are
to be a spiritual house offering themselves to God.[37] But the
invitation to holiness is not without explicit content. In fact, it
is God's holiness which becomes the model for God's people as
the author spells out the details of the Christian life.

Christians in a Hostile Society

The *Haustafel*

The main theme of the letter of 1 Peter is focused in the
Haustafel (2:11-3:12). What has been said so far in the letter is
preparatory. The *Haustafel* itself is shaped by a specific problem:
how are Christians to live amongst a hostile population? It is
addressed to those who are being persecuted and focuses
particularly on the plight of the Christian slave who is, no doubt,
in the most helpless and seemingly powerless situation.

---

[37]In other parts of the New Testament as well as in 1 Peter the material
offering in the temple is replaced with the spiritual offering of the body (Romans
12:1; Hebrew 10:5-10; 1 Peter 2:5). See O. Procksch, "*hagios* in the NT," 108.

Early in the mission to the gentiles, the apostles would begin by preaching in the synagogue. It is here that well-to-do gentiles, Godfearers attending the synagogue, would convert to Christianity. Oftentimes the whole household would accept the faith together (Acts 10:2; 16:33). Thus a house church would be formed. The house church in turn would offer hospitality to slaves and servants travelling on behalf of other houses. As a result, persons who converted to Christianity would need to return to their own houses which were not Christian and which in time became hostile to such Christians.[38] The *Haustafel* speaks to the latters' situation and plight.

The *Haustafel* is organized in an "a, b, b, a" pattern. It begins with a general exhortation (2:11-17) followed by two specific focused exhortations (2:18-25; 3:1-7), then returns to a general exhortation to all (3:8-12). The counterparts to those addressed—masters, husbands, wives—are not mentioned because they do not belong to the people of God.[39] It is because of their hostile attitude that problems have arisen for the Christians.

The General Exhortation

The general exhortation (2:11-17) is given in two parts. The first has to do with nonconformity to the world and makes reference to maintaining good conduct among the gentiles (2:11-12). The readers are reminded once more that they are exiles and aliens in the midst of people who are intolerant toward them. Since they are God's people they should refrain from responding to this situation the way they were accustomed to, that is, by fighting back in kind. To act that way would be self-defeating,[40] and a denial of who they are in Christ.

Rather, they are to maintain good conduct among the gentiles. They are not to withdraw from the problem but to meet it with conduct that befits who they are as God's people. That is

---

[38]Some of this has now been documented by Klauck, *Hausgemeinde und Hauskirche im frühen Christentum*, but it still needs to be applied more directly to the situation in Asia Minor.

[39]In Colossians 3:18-4:1 and in Ephesians 5:21-6:9 husbands and masters are included because they are Christian.

[40]The term *stratuomai* is a military term and is translated as "war against the soul" in the Revised Standard Version Bible.

really to be their basic concern: not to betray who they are, but to live truthful, transparent lives before those who see them as wrongdoers (2:12).

The second part of the general exhortation (2:13-17) is given in a sequence of five exhortations. (It is a sad commentary on the church that it has by and large heard only the first of these.) The first exhortation is determined by what could be considered an entirely unjust situation. Christians live in a society where the very "order" of society not only fails to recognize them, but actually sees them as "wrongdoers." This is not an accident. It is so because of who they are: strangers and exiles, people of God.

How are they to live in this kind of structured society? They are told to "be subject" to every human institution.[41] Are they to do so because they have no power over the structures of society in the first place? Any power they have to change the structure could come only in the way it was suggested in the first general exhortation: through the providence of God. Thus the writer could have given this as a reason: "The point is, you have no power, so be subject!" But he doesn't, because, in fact, they are not without power. The author exhorts them to be subject out of Christian conviction,[42] out of the knowledge that they are God's people in the world, out of obedience to God who is sovereign over all.

What is enjoined here, however, is not to be *obedient* to the human institutions of order, but to be *subject* to them. Obedience belongs to God and to Christ alone,[43] never to the world or its structures. However, to be subject is to recognize that these structures of order, which are intended to respect what the world considers to be right, have power over all people. Christians

---

[41]The term *ktisis* is to be interpreted broadly to include every human institution. It is clear from the reference to the emperor and to the task of encouraging the good and restraining the evil that institutions of order are intended.

[42]It is a given in this setting that all aliens and sojourners were subject to the emperor, but they are now encouraged to be subject "for the Lord's sake," that is, willingly.

[43]"Obedience" in 1 Peter is always spoken of in relation to God or Christ, never in relation to those who are over them in society. In 1 Peter 3:6 it is used of Sarah in her relation to Abraham, but this is a reference to an Old Testament story and represents a relationship in the same faith.

cannot pretend that they live in a separate material world, or that the world will necessarily change to accommodate them. They are to be subject not because they have to, not because they could not fight back, but because they belong to God, and want to do God's will. God in divine providence has seen fit to call people out of the world, but in doing so has not destroyed the world. Rather, it is precisely through the faithful that God wishes to save the world from self-destruction.

Equally significant is the second exhortation: to do good or to do what is right (2:15). This is the counterpart to being subject. This is what gives them as Christians power in situations where they seemingly have no power. They are simply to be the people of God and do what is right or just, because God is righteous. This action is powerful because God can use it to bring to silence the ignorance of foolish people (2:15); God can use it to bring to an end the false notions of right and wrong that now govern the structures. Acting rightly in even the worst situations is powerful and can hasten the opportunity for God's redemptive activity. Christians often do not know how powerful they are when they do what is right, thereby demonstrating the truth of God.

The fact that the Christian is exhorted to do good already implies that Christians are free and responsible persons. In the third exhortation they are called to live as free persons (2:16). Christians have been set free, redeemed by the blood of Christ (1:18) and are now called upon to use their freedom responsibly. Freedom can be used for evil, but to do so would be a betrayal of who they are, a betrayal of their life in Christ. They might think they are not free, but they are, despite the power of the structures of false order over their lives. As free persons they are exhorted to act responsibly.

Given who they are, the only thing that makes sense is for them to live as God's servants. This is the fourth exhortation (2:16). They have been separated from the world, sanctified by God's spirit, and now they are to live as God's servants. No more and no less could be expected of the people of God.

Finally, they are exhorted to honour all people, including the emperor (2:17). The emperor represents the people who are in positions of power in the structures of society. Christians are to honour all persons, even those who exercise power over them and may make life painful for them as well as those who are potentially the enemy. Towards fellow Christians they are to show love; to God they are to show the respect (fear) that is due God alone. Again the exhortation is for them to be who they are as God's people, to be no respecters of persons (1:17).

In the past, this general exhortation has been interpreted far too exclusively as speaking about the relationship of Christians to the state. It does include that relationship, but it encompasses much more. The exhortation is a general statement about how to live within the structures of order in society. By such structures of order, each society seeks to encourage what is right and to restrain what is evil. What is considered to be good or evil, however, is not to be equated with what the Christian holds to be right and wrong. It is because of this dichotomy that the Christian walk may be termed as evil rather than as good. The reference to the emperor as supreme and to the governors under the emperor serve to make the reader aware of a complexity of interrelated structures of order—structures that govern social, political, economic, educational and all other aspects of life. One such structure is the institution of slavery.

The Admonition to the Slaves

The admonition to the slaves (2:18-25) serves as an ethical paradigm for the author. It illustrates what it means to be holy as God is holy and to be subject as Jesus was subject. The author knows how his general admonition would be understood. It would be seen as applying to those who are free, but hardly to those who are slaves. Anyone could see that for the slave to be truly responsible as a Christian would place his life in danger. For the slave to act out of personal responsibility would bring disorder into the house and would be seen as a threat to society. Such action would promptly be stopped by the master. The author knows this line of thinking and thus addresses the slave as a free and responsible person.

The slave is told to be subject (3:18) not only to the

Christian master but also to the perverse[44] one who would not give him fair consideration. The author has in mind a genuine, voluntary response to the master and not one of reluctant compliance. If carried out this exhortation could well include suffering. Slaves were no strangers to suffering. Often they suffered for their own evil deeds; at other times because of the injustice of the master.[45] Christian slaves are advised to have the right attitude of respect for the master (2:18) and to make sure they do what is right. If they do what is right and then suffer for it, they have God's approval (2:19). The general exhortation applies even to slaves who are to be subject, to do good, to live as responsible servants (slaves) of God and to honour and respect those who have power over them.

But the author amplifies the admonition in an interesting way. It is precisely to suffering that they have been called. This is what it means to be holy as God is holy and to be the people of God in the world (1:15-16). That is why those who suffer for doing what is right have God's approval (2:20). Christian slaves are opposed as wrongdoers precisely because the world feels threatened when the "powerless" begin to act as responsible persons. Their actions upset the system! But Christians may have no other choice but to suffer if they are to be Christian in the world. That is what the writer is saying "to this you have been called" (2:21). It comes with the territory. It is part and parcel of what it means to be God's people in the world. Thus to be holy as God is holy is in fact to be subject as Jesus was subject. This is basic to the exhortation.

Be Subject as Jesus Was Subject

The heart of the message of 1 Peter to the slave is a

---

[44]*skoliois* (crooked, perverse) is to be taken together with *adikós* (unjust) in 2:19.

[45]The lot of the slave in Roman society has received considerable attention of late. See M. I. Findley, *Ancient Slavery and Modern Theology* (London: Chatto and Windus, 1980); Henneke Guelzow, *Christentum und Sklaverei in den ersten drei Jahrhunderten* (Bonn: Rudolf Habelt Verlag, 1969); Gerhard Kehnscherper, *Die Stellung der Bibel und der alten christlichen Kirche zur Sklaverei* (Halle: Max Niemeyer Verlag, 1957); Keith Hopkins, *Conquerors and Slaves* (Cambridge: Cambridge University Press, 1978); Thomas Wiedemann, *Greek and Roman Slavery* (London: Croom Helm, 1981).

reference to the example of Jesus in 2:21-25.[46] The story of
Jesus' life, death and resurrection was all important to the
suffering Christian. Christ himself had been true to what the
slave was exhorted to be in the world. Jesus' life was an example
of how to live within the structures of society (2:21). In his
typical way, the writer lifts up as example those situations in
which Jesus could have fought back against his accusers and
prosecutors. Jesus could have worked toward a material kingdom—then his servants would have been called on to fight—but
he chose rather to be the servant (slave) of God (2:16), to suffer
and to give his life as a ransom for many (Mark 8:45). Jesus
could have called on legions of angels to protect him (Matthew
26:53), but he chose rather to remain subject to the powers that
be and to accept the way of suffering and death as a servant of
God. The author knows that, by pointing out that Jesus did not
respond in kind to those who reviled him, he would bring to
mind the whole story of Jesus' ministry and passion.

The author says it most powerfully in a poem which is
clearly set up in the form of a chiasm.[47] The two aorist passive
clauses at the beginning and end, "you have been called" (2:21)
and "you have been healed" (2:24), are related. So also are the
two *hina* clauses, "that you should follow in his steps" and "that
you might die to sin." In the middle are three *hōs* clauses (vv. 22,

---

[46]This is documented most clearly by Mary Schertz in a yet unpublished
article entitled "The Pursuit of Peace and the Rhetoric of Oppression: Nonretalia-
tion and the *Haustafeln* in 1 Peter" (March 1988). She sees 2:23 as the heart of
a chiastic poem in 2:21-24. The poem itself is central in the *Haustafel*.

[47]21 For to this you have been called,
  because Christ also suffered for you,
   leaving you an example,
    (*hina*) that you should follow in his steps.
22   (*hōs*) He committed no sins;
     no guile was found on his lips.
23   (*hōs*) When he was reviled, he did not revile in return.
    when he suffered, he did not threaten;
     but he trusted to him who judges justly.
24   (*hōs*) He himself bore our sins
     in his body on the tree,
    (*hina*) that we might die to sin
    and live to righteousness.
   By his wounds we have been healed.
25 For you were straying like sheep, but have now returned to the
  shepherd and guardian of your souls.

23, 24) suggesting, as Mary Schertz has argued, that the *hōs* clause in the middle "when he suffered, he did not threaten" (2:23) is the central concern of the poem, the illustration of what it means to be subject to the structures of order that consider the righteous to be wrongdoers. This relates directly to the treatment which Christian slaves received under perverse or unjust masters (2:15-19).

Jesus was subject the way Christian slaves were to be subject. He was free and used his freedom to be a servant of God. He did no sin but rather did what was right. And he suffered unjust treatment under the powers of the world. But he also knew that God was just and that God was in charge of human history. Jesus was free to suffer because he related to God and God's reign. In the end all angels, authorities and powers would be subject to God (3:22). Therefore, the only way to appreciate and to fully know what being subject meant was to tell the story of Jesus who lived the life of obedience to God. He was subject to the powers of the structures, yet committed himself to God who judges justly. This is also what it meant for the slave to be what he was in Christ.

Wives Be Subject

The general exhortation applies also to wives whose husbands are not Christian. Wives of men who are heads of households would have experienced this in one way; wives of husbands who are members of a larger household would have experienced it in another way. The wife of a slave, where such a relationship was allowed by the master, would represent still another case. It is most likely that the first or second instance is the one considered by the author.

The head of the house determined to what extent religious liberty would be permitted and which deities would be allowed to be worshipped. Worship of a deity which would threaten the order of the whole house, and therefore society, was forbidden. This explains why, if slaves and wives become Christians, they would threaten the order of the house. For slaves or women to act as free persons and do what was right but refuse to do what was wrong would bring a quick response. Women are thus not allowed to speak, to propagate the faith or to manifest public forms of worship.

Here too the admonition is to "be subject." The same concern remains: they are to act in such a way (2:12) that God can use their chaste behaviour to win their non-believing husbands. They are to cultivate not the outward adorning but the inner hidden character, the gentle spirit. They are to be what they are in Christ. Their character is to manifest Christ. It is illustrated in the way Sarah obeyed Abraham. They are, in any case, to do what is right, to let nothing terrify them, but rather to fear God. They are to keep the faith. They are addressed as responsible persons and given power to be Christian.

The Christian husband is addressed in even fewer words. He is obviously not the counterpart to the wife in 1 Peter 3:1-6 because there the husband does not obey the word. One of two cases has to be considered. It is usually understood in terms of the husband of a Christian wife. Then it speaks of their mutual relationship as Christians (Colossians 3:18f; Ephesians 5:21ff). In such a case the husband is to live considerately with his wife and to recognize that they are joint heirs of the grace of life (3:7).[48] However, it is more likely that his wife was not Christian. This made it as difficult for him in the non-Christian house as it was for the Christian wife in the same larger household. The wife then is overtly opposed to his religion because she has not followed her husband into the Christian faith.

The temptation for the husband here would be to place pressure on his non-Christian wife the way the non-Christian husband did on his Christian wife. But to act thus would be to betray who he was as a Christian. Such use of power, force and compulsion is no longer open to him in Christ. He is thus admonished to live considerately with his wife and not to exploit the fact that she is the "weaker" person in that context. He is to suffer and bear the situation of possible loss of face, yet honour his wife in spite of the possibility that she is exploiting this situation against him. Interpreted in this way it is easier to understand the clause "in order that your prayers may not be

---

[48]Carl D. Gross, "Are the Wives of 1 Peter 3:7 Christians?" *Journal for the Study of the New Testament* 35 (February 1989): 89-96.

hindered" (3:7).[49] To act in a way contradictory to the general exhortation would be counterproductive and would not allow his prayers to be answered.

In these specific exhortations it is clear that every person who has been born anew to a living hope in Christ is a free and responsible person. All are equally responsible. No one can say that circumstances do not permit him or her to be Christian. They belong to the people of God; all are to live as God's people in the world.

The General Exhortation

The final section (1 Peter 3:8-12) of the *Haustafel* is again a general exhortation. In this case the author gives some character traits that they are to strive for and learn. These traits relate to the spirit of unity, love for fellow Christians, a tender heart and a humble mind (3:8). All are in harmony with the character of Jesus. It is again underlined that Christians are to be like Christ in not returning evil for evil and reviling for reviling (3:9). They are called to bless rather than curse (3:9 and 2:23) so that they may be blessed of God.

The emphasis is placed on Christian virtues which express the character of God as revealed in Christ. These virtues need to be learned and exercised in the community of faith. Christians are to be God-like and Christ-like in character. This character will then be expressed in deeds and in words in many different but specific situations.

In typical fashion the author closes the exhortation with a reference to the Psalms: "Come . . . I will teach you the fear of the Lord" (Psalm 34:11) ending with the words, "When the righteous cry for help the Lord hears and delivers them out of all their troubles" (Psalm 34:17). This is an amplification of what the author had in mind when earlier he exhorted them to conduct themselves with fear throughout the time of their exile (1:17). It is a fitting close to and summary of the *Haustafel*: turn away from evil in word and deed; do what is right; seek peace and justice and bring your prayers to God whose eyes are upon

---

[49]The plural here refers not to husband and wife but to Christian husbands who alone are addressed.

the righteous.

The Eschatological Perspective

As mentioned earlier, 1 Peter offers a unique approach to
ethics which is often misunderstood. This approach also changes
the way the matter of eschatology is put. The ethic of subjection
is not based on utility, nor on the gradual development of
goodness towards perfection via progressive improvements of
social structures. 1 Peter 3:13-4:11 develops an eschatological
base for the *Haustafel*[50] which brings the ethic of subjection into
proper perspective by linking the future reign of God to the
reign of the suffering Christ and his followers. Significantly, the
essential link between our obedience and God's triumphant reign
is the same as the link between the suffering of Christ (cross)
and the blessing of God to the faithful (resurrection). The way
of the future reign of God is characterized by God's creative
blessedness, not by laws of history rooted in power struggles of
the dominant ones.

First Peter 3:13-17 is transitional and reiterates what has
already been said in the general exhortation (1 Peter 2:11-17).
The admonition to do what is right (2:15) frames the paragraph
3:13-17. Suffering for what is right (2:15, 20) is again mentioned
(3:14). The readers are told to sanctify or reverence Christ ("fear"
God in 2:17). Now they are also told to be prepared to give an
answer to those who call them to account and challenge the
hope that is in them (3:15). They are not to be hesitant in giving
an apology for the faith which is, after all, the truth of God.
They have already been told to proclaim the "deeds of him who
called you out of darkness into his marvellous light" (2:9).[51] Yet

---

[50]We cannot give detailed attention to the remaining two sections of 1 Peter
but we do need to show how 1 Peter 3:13-4:11 relates to the *Haustafel* and how
1 Peter 4:12-5:14 relates to the theme of the letter as a whole.

[51]Elliott and Balch argue whether a mission strategy is suggested in 1 Peter.
Elliott sees such a strategy given in 1 Peter 2:9, "that you may show forth him
who has called you out of darkness into his marvellous light." Balch counters this
thesis. There is a sense in which Elliott is correct. Christians are to proclaim the
story of God's people; they are to be Christian in their conduct and thus witness
to the grace of God. But it is God who uses their words and deeds to bring

even this has to be done in harmony with who they are as God's people. They are to respond in meekness or gentleness and with reverence or fear (2:17) and in good conscience. Here, as in 2:12, it is indicated that God may use this way of responding to put those who abuse them to shame (2:6).

The appropriateness of the *Haustafel* ethic is embodied in Christ (3:18-22). Humans responded to Jesus by putting him to death. This was the most that human sin could do. But Jesus died as the righteous for the unrighteous. He was subject to the structures of order by doing what was right before God. Consequently he was put to death in the flesh but made alive in the spirit (3:18). Sin could not destroy life. By obeying God, he participated in the blessing of life, not death. Jesus went this way in order to invite all into the way of obedience to God, so that all might live. This is the blessing God gives to the faithful. Since this is the truth of God, in the final analysis all angels, authorities and powers will be subject to the power of God. Jesus, the Son of God, was subject to the authorities and powers here on earth because of his obedience to God even unto death. Hence, in the end all powers will be subject to him (3:22). This is what provides hope for those who even now suffer.

Because God's people already know of the victory over evil through Christ's suffering they are to prepare themselves for the same (4:1-6). To be Christian may bring suffering, but it will also bring sanctification, freedom from sin (4:1) and new life (4:2). The world will not understand Christians who no longer conform to society's norms, hence will abuse them (4:4). But non-Christians will need to give an account to God for their actions (4:5) where they will be dealt with impartially (1:17; 4:5). This is why the gospel was preached even to those who have already died so that they might share in the sufferings of Christ and through him "live in the Spirit like God" (4:6).[52]

---

people to God. The strategy, if any, belongs to God. The focus is on God and on Jesus Christ and not on what Christians are to accomplish. In that sense Balch may be right in saying the focus is not on a strategy for mission work. See John H. Elliott, "1 Peter, Its Situation and Strategy: A Discussion with David Balch" and the literature mentioned in Charles H. Talbert, ed. *Perspectives on First Peter* (Macon, GA: Mercer University Press, 1986), 61-78.

[52]An excellent exegetical article on the difficulties posed by 1 Peter 3:18-22

The coming end of all things adds a sobering perspective to the ethic (4:7-11). If their prayers can at all be answered Christians need to remain true to who they are. At this point the character traits mentioned at the end of the *Haustafel* are reintroduced. Love and ungrudging hospitality are important. Each person has received a variety of gifts (4:10) which are rooted in the very being of God. Therefore, by being good stewards of these gifts, God will be glorified. To Christ be the glory (4:11).

The Final Exhortation

The third major section of 1 Peter (4:12-5:14) returns to the theme of suffering from a different perspective. The concern is no longer how to live in a hostile society or how to respond to the persecutors. Now the theme is the suffering itself and how to respond to it. How is one to be Christian in the community of faith in light of the "fiery ordeals" that are yet to come?

First of all, they are to see suffering as the normal outcome of being holy as God is holy and of being subject as Jesus was subject. They are not asked to seek suffering. Yet suffering is not something strange or foreign to the church (4:12). It occurs when the world sees the Christian walk as an evil to be overcome. Secondly, they are to rejoice in their suffering (1:6) since they share the sufferings of Christ (Colossians 1:24) and will share in the victory (glory) of Christ (4:13). If they suffer for the "name of Christ" (4:14) or for being "Christian" (4:16), they will be blessed of God (4:11). But they will not be blessed if they suffer as wrongdoers (4:15).

They can have confidence in their walk because judgement has begun with the household of God (4:17). Those who belong to Christ have been sanctified by the Holy Spirit (1:2). By the grace of God they have been born anew to a living hope (1:3). They have been made righteous, not through their works but

is given by R. T. France, "Exegesis in Practice: Two Samples," in I. Howard Marshall, ed. *New Testament Interpretation: Essays on Principles and Methods*, (Grand Rapids, MI: Eerdmans Publishing Company, 1977), 252-281.

through the grace of God, hence have become obedient to Christ
and share his suffering. If those who have been separated from
the world and its worldly ways are declared righteous by the
grace of God, what will be the end of those who have chosen to
reject the word that leads to life (1:23-25)? This question posed
by Proverbs 11:31 is left to speak its own message. Such people
are most to be pitied. Christians, however, are to suffer according
to God's will and entrust their souls to a faithful God (4:14).

But the church represents not only a "spiritual" house but
also a structure of order. The church is not taken out of the
world. It too will have structures that may be contradictory to
what it means to be God's people. This issue is addressed in 1
Peter 5:1-14.

The writer first of all appeals to his apostleship (5:1). He
speaks as a witness of the sufferings of Christ, as a fellow elder,
as one who will share in the glory yet to be revealed (5:1). As
such he exhorts the church in terms that relate to the *Haustafel*.
They are to "lead the flock" ("be servants of God," 2:16); "not by
constraint but willingly" ("live as free men," 2:16; 4:7); "not for
shameful gain but eagerly" ("passions which war against the soul,"
2:11); and, most importantly, "not as domineering" but by being
"examples" to the flock, that is, as those who themselves are
subject to and servants (slaves) of the community of faith.

The main danger in the church is not for those who are
subject but for those who are in leadership. The danger is that
they will forget who they are; that they will import the ways of
the world into the governance of the church and impose
themselves on the church. In asking them to be examples to the
members of the church the author is asking the elders to be to
the church what Christ is to them as illustrated in 1 Peter 2:21-
25. They are to be subject to the church (or the structures of the
church) as Jesus exemplified. All domineering ways, and all
attempts (or efforts) to determine agenda from above are gone.
Christians are not to lord it over others, not even in the church.

In the church there should be mutual subordination. The
term "likewise" and the phrase "all of you" in 1 Peter 5:5 indicate
that this applies to everyone in the church—all are to be subject.
The policy is stated in terms of older (elder) and younger

patterns of organization known to Judaism[53] but it actually refers to the relationship between the elders and the rest of the members of the church.

They are not only to be mutually subject to each other but also to manifest Christian humility on the basis of Job 22:29. All are to recognize that they are subject to God who governs all of history, who looks after their future (5:6) and who cares for them (5:7).

The last admonitions (5:8-10) recall the seriousness of the conflict. They are in the world, under pressure to conform to the world, but they are to resist the temptation to return to their former ways (5:8). They could avoid the sufferings of the moment, but doing so would be a denial of who they are in Christ. This they are to resist (5:9). The suffering they experience now will be only for a little while (1:6, 7); it will be shared by many fellow Christians (Revelation 6:11) but God will strengthen them and establish them (5:10). The God of all grace will be with them in all eternity. In the end the writer can say, "Peace to all of you that are in Christ" (5:14).

Theological Implications

Be Subject

The admonition to "be subject" in the *Haustafel* of 1 Peter has become a "stone of stumbling" for most of the church today. It is rejected by those who hold to a sweet, loving, spiritual and apolitical Jesus because it does not permit their belief in Jesus and their involvement in the world to be kept neatly separate. It is rejected by liberation movements because it does not allow for the degree of violence thought necessary to overcome oppression. It is rejected by feminists and egalitarians because it is seen as betraying the ethic of Jesus and Paul. But, above all, the ethic of the *Haustafel* has been rejected because it has not been seen as

---

[53]The exhortation in terms of younger and older (elders) is characteristic of the Qumran community. It was taken to be the proper structure for the community of God's people. It is also used in the Pastoral Epistles. See David Schroeder, "Anhang," in *Haustafeln*, 188ff.

being at the heart of the gospel. This is because the gospel itself is read with false assumptions.

When the *ruling* model of equality[54] is used, it does indeed appear as if the husband rules over the wife and the master over the slave; then it does appear as if the values of society and its structures are affirmed and the Christian ethic is negated. But this is not the model of the *Haustafel* of 1 Peter. The model used is precisely that of Christ. As Christ manifested the character of God so Christians are called on to manifest the same character in the world. The model of the *Haustafel* is the Suffering Servant of Isaiah as demonstrated in Jesus' life and death. He came to serve and to give his life a ransom for many. On this model all are servants; all are subject to one another. There is no more ruling over each other in the church or outside the church. But there is equality; there is mutuality and the gifts of each person (4:10) are honoured.

The way in which Jesus was subject to the structures of order in the world is the way in which God works in the world. God is like that, for God is revealed in Christ. Not to see this is to misunderstand the nature of God's sovereignty. God is sovereign Lord in the way that Jesus is sovereign. God acts in harmony with God's own being and so chooses not to act in a despotic, high-handed way with creation. God does not come as a king lording it over people and compelling them to do God's bidding. God comes rather as the righteous king of the prophet Isaiah, as the Suffering Servant. He comes to us in Jesus in whom we see how the sovereign God of the universe acts.[55] Jesus subjected himself to the structures of order; he suffered and died, the righteous for the unrighteous. Through Jesus God acts in character with God's being. This is why the reference to Christ's suffering is at the heart of the *Haustafel*.

Only as we understand more fully the scandal of the cross

---

[54]This is the prevailing notion where equality between women and men is discussed. Who is in authority? Who has power over others? Who is in executive positions? Who rules over people?

[55]What we call the judgements of God then need to be seen in a different light. The judgements of sin reveal the character of the sinner, and the saving acts of God reveal the character of God in that God uses even judgements to draw people to God. It is really the truth and the love of God once revealed that judge all falsehood and all evil.

can we appreciate the theology of the *Haustafel*. What it means to be what we are in Christ has not changed. Jesus said, "If any man would come after me, let him deny himself and take up his cross and follow me" (Mark 8:34).

Structures of Order

It is simply a given that there are structures of order in society. Each particular society calls new structures into being because God has given humans dominion over what God has created. The structures of order are in this sense human creations (*ktisis*). As humans we order the world by naming what we value and despise. On the basis of these values we act and call into being a material and cultural world; we create a structure of order that encourages what we hold to be good and discourages what we have named as evil. No clan or nation is thus without such structures of order.[56]

The "good" sought by any such human structure of order need not be the good that is revealed in Christ; it need not be true; it need not participate in God. When Christians act in harmony with who they are in Christ they may well act contrary to what is held to be right and good in that society. In this situation Christians are to be *obedient* to Christ and *subject* to the structures of order. All Christians must know that there may come times when civil disobedience will be their only option if they remain true to what they are in Christ. Every structure of order calls into being some form of civil religion, or a set of beliefs that justifies the values enshrined in that particular structure of order. But Christians cannot serve two masters. To follow Christ will mean for them to take up the cross. To follow Christ will mean for them to be what they are in Christ and to commit themselves to God who judges justly. This is the way it always has been. This is why the story of God's people and the story of God working in and through Christ has to be told over and over again.

---

[56] It is important to recognize the interrelatedness of the structures of order. These structures include not only governments, but also other political, social, economic and educational aspects of society. Even the church as an institution represents such a structure of order.

Conclusion

The ethic of the *Haustafel* in 1 Peter is an ethic rooted in God. It assumes as basic the revelation of God's character in God's people. This revelation or story has shaped and formed the people of God through the ages. This story has enabled the early followers of Jesus to recognize him as the Messiah, the Prince of Peace and the Suffering Servant of God (Isaiah 9 and 53). These disciples believed that Jesus manifested the very character of God and did the work of God here on earth. Consequently, as followers of Jesus, they saw themselves as full participants in the peoplehood of God. Even those who earlier were not the people of God (the gentiles) could now see themselves as God's people.

This identification of the people with God became possible because of God's identification with the people in Christ Jesus. Jesus was the new Adam. He revealed what a human life lived in full obedience to God was like. The way Jesus lived his earthly life became normative for his followers who became his disciples. The way in which Jesus lived in the world and the character which he manifested in his earthly ministry exemplified the character of God. Jesus went the way of the cross, the way of suffering and death in order to be and to remain a faithful servant of God. But Jesus also called on his followers to take up the cross and follow him in life.[57] The way in which Jesus rejected power and might, dominion and the way of the world, is a model for those who would follow after him. The way Jesus was subject to the authorities of the world and yet did what was right is a model for all Christians and for all who seek life.

---

[57]See Harry Huebner, "Christology: Discipleship and Ethics" in the forthcoming publication of the papers presented at the Study Conference on Christology, Normal, Illinois, August 4-6, 1989.

II. Historical Theology

Adolf Ens*

THEOLOGY OF THE HERMENEUTICAL COMMUNITY IN ANABAPTIST-MENNONITE THOUGHT**

At first glance this theme does not appear to have been a prominent one in sixteenth-century Anabaptism. One does not expect the expression "hermeneutical community" to have been used by Anabaptist writers, nor, given the general absence of a formal theology among them, for them to have developed the concept as a clear theological position. Most secondary treatments of Anabaptist hermeneutics are preoccupied with other aspects, such as the relationship of the Old and New Testaments, of Word and Spirit and of outer and inner word, and give only marginal, if any, attention to the hermeneutical community.[1] Historical evaluations of community in Anabaptist thought, on the other hand, rarely even mention biblical interpretation as one of its collective functions.

Nevertheless, there was a remarkably pervasive consensus among most of the leaders of the movement in the sixteenth century about the importance of all members of the church studying the scriptures and participating in the process of understanding their meaning in and for the contemporary church. According to George H. Williams, "There is one principle or practice—group study and reverent disputation—common to the entire Radical Reformation which goes far to explain the spirit

---

*Adolf Ens is Associate Professor of History and Theology, Canadian Mennonite Bible College, Winnipeg, Manitoba.

**The author wishes to thank Abe Dueck, Academic Dean, Mennonite Brethren Bible College, Winnipeg, Manitoba, and Harry Loewen, Professor of Mennonite Studies, University of Winnipeg, Winnipeg, Manitoba, for their critical responses to this essay at the Symposium.

[1]Walter Klaassen, "Anabaptist Hermeneutics: Presuppositions, Principles and Practice," in *Essays in Biblical Interpretation: Anabaptist-Mennonite Perspectives*, ed. Willard Swartley (Elkhart, IN: Institute of Mennonite Studies, 1984), 5-10, for example does not include it among his four "hermeneutical principles of Anabaptism" although "the community interprets" forms the bulk of his short section on "Anabaptist hermeneutics in practice."

of the movement as a whole."[2] This emphasis, furthermore, was given, in some cases quite overtly, over against other prevailing models of scriptural interpretation.

It may be helpful to identify briefly the contemporary hermeneutical "schools" to which Anabaptists had ready access, and against which they developed their own method.

First, the Protestant model is characterized by Robert Friedmann, perhaps a bit unfairly, as follows:

> The clergy had to study at theological schools in order to know how to expound the Scriptures. "Hear the sermon" was the prime requirement of a good Protestant, for "faith comes by hearing" (as Paul said); and only the learned minister is certified to expound Scriptures properly to the helpless layman.[3]

Whereas the Anabaptist understanding of community recognized the importance of leaders, including teachers, it was not inclined to acknowledge that kind of sharp division between clergy and laity.

Second, the Spiritualists tended to place too little emphasis on study. Included in Thomas Müntzer's sevenfold gift of the Spirit was "the reception of direct instruction from the Holy Spirit in the form of vision, dream, ecstatic utterance, or inspired exegesis."[4] Melchior Hofmann considered himself "in his oracular ecstasy authorized to interpret scripture and to resolve" even the complex contradictions involved in his exegetical principle of the two clefts.[5] Andreas Carlstadt, like Müntzer at the end, took the

---

[2]George Hunston Williams, *The Radical Reformation* (Philadelphia, PA: Westminster Press, 1962), 828.

[3]Robert Friedmann, *The Theology of Anabaptism: An Interpretation* (Scottdale, PA: Herald Press, 1973), 23.

[4]Williams, *The Radical Reformation*, 49.

[5]Ibid., 831. Hofmann held that the Old and New Testaments "were one from God, as two clefts constitute the one hoof of a clean cloven-hoofed beast" (Leviticus 11:3; Deuteronomy 14:6). All Old Testament events, according to this theory, are images to which happenings in the New Testament, or those yet to take place, correspond.

While Hofmann urges all "lovers of truth" to hold themselves "solely to the straightforward words of God in all simplicity," he quickly goes on to add that only those who have the "Key of David" (Isaiah 22:22) can understand the "cloven claws and horns." To explicate the scripture "is not for everybody—to unravel all such snarls and cables, to untie such knots—but only for those to whom God has

role of the Spirit to the extreme that the "outer witness" of scripture was not even required. "As far as I am concerned, I do not need the outward witness. I want to have the testimony of the Spirit within me, as it was promised by Christ."[6] Sebastian Franck, and perhaps other spiritualist leaders, also held direct revelation from the Spirit above the scriptures.

While the Anabaptists by no means minimized the importance of the Holy Spirit in the process of interpretation, they were clearly committed to the witness of the "outer word" of scripture which must be interpreted, not bypassed. Marpeck, according to William Klassen, held that "within the context of history the Holy Spirit is restricted to the use of external means, which are the antecedents of the real work of the Spirit just as the physical words of Christ served to prepare the way for the coming of the Spirit."[7] Study of the written word could thus not be avoided.

Third, the Roman Catholic model of the church, which arrived at a binding doctrine through the deliberations of a representative council, was more acceptable to Anabaptist thought.[8] However, because Rome held to the equal authority of tradition and scripture and prevented direct access of the majority of church members to either, two serious stumbling blocks were placed in the way of a ready acceptance of this process by Anabaptists.

Fourth, the model of public disputation, especially common in the Swiss Reformation, initially seemed promising. Where both sides agreed to the sole authority of the scriptures, and as long as the judges allowed all those who would agree to the basis of scripture alone free access to the debate, this process held great promise as a hermeneutical method. In Switzerland

---

given (the power)." "The Ordinance of God" (1530) in *Spiritual and Anabaptist Writers,* ed. George Hunston Williams and Angel M. Mergal (Philadelphia, PA: Westminster Press, 1957), 202-203.

[6]Quoted in Williams, *The Radical Reformation,* 823.

[7]William Klassen, *Covenant and Community: The Life, Writings and Hermeneutics of Pilgram Marpeck* (Grand Rapids, MI: Eerdmans Publishing Company, 1968), 72.

[8]Ben C. Ollenberger, "The Hermeneutics of Obedience: Reflections on Anabaptist Hermeneutics," in *Essays in Biblical Interpretation,* ed. Swartley, 48.

and the South German regions Anabaptists continued to participate in such disputations whenever possible as long as their opponents permitted them to do so.[9] The difficulty with this approach, as the usual designations of "disputation" and "debate" suggest, is that these conversations very often became polarized because of political vested interests. The central task of interpreting and understanding scripture was seriously undermined by this mixing of interests. Hence, in the end the disputation model too was found lacking.

The Congregation as Hermeneutical Community

Sola Scriptura

A commitment to the Reformation principle of scripture as the sole authority was shared by all Anabaptists.[10] But to call them biblicists, as if to imply that the rest of European Christendom was not, is misleading. In the sixteenth century everyone was a biblicist. As John Howard Yoder observes, "Even the spiritualists and rationalists took Bible authority for granted and used proof texts to make their points. Even when their point was the insufficiency of the letter of scripture, they proved it with a proof text."[11]

Whether the Anabaptists were "more radical and consistent in their application of the principle of sole Scriptural authority" than the Protestant reformers, who were "led at times by theological and practical considerations to depart from the strict teaching of scripture,"[12] is debatable. But that they repeatedly

---

[9]John Yoder, *Täufertum und Reformation in der Schweitz: I. Die Gespräche zwischen den Täufern und Reformatoren 1523-1538* (Weierhof: Mennonitischer Geschichtsverein, 1962), analyzes the first 15 years of those "conversations."

[10]It may be argued that some of the Melchiorite and Batenburger leaders increasingly depended on immediate revelation for their teaching and for the organization of their faith communities. In most cases, however, dream, vision or other direct enlightenment were attached to some passage of scripture which was thereby "properly" interpreted.

[11]John Howard Yoder, "The Hermeneutics of the Anabaptists," *Mennonite Quarterly Review* 41 (October 1967): 295.

[12]H.S. Bender, "Bible," in *Mennonite Encyclopedia*.

appealed to scripture as the sole authority for all matters of Christian faith and life has been amply documented.[13] Given this commitment to the central importance of scripture, its interpretation and application to the life of the Christian was of utmost importance to them. Their search, accordingly, was for a process of interpretation that would ensure correct understanding and proper application.

The Place of Scholarship

Since access to scripture had for so long been denied to the membership of the church, its interpretation had naturally been taken over (or retained) by the clergy and the scholars. In the minds of many, therefore, it was assumed that these were the only ones capable of understanding the Bible properly. Luther could indeed say, in one of his not infrequent rhetorical flights, that any German shepherd boy with the assistance of the Holy Spirit could interpret scripture better than the pope. But in his more considered statements Luther made it clear that only authorized persons could in fact be trusted with this task.[14]

In the Swiss regions, where the renaissance emphasis on a return to the sources was prominent, scholarly qualifications included knowledge of the original biblical languages and of

---

[13]See for example John Horsch, "Authority of the Scriptures," chapter in *Mennonites in Europe* (Scottdale, PA: Mennonite Publishing House, 1950); Bender, "Bible;" and John C. Wenger, "The Biblicism of the Anabaptists," in *The Recovery of the Anabaptist Vision*, ed. Guy F. Hershberger (Scottdale, PA: Herald Press, 1957).

[14]For expressions of Luther's rejection of the clergy-laity distinction see "The Freedom of a Christian" (1520), in *Martin Luther: Selections from His Writings*, ed. John Dillenberger (Garden City, NY: Doubleday and Company, 1961), 65; and "An Appeal to the Ruling Class of German Nationality" (1520), ibid., 407-408, 409. For his denunciation of Anabaptists and other "schismatic spirits" who have "no calling to the ministry," see his commentary on the Sermon on the Mount in *Luther's Works*, vol. 21, ed. Jaroslav Pelikan (Philadelphia, PA: Muehlenberg Press, 1960), 5, 63, and especially his "Von den Schleichern und Winkelpredigern" (1532), translated as "Infiltrating and Clandestine Preachers," ibid., vol. 40, ed. Conrad Bergendoff (Philadelphia, PA: Fortress Press, 1958), 383-94. "I have often said and still say, I would not trade my doctor's degree for all the world's gold. For I would surely in the long run lose courage and fall into despair if, as these infiltrators, I had taken these great and serious matters without call or commission," 387f.
Menno Simons occasionally complained about being called a *Winkelprediger*. See for example "The True Christian Faith" (1541), in *The Complete Writings of Menno Simons*, trans. Leonard Verduin, ed. John Christian Wenger (Scottdale, PA: Herald Press, 1974), 400; and "Reply to Gellius Faber" (1554), ibid., 674.

Latin.[15] Most Anabaptists, even most of their leaders, did not know Greek or Hebrew,[16] and rejected the idea that this was essential for understanding the Bible. Balthasar Hubmaier, perhaps the most complete scholar in their ranks, admitted a limited usefulness of such knowledge. "Although I do not despise the use of languages for the exposition of difficult passages of scripture, for the sunny, luminous words one needs neither tongue nor lung."[17] Since most of the Bible is clear and readily understood, Hubmaier rejected knowledge of Greek and Hebrew as prerequisites, for that would mean that "instead of the infallible pope and councils to interpret scriptures we must now wait for the learned experts who know three or four languages."[18]

There was indeed some suspicion among a number of Anabaptists that learning, or at least too much trust in learnedness, could hinder rather than help one to understand scripture. Marpeck, writing to Caspar Schwenckfeld (1544), warned that

> God captures the wisdom of the wise in their treachery; He entrusts His truth to the faithful and truly innocent ones but conceals it from the highly learned, wise, sly, and obstinately independent ones. . . . Such wisdom, with its artistry and mastery, presents itself to the Holy Spirit, as if the Holy Spirit could not instruct anyone except through artistry and wisdom.[19]

Like Hubmaier, Marpeck much preferred "true and faithful simp-

---

[15]Walter Klaassen, "The Bern Debate of 1538: Christ the Center of Scripture," *Mennonite Quarterly Review* 40 (April 1966): 151.

[16]Ludwig Hätzer and Hans Denck translated the prophets from Hebrew; Conrad Grebel and Felix Mantz had studied both Greek and Hebrew and were respected by Zwingli as scholars; those who had been priests or religious in the Catholic church knew at least rudimentary Latin.

[17]Balthasar Hubmaier, "Gespräch auf Zwingli's Taufbüchlein" (1525), quoted in Walter Klaassen, "Speaking in Simplicity: Balthasar Hubmaier," *Mennonite Quarterly Review* 40 (April 1966): 147.

[18]Ibid., 142. See also William Klassen and Walter Klaassen, trans. and eds. *The Writings of Pilgram Marpeck* (Scottdale, PA: Herald Press, 1978), 371.

[19]Marpeck, *Writings*, 370. Schwenckfeld himself showed an anti-intellectualism when faced by what he considered the arrogance of the highly educated Lutheran ministry. R. Emmet McLaughlin, "Spiritualism and the Bible: The Case of Caspar Schwenckfeld (1489-1561)," *Mennonite Quarterly Review* 53 (October 1979): 289f.

licity." "Just as God has always begun so will God conclude: with the faithful and simple people."[20]

For Menno Simons it was not the intellect but the heart which enables a person to understand scripture. Formal education was thus not a prerequisite.[21] While not despising knowledge of languages and education, he nevertheless preferred "heavenly wisdom" to human wisdom. "Now this wisdom which effects such power and yields such fruits, I consider to be the very finest that can be named, even if it is taught and recovered by an ignorant teamster or hod carrier."[22]

But if education and the knowledge of biblical languages could not ensure correct understanding of scripture, neither could their absence.

The Role of the Spirit

In their discussion of the relationship between letter and Spirit, it is clear that Anabaptists strongly affirmed that without the Holy Spirit the scriptures cannot be explained or interpreted. For Marpeck at least the designation of the Spirit as the One who was to lead Christians into all truth is the primary one.[23] Yet, "the Holy Spirit was not considered to be a separate and independent 'inner light' or 'inner Word' as the Spiritualists taught."[24] Rather, as the true author of scripture the Holy Spirit is also the true interpreter.

While emphasizing the importance of the Spirit as essential for understanding scripture, in some sense over against the Protestant reformers' emphasis on education, the Anabaptists realized the danger of antinomianism inherent in simply allowing everyone to interpret a passage in accordance with some internal impulse ascribed to the Holy Spirit. Hence, the need arose for some kind of "testing the spirits" to ensure that the one Spirit

---

[20]Marpeck, *Writings*, 371.

[21]Henry Poettcker, "Menno Simons' Encounter with the Bible," *Mennonite Quarterly Review* 40 (April 1966): 115.

[22]Menno Simons, "The Incarnation of our Lord" (1554) in *Complete Writings*, 791.

[23]Klassen, *Covenant and Community*, 67-77.

[24]Erland Waltner, "Holy Spirit," in *Mennonite Encyclopedia*.

would not appear to be giving occasion for conflicting interpretations of the Word. The congregation became the locus for that kind of testing.

Interpreting in the Community

In the late summer of 1524, Balthasar Hubmaier, designating himself "a brother in Christ of Huldrych Zwingli," presented twenty-six theses to Dr. John Eck in response to Eck's challenge of certain aspects of the Swiss Reformation. Two of the theses identify the foundation of the later Anabaptist concept of the congregation as hermeneutical community.

> I. Every Christian is obligated to give account of his hope and thereby of the faith which is in him to whoever desires it (1 Peter 3:15).
> V. Further, the decision which of two understands it more correctly is conceived in the church by the Word of God and born out of faith. When you come together, etc., the others should judge (1 Corinthians 14:30).[25]

Two underlying assumptions in these statements are: that every member of the church must have a sufficient understanding of the faith to be personally able to defend it, and that the gathered community was the appropriate body to discern the right interpretation.[26] Zwingli designated this view as the "Rule of Paul."[27] Williams refers to it as the *lex sedentium* (*Sitzrecht*), "the right of the whole Christian congregation, the laity with the divines, to judge difficult passages of scripture together, not

---

[25]H. Wayne Pipkin and John H. Yoder, trans. & eds. *Balthasar Hubmaier: Theologian of Anabaptism* (Scottdale, PA: Herald Press, 1989), 51.

[26]That many Anabaptist members were not literate no doubt presented something of a handicap to the congregation seeking to be a community of interpretation. But there were always literate members present, and many who were unable to read had memorized large portions of the Bible.

[27]Yoder, "The Hermeneutics of the Anabaptists," 301. Luther, in "An Appeal to the Ruling Class" (1520), like Zwingli at this early stage, affirms this "Rule of Paul," commenting as follows on 1 Corinthians 14:30, "What would be the virtue of this commandment if only the speaker, or the person in the highest position, were to be believed? Christ Himself says, John 6[:45], 'that all Christians shall be taught by God,'" Dillenberger, ed. *Martin Luther,* 413. In "Concerning the Ministry" (1523), he clearly affirms that "each one of us, one by one, may prophesy;" the *Sitzrecht* is a "general right common to all Christians described in 1 Corinthians 14[:30]." *Luther's Works,* 40:33, 37.

individualistically or professionally."[28] This conviction was thus already present in circles where Anabaptism came into being. It not only became widespread among them but was also continued by them when leaders of the Protestant Reformation abandoned it.[29]

At almost the same time as Hubmaier sent his theses to Eck, Grebel and associates wrote to Thomas Müntzer. Having moved from listening to and reading the "evangelical preachers" to taking scripture in hand and studying it together, they addressed Müntzer on a number of points of interpretation and application. As the multiple signature attests, their conclusions were clearly the result of group study of the Bible. Still, they were willing to be corrected: "If we are not in the right, teach us better. And do thou . . . act in all things only according to the Word, and bring forth and establish by the Word and the usage of the apostles."[30] They asked whether he and Carlstadt were of one mind, continuing "We hope and believe it. . . . And if thou couldst visit Carlstadt, so that ye could reply jointly, it would be a sincere joy to us."[31] They would rather dialogue with a hermeneutical community in the radical wing of the Lutheran Reformation than with Müntzer as an individual.

Both Hubmaier and the Grebel circle were at this time still active in the debates with Zwingli and colleagues. As Williams summarizes it,

Confidence that the Holy Spirit would infuse their exegetical

---

[28]Williams, *Radical Reformation*, 829.

[29]John H. Yoder, "Radical Reformation Ethics in Ecumenical Perspective," *Journal of Ecumenical Studies* 15 (Fall 1978): 657. By 1532 John Campanus, in *Restitution göttlicher Schrift* ". . . accuses Luther of having deprived the Christian laity of their right to sit in judgement (1 Corinthians 14:23ff) when Scripture is being interpreted (*Sitzrecht*)." Williams, *Radical Reformation*, 272-73. By that time Luther commented as follows on 1 Corinthians 14[:30]: "In this passage Paul is speaking of the prophets, who are to teach, not of the people, who are to listen. For prophets are teachers who have the office of preaching in the churches." If everyone were allowed to speak in the gathered congregation, drunks from the tavern and "at last the women too would claim the right of 'sitting by,' telling the men to be silent." *Luther's Works*, 40:388.

[30]"Letters to Thomas Müntzer," in *Spiritual and Anabaptist Writers*, ed. Williams and Mergal, 77.

[31]Ibid., 82.

deliberations and also that the same Spirit would bridge the gulf between them and their Protestant opponents accounts for the frequency of the biblical colloquies or disputations (*Gespräche*) so eagerly attended by the Anabaptists. Confident in the ultimate unity of the true church of Christ, the sectarians long persisted in the hope that the colloquies with the magisterial divines would be eventually consummated by some fresh illumination leading to oneness of mind and heart.[32]

Long before the formula *cuius regio, eius religio* (the religion of the ruler determines the religion of the region) became formal in 1525, its principle was already operative among the Protestant leaders. This meant that biblical discussions were frequently conditioned by political and theological considerations. Only the Anabaptists, in their rejection of any ecclesiastical authority of the government, kept the disputations going.[33] That they were serious in their expressed willingness to be corrected in their understanding ("sich 'berichten zu lassen'") is evidenced by the fact that some were "converted" during the course of a debate.[34]

Michael Sattler, both in dialogue with the Reformed leaders in Strasbourg and within the recently formed circle of Anabaptists, also held to this principle of the hermeneutical community. To Capito and Bucer he wrote in 1527:

> I recently spoke to you in brotherly moderation and friendliness on several points, which I together with my brothers and sisters have understood out of Scripture, namely out of the New Testament, and you for your part as the ones asked answered in similar moderation and friendliness.[35]

The Schleitheim "Brotherly Union" articles represent the product of what was apparently an intensive application of the principle. Each of the seven articles is preceded by the affirmation, "we have been united."[36] As the cover letter indicates,

---

[32]Williams, *Radical Reformation*, 829.

[33]Yoder, *Gespräche*, 153.

[34]Ibid., 159.

[35]John H. Yoder, trans. & ed. *The Legacy of Michael Sattler* (Scottdale, PA: Herald Press, 1973), 21-22.

[36]Ibid., 36-41.

these are the articles which some brothers previously had understood wrongly and in a way not conformed to the true meaning. Thereby many weak consciences were confused, whereby the name of God has been grossly slandered, for which reason it was needful that we should be brought to agreement in the Lord, which has come to pass. To God be praise and glory!*37*

The "Congregational Order" which apparently accompanied the articles enjoins that the process of congregational study of scripture continue.

1. The brothers and sisters should meet at least three or four times a week, to exercise themselves in the teaching of Christ and His apostles and heartily to exhort one another. . . .
2. When the brothers and sisters are together, they shall take up something to read together. The one to whom God has given the best understanding shall explain it. . . .*38*

Pilgram Marpeck, who had less theological training than any of the leaders mentioned above, similarly promoted and practised biblical interpretation in the congregation. To the Swiss Brethren he wrote:

I gladly submit my mind to a clear and more lucid understanding, which is given by the Holy Spirit, and I would also gladly submit to the least among Christ's own, and thank my Lord Jesus Christ if I find witness in my conscience. . . . If I am in error, I desire to be taught by God, through his Holy Spirit and the Scriptures. If I testify to the truth (by grace), I desire confirmation of it from those who truly believe.*39*

The Marpeck circle placed much stress on this *Mitzeugnis* (co-

---

*37*Ibid., 42; cf. Yoder, *Gespräche*, 98.

*38*Yoder, *Legacy of Michael Sattler*, 44. The fifth article of Schleitheim specified that one who was chosen to the office of shepherd would need "to read and exhort and teach, warn, admonish." The study process described above may thus not be quite as open as it appears; that is, the one with the "best understanding" may refer to the congregational leader. Yoder, ibid., 54, note 104, offers some additional possible interpretations.

*39*Marpeck, "Judgement and Decision" (ca. 1541) in *Writings*, 313. Similarly Menno Simons: "if I err in some things . . . I pray everyone . . . that if anyone has stronger and more convincing truth that he through brotherly exhortation and instruction might assist me." "Meditation on the Twenty-fifth Psalm" (ca. 1537) in *Complete Writings*, 65.

witness) from fellow believers to confirm their right understanding, just as they desired correction when they were wrong.[40] This was necessary because "once one is in Christ, the Law is gone, and the Christian is driven by the Spirit. . . . To keep this from degenerating into any subjective individualism Marpeck insisted that each motive, each drive of the Spirit be shared in the community of the Spirit where it would receive correction and purification."[41]

This kind of guidance by the Holy Spirit is illustrated in the case of Countess Helene von Freyberg who refused at first to participate in the congregation in this way. In her Confession, submitted to the Marpeck circle, she admitted: "I wanted to instruct and punish my brother, but was not teachable or punishable myself." But now, she concluded, "I submit to the discipline and punishment of my heavenly Father, of his holy community (*Gemein*) and Christian church as long and as often as it pleases the Holy Spirit."[42]

According to Menno Simons, the prerequisites for gaining a proper understanding of the Bible include an attitude "marked by obedience (willingness to submit to the cross) [and] a willingness to be instructed both by the Spirit and by the brethren."[43]

Regarding Dirk Philips, a recent essay concludes that more study was needed of "the role of the hermeneutical community in interpreting scripture."[44] His view of the church, as argued below, seemed to place interpretation within the mandate of the congregation.

Littell's summary confirms that interpretation by the congregation was in fact a widely accepted principle in the sixteenth-century Anabaptist movement.

---

[40]Klassen, *Covenant and Community*, 80, note 38.

[41]William Klassen, "The Relation of the Old and New Covenants in Pilgram Marpeck's Theology," *Mennonite Quarterly Review* 40 (April 1966): 104-105.

[42]Quoted in Klassen, *Covenant and Community*, 79, note 36; see also "The Relation of the Old and New Testaments," 105.

[43]Poettcker, "Menno Simons' Encounter," 115.

[44]Douglas H. Shantz, "The Ecclesiological Focus of Dirk Philips' Hermeneutical Thought in 1559: A Contextual Study," *Mennonite Quarterly Review* 60 (April 1986): 127.

As the groups took definite form, the key which unlocked Scripture and made possible true interpretation of Biblical teaching became a collective rather than an individual possession. The right of private interpretation, still asserted against the monopoly of the "Roman doctors" in public life, became the obligation to test one's findings with those of others within the fellowship.[45]

The early excommunicating of each other by some groups of Dutch Anabaptists interrupted the dialogue as effectively as imprisonment by the authorities and prevented the reaching of a broader consensus.[46]

Theology of the Church

The church as a whole, rather than individuals within it or the clergy or the scholars, was thus seen as being responsible for scriptural interpretation. Undergirding this understanding was the concept of "the keys." Dirk Philips stated it succinctly:

what the congregation of the Lord determines with his Word, the same is judged [confirmed] before God, for Christ gave his congregation the keys of the Kingdom of Heaven (Matthew 16:19). . . . What the congregation binds upon earth shall be bound in heaven. . . . the congregation has received the Holy Spirit and the gospel from Jesus Christ. . . . This word, together with the Holy Spirit, is the judge in the congregation over all false brethren (Titus 3:10), over all heretical people (Romans 10:16) and all disorderly and disobedient persons who after sufficient warning do not better themselves.[47]

---

[45]Franklin H. Littell, *The Origins of Sectarian Protestantism: A Study of the Anabaptist View of the Church* (New York, NY: Macmillan, 1964), 85-86.

[46]Perry Yoder, "The Role of the Bible in Mennonite Self-Understanding," in *Mennonite Identity: Historical and Contemporary Perspectives*, ed. Calvin Wall Redekop and Samuel J. Steiner (Lanham, MD: University Press of America, 1988), 76, identifies as "a central characteristic of interpretive communities that those who read the text the same way are in and those who read the text differently are out."

[47]Dietrich [Dirk] Philips, "The Church of God," in *Spiritual and Anabaptist Writers*, ed. Williams and Mergal, 247-48. Cf. Menno Simons: "the key of binding is nothing but the Word and the righteousness of God. . . . this binding key of Christ is given to His ministers and people," in *Complete Writings*, 989; Marpeck: "The Saints of God have been charged by the Lord to exercise judgement through the Holy Spirit. . . . the Holy Spirit is the key of heaven, through which sin is retained or forgiven in the community of the saints," *Writings*, 334; Peter Rideman: "this power and key is given to the Church and not to individual

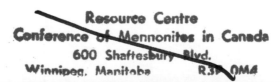

Philips, like most other Anabaptists, did not limit the role of either scripture or church to teaching, faith and doctrine, but freely included also obedience, living and ethics. Anabaptists usually cited not Matthew 16 but rather Matthew 18 when they referred to the power of binding and loosing. The latter context places the "Rule of Christ," as it is usually referred to, at least since the 1524 Grebel letter to Müntzer, directly in the context of ethical admonition and correction. But for Anabaptists discernment in both doctrine and ethics came from the understanding of scripture. Interpretation of the Bible thus involved its practical application in life. Such interpretation-application could only be done by the community. This concept brought together scripture (sole authority), Spirit (essential interpreter-teacher) and church (discerning body).[48]

When an understanding of scripture had been reached by the church in this manner, then it became binding. Thus Sattler, writing to the church at Horb (1527), could say: "Be mindful of our meeting, and what was decided there, and continue in strict accordance therewith."[49] Yoder, commenting on this exhortation, found it "of theological significance that a leader calls for faithfulness to the conclusions reached by the brotherhood *at a past meeting*, rather than appealing to a law, to his credentials, to a Bible text, etc."[50]

Rideman accordingly identifed the church as the locus of truth:

> the Church of Christ is, and continueth to be, a pillar and ground of truth, in that truth itself sheweth and expresseth itself

---

persons," *Confessions of Faith: Account of Our Religion, Doctrine and Faith* (Rifton, NY: Plough Publishing House, 1970), 44; Hubmaier, in *Balthasar Hubmaier,* trans. and ed. Pipkin and Yoder, 412, 545. Luther also argues against Rome that "the keys were not given to St. Peter only, but to the whole Christian community," but maintains that "the keys have no reference to doctrine or policy." "An Appeal to the Ruling Class," in *Martin Luther,* ed. Dillenberger, 413.

[48]Yoder put it this way: Anabaptists "affirmed that the way God leads is that the Spirit gathers believers around Scripture. The Spirit, the gathering, and the Scripture are indispensable elements of the process, "Radical Reformation Ethics," 657."

[49]Yoder, *Legacy,* 62.

[50]Ibid., 65, note 34.

in her, which truth is confirmed, ratified, and brought to pass in her by the Holy Spirit.[51]

That Rideman was speaking not of the institutional church of Rome, but of a congregation gathered under the Holy Spirit, is obvious in his entire *Confession*. For Marpeck this concept ensured that the Christian is "guided not by any legalistic biblicism but by the Spirit working through the body of believers in the church."[52] Hubmaier, on the other hand, seemed to have contemplated the possibility that the congregation, faithfully pursuing this process, might still err. In his final *Rechenschaft* he accordingly expressed willingness to submit to a truly universal council. According to Williams, this was

> in keeping with his conviction that the universally operative Holy Spirit, the divine which, according to his trichotomous scheme, moved freely in each redeemed person, would operate most effectively in a universal enclave where the divisiveness and partiality of fleshly wills could be offset by the dynamic presence of God in force.[53]

For Millard Lind the "epistemological dimension" of the concept of the hermeneutical community lies in the way it shifts the emphasis from the Bible as book for private devotions to seeing it as "a *public* book." If "it is assumed that there is no twentieth century context in which the Bible is truly at home" then the hermeneutical process is "largely meaningless. It is only within the life situation of the hermeneutical community that the fundamental analogies are experienced which make the Bible historically credible."[54]

Hermeneutics and Discipleship

If the "Rule of Christ" involves interpreting and applying the Word to the life of the disciples, then the life of the disciples

---

[51]Rideman, *Confession*, 40.

[52]Klassen, "The Relation of the Old and New Covenants," 104.

[53]Williams, *Radical Reformation*, 223.

[54]Millard Lind, "Reflections on Biblical Hermeneutics," in *Essays in Biblical Interpretation*, 153f.

also becomes one of the qualifications for proper interpretation.

Hans Denck's oft-quoted expression immediately comes to mind: "No one can truly know Christ unless he follows after him in life."[55] But others expressed themselves in very similar ways. Hans Hut wrote: "For no one can reach the Truth unless he follows in the footsteps of Christ and His elect in the valley of suffering, or in part at least has decided to follow. . . ."[56] Bernhard Rothmann put it this way: "And as we (with constant diligence) earnestly put into practice what we understand, God teaches us further every day."[57]

While expressions like this have usually been cited to emphasize the concern for obedience and commitment in discipleship, Yoder points out that the important thing is "rather the limitations it places upon knowledge."[58] The concept of discipleship (*Nachfolge Christi*) "thus has epistemological importance in connection with right thinking (*vera theologia*) and is thus more than a question of piety and ethics."[59]

Rideman explicitly applied this "limitation to knowledge" principle by denying the authority of priests to teach. They "have presumed to take upon themselves the proclaiming of the gospel, yet teach only the literal word, law and doctrine. . . . That they preach not the gospel but only the literal word is shown by their own deeds."[60] In Strasbourg the reformers found that the same strictures applied to them, as Wolfgang Capito reflected in a letter of 1527. Referring to Sattler, he wrote that "it may well be shortcomings among the people who claim to be Christian, a life found to be offensive, it was for this reason, if I understand, that he took so little to heart what we basically argued to clarify

---

[55]"Das mittel aber ist Christus, welchen nyemandt mag warlich erkennen, es sey dann, das er im nachvolge mit dem leben. Und nyemandt mag im nachvolgen, dann sovil er in zuvor erkennt." Hans Denck, *Schriften*, 2. Teil, ed. Walter Fellmann (Gütersloh: C. Bertelsmann, 1956), 45.

[56]Quoted in Littell, *Origins of Sectarian Protestantism*, 81.

[57]Bernhard Rothmann, "A Restitution of Christian Teaching . . ." (1534), in *Christianity and Revolution: Radical Christian Testimonies 1520-1650*, ed. Lowell H. Zuck (Philadelphia, PA: Temple University Press, 1975), 99.

[58]Yoder, "Hermeneutics of the Anabaptists," 307.

[59]Irvin B. Horst, quoted by Yoder, ibid., note 13.

[60]Rideman, *Confession*, 95-96.

the truth."[61]

For Anabaptists right living was thus a prerequisite to or concomitant of right knowing. This applied especially to teachers. Dirk Philips wrote: "true ministers of the divine Word are easily recognized by the saving teachings of Jesus Christ, by their godly walk . . . the fruits which they bear and . . . the persecution they must suffer."[62]

The Process of Interpretation

One is tempted to combine all the scattered bits and pieces from the various writers cited and create an outline of the process of an Anabaptist congregation functioning as hermeneutical community. Yet such a construct would be artificial. No historical group would likely have thought of itself in that way or functioned in that precise manner.

It may therefore be more helpful to look in detail at the model proposed by Hubmaier in his 1524 "Theses Against Eck."[63] Numbers in parentheses in the following summary indicate references to Hubmaier's twenty-six theses.

1. The judgement shall fall according to "the plumb line of scripture" (VIII), "the discourse which Christ spoke," not "papal law, not councils, not fathers, not schools" (IX).

2. Every Christian is accountable for his faith and hope (I).

3. Belief is a condition for understanding. "Unless you believe you will not understand it" (IV).

4. So that order may be maintained, three or four judges are to be elected. "Not that they should stand in judgement over the truth of the Word . . . but to [judge] which party comes closest

---

[61]Wolfgang Capito, to "Bürgermeister and Council at Horb," 31 May 1527, in Yoder, *Legacy of Michael Sattler*, 87.

[62]Dirk Philips, "The Church of God," in *Spiritual and Anabaptist Writers,* ed. Williams and Mergal, 241. For a fuller discussion of this theme in Anabaptism, see Cornelius J. Dyck, "Hermeneutics and Discipleship," in *Essays in Biblical Interpretation*, ed. Swartley, 29-44. Dyck uses the expression "epistemology of obedience."

For a study of its similarities to and differences from Latin American liberation theology, especially the latter's praxis approach to reading the Bible, see LaVerne A. Rutschman, "Anabaptism and Liberation Theology," in *Freedom and Discipleship: Liberation Theology in an Anabaptist Perspective*, ed. Daniel S. Schipani (Maryknoll, NY: Orbis, 1989), 58-60.

[63]Pipkin and Yoder, eds. *Balthasar Hubmaier,* 49-57.

to the intent of the divine Word" (VI). They should be "God-learned and God-inspired" (*theodidactos* and *theopneustos*; *gotglernig* and *gotsgeystig*) (X). They should be theologians (*theologi, gotzglernig*), "not hooded or capped" (that is, neither monks nor doctors) (XXIV).

5. The Bible is opened with a prayerful spirit; "like the learned scribe they are bringing forth new and old, to which they submit themselves without any speculation or disputation" (XI). This searching of scripture does not take place with "unspiritual chatter" nor with "wordy warfare until one is hoarse" (XII). Nevertheless, the judges will apply 1 Corinthians 14:30 so that "one who is seated, to whom something is revealed" may have the floor while the former speaker is silent (XIV), so that all persons may prophesy one by one (XVII).

6. The gathered congregation decides "which of the two understands it more correctly" (V), setting aside "all human motivation" (XI), guarding against false prophets and testing the spirits "whether they are from God" (XIX). Those "who do not read the Book of the Law and the Prophets" are not eligible to "hear" the process nor to serve as judges (XXVI). Women are permitted in the gathering but "shall be silent" (1 Corinthians 14:34) (XXII), but where the men are afraid then "the women should speak up" (XXIII).

7. When all are silent "then the judgement of the umpires is confirmed through the silence of the church" (Acts 15:12) (XV).[64]

8. According to the precedent of Acts 15, the purpose of this process is more to maintain unity than "for the sake of the doctrine of faith" (VII).

Implications

Informed members of believers' churches will not find much

---

[64]A minister ("Diener des Wortes") explained the communal process in a Dakota Hutterite Bruderhof as follows: "I put questions to the members. If anybody is against it, he is to say so. They talk it up in small groups. If the (whole) group gets quiet, then it means 'yes.' I can tell by the quietness whether they are for it." Reported in Franklin H. Littell, "The Work of the Holy Spirit in Group Discussions," *Mennonite Quarterly Review* 34 (April 1960): 81f.

that is new in this sifting through of the historical documents of the Radical Reformation. Mennonite, Amish, Hutterite, Baptist and other groups who see themselves in some historical sense as descendants of Anabaptism may well consider that their congregations or synods are today functioning as hermeneutical communities. Yet in most instances this happens not because the groups are consciously planning it, but because it is an inherent aspect of the nature of a believers' church. For this aspect to be recovered more fully, it may be helpful to consider the following specific implications.[65]

First, biblical literacy would be expected of individual members of the congregations. It is ironic that with the widespread availability of the Bible in many translations and with many good study aids readily accessible, biblical knowledge among church members today is probably less adequate than it was among sixteenth-century Anabaptists.

Second, scholars, especially biblical specialists, would see themselves "as part of a team concerned with the larger hermeneutical question." Not only would they be expected to submit their interpretations to the church, the community would also help to discern agenda, thereby possibly delivering the specialists "from trivial and unprofitable questions in research."[66] There is a tendency today to think that the community of scholars, either in annual meeting or through learned journals, is the most appropriate place to test one's findings. On the other hand there is a widespread sense that a considerable gap exists between what is being preached in church and what is being taught in seminaries, Bible colleges and university religion departments. Erland Waltner suggests that preaching too take seriously the hermeneutical community, so that "those who speak from pulpits and those who listen are engaged in authentic Christian dia-

---

[65]John H. Yoder, "The Hermeneutics of the Anabaptists," is especially helpful in this discussion. Yoder proposes a somewhat different application of "this congregationalism of the earliest Reformation," in "Is There Historical Development of Theological Thought," in *The Witness of the Holy Spirit: Proceedings of the Eighth Mennonite World Conference*, ed. Cornelius J. Dyck (Elkhart, IN: Mennonite World Conference, [1967]), 387-388.

[66]Millard C. Lind, "Reflections on Biblical Hermeneutics," in *Essays in Biblical Interpretation*, ed. Swartley, 153; see also Ross T. Bender, "Teaching the Bible in the Congregation," ibid., 298.

logue."[67]

Third, congregations would more consciously become hermeneutical communities. That is, in taking seriously the premise that a text is best understood in a congregation, they would need to find occasions where they would structure themselves consciously to "sit in judgement" on an interpretative process. Doing this quite consciously and deliberately at specific times would probably result in regular meetings of the congregation which would more frequently take on the characteristics cited in 1 Corinthians 14.

Fourth, the church or denomination would give more attention to the importance of unity of understanding of the Bible. Division (schism) is taken rather matter-of-factly in much of Christendom, including the Mennonite church which is divided into an embarrassingly large range of groups. Marpeck wrote to the Swiss Brethren:

> there is nothing lacking in the Spirit. Our schism has sprung only out of the weakness and ignorance of our consciences and understanding. If, by acknowledging ignorance on my part, I could liberate your understanding so that . . . an exposition of the gospel of the creatures might bring us together . . . I would gladly do so.[68]

In resuming the ecumenical *Gespräche* that broke off during the sixteenth century, one would need as much as possible to come to scripture without being tied to particular traditions and historical creedal statements.

Fifth, in the ongoing discussion of biblical authority the focus would shift from infallible text to hermeneutical community.[69] This is reflected in the nature of the article on "Scripture" in sixteenth- and seventeenth-century Mennonite confessions of faith (or on the absence of such an article).[70]

---

[67]Erland Waltner, "Preaching the Bible in the Church," ibid., 319.

[68]Marpeck, *Writings*, 353. William Klassen, "Anabaptist Hermeneutics: The Letter and the Spirit," *Mennonite Quarterly Review* 40 (April 1966): 92f, comments on Marpeck's concern for unity.

[69]Littell, "The Work of the Holy Spirit in Group Discussions," 90-91.

[70]Norman Kraus, "American Mennonites and the Bible," in *Essays in Biblical Interpretation*, ed. Swartley, 133-138.

Sixth, scholarly gatherings like this Symposium would need to take themselves more seriously as Christian congregations, that is, as hermeneutical communities. Ecumenical gatherings like the annual meetings of the Society of Biblical Literature or American Academy of Religion may not share these presuppositions, but Mennonite "scholarly" meetings at least should find it possible.

John Yoder began his address to regional meetings of Goshen College Biblical Seminary alumni some years ago with the words:

> As has always been the case in any stable society, a meeting cannot properly begin without a gesture of reverence toward the ancestors. I have therefore been called in, as one of those men assigned to the study of ancient monuments, to lead the congregation in its ritual nod to the past.[71]

Unless we are gathered here during these days to *be* a hermeneutical community, to work together toward a common understanding of biblical truth, then this "gesture of reverence" might just as well have been omitted from the agenda.

---

[71] Yoder, "The Hermeneutics of the Anabaptists," 291.

Waldemar Janzen*

A CANONICAL RETHINKING OF THE ANABAPTIST-MENNONITE NEW TESTAMENT ORIENTATION**

The preference of authority given by sixteenth-century Anabaptism to the New Testament over the Old will be assumed rather than argued in this paper. It has been documented in several scholarly studies[1] and is frequently acclaimed by its modern heirs as "one of our Mennonite distinctives." Nuances on this point among early Anabaptists are less important for our purposes than the general Anabaptist belief that "where the Old Testament is superseded by the New it is no longer authoritative for Christians,"[2] together with the assumption that the Old has indeed been replaced by the New in most matters of greatest importance.

It has often been pointed out, and must be acknowledged here, that the early Anabaptists did not reject the Old Testament in an overtly Marcionite fashion.[3] They accepted it as true divine revelation for its own time and believed that it retained "a certain authority 'outside the perfection of Christ'."[4] This understanding, however, does not outweigh the fact that the early

---

*Waldemar Janzen is Professor of Old Testament at Canadian Mennonite Bible College, Winnipeg, Manitoba.

**The author would like to thank Walter Klaassen, Research Professor, Conrad Grebel College, Waterloo, Ontario, and Ben C. Ollenburger, Associate Professor of Old Testament, Associated Mennonite Biblical Seminaries, Elkhart, Indiana, for their critical responses to this essay at the Symposium.

[1]Key essays on this subject have been helpfully collected in Willard Swartley, ed. *Essays on Biblical Interpretation: Anabaptist-Mennonite Perspectives* (Elkhart, IN: Institute of Mennonite Studies, 1984), hereafter cited as *Essays*.

[2]Walter Klaassen, "Anabaptist Hermeneutics: Presuppositions, Principles and Practice," *Essays*, 8.

[3]William Klassen, "The Relation of the Old and the New Covenants in Pilgram Marpeck's Theology," *Essays*, 26.

[4]Klaassen, "Anabaptist Hermeneutics," *Essays*, 8. See also John H. Yoder, "The Hermeneutics of the Anabaptists," *Essays*, 26.

Anabaptists drew a clear line of separation between the Testaments and subjected the Old Testament to the overriding authority of the New in all important matters that dominated theological discussion during the Reformation era.

The practice of drawing a distinction between the Testaments is such a hallmark of early Anabaptism that John H. Yoder lists it, along with the hermeneutical community, as one of the two distinctives of Anabaptist hermeneutics when compared to the hermeneutics of the mainline reformers.[5] He attributes to this distinction a highly positive valuation, a "fundamental exegetical importance, as one of their century's few ways of focusing the historical character of revelation."[6] He sees in the Anabaptist position an incipient understanding of salvation history, "a meaningful movement from the Old Testament to the New," as compared to a Greek understanding of timeless truth underlying the synoptic view of the Testaments that marked Zwingli and the mainline Reformation.[7] More than that, Yoder makes the claim that these two distinctives of Anabaptist hermeneutics, that is, the hermeneutical community and the historical relationship of the Testaments, "have been confirmed by further theological research and by experience."[8] These assessments will require our further attention.

In his "Afterword" to *Essays on Biblical Interpretation*, entitled "Continuity and Change in Anabaptist-Mennonite Interpretation," Willard Swartley comments extensively and approvingly on the extent to which the Mennonite interpretation

---

[5]Yoder, ibid., 28. I gratefully acknowledge the following observations of my respondent, Walter Klaassen: 1) The relationship between the Testaments broke open anew for all Reformation parties after the medieval four-level interpretation of scripture was abandoned. 2) All reformers tended to give precedence to the New Testament in some fashion. 3) The diverging positions between the mainline reformers and the Anabaptists were generated by controversy. This underscores the fact that the problems addressed in the present paper, though focused on the Anabaptist-Mennonite situation, are wider Christian problems.

[6]Ibid.

[7]Ibid., 27. See also Klassen, "The Relation of the Old and the New Covenants in Pilgram Marpeck's Theology," *Essays*, 100 and 103.

[8]Yoder, ibid., 27. See also Ben C. Ollenburger, "The Hermeneutics of Obedience," *Essays*, 49, where he characterizes the "sharp distinction between the Old and the New Testaments" as a "preunderstanding, because it stands as a principle of interpretation, not as a result of it."

of the Bible has preserved the first of Yoder's distinctives of Anabaptist hermeneutics, the hermeneutical community.[9] One looks in vain, however, for a comment on Yoder's second distinctive, the relationship between the Testaments.

My impression, gathered over thirty years of Bible teaching in the context of Mennonite schools and churches, is that the formal continuity between early Anabaptists and present-day Mennonites in this area, by far exceeds that of an emphasis on the hermeneutical community.[10] The belief that the Old Testament has been superseded by the New flows easily from Mennonite lips, learned and unlearned alike. Coupled with this understanding is a disdain for the mainline churches which are seen to have somehow stayed back in the lesser fullness of the Old Testament in the areas of laws, politics and war.

However, the continuity between early Anabaptists and present-day Mennonites in this respect is merely formal and superficial. Both the motivation and its function are vastly different then and now. In 1966, Yoder could say that "the origins of Anabaptist originality on this point [the relationship between the Testaments], already visible in September of 1524, have not yet been traced."[11] Meanwhile, James A. Sanders[12] and other proponents of canonical criticism have taught us much about the mutual interaction of canon and community. A religious community expresses its identity in the story it adopts as canonical, and is shaped, in turn, by that canon. It appears that the early Anabaptists were people who, in that eschatologically sensitive century, were especially imbued with the reality of the rule of Christ over his Messianic flock.[13] Obedience to the

---

[9]*Essays,* 328-330.

[10]It is instructive in this connection to consult "Scripture in Individual Confessions," in Howard John Loewen, *One Lord, One Church, One Hope, and One God: Mennonite Confessions of Faith in North America, An Introduction* (Elkhart, IN: Institute of Mennonite Studies, 1985), 333-369. Even a quick glance will reveal the vastly greater use of the New Testament in these confessions. In the Ris Confession, for example, the ratio of Old to New Testament references is approximately 1:4.

[11]Yoder, "The Hermeneutics of the Anabaptists," *Essays* 28.

[12]See the section below on "The Promise of Canonical Criticism."

[13]The events at Münster have attracted attention in this respect, due to their violent and excessive nature, but the Münsterites should not be isolated or set in

Lord at all cost, and regardless of consequences for self or the structures of society, was paramount. They were repeatedly distracted from this quest for obedience by apparently compromising positions that found scriptural support in the Old Testament: support for infant baptism and people's church, for the oath and for the use of violence and war. Theologically inexperienced and unsophisticated as they were, they confronted these challenges to obedience with a hermeneutical *tour d'force*, namely, the neutralization of the Old Testament as authoritative canon.[14] Whether right or wrong, it was a bold and, to them, costly move in the interest of obedience.[15]

For most Mennonites in the Western world, on the other hand, an eschatological urgency towards costly obedience in the context of the Messianic community has hardly been the stamp shaping our existence. We have become largely acculturated rather than separated. And we have come to accept as legitimate Christian goals such concerns for this world as the liberation of the politically and economically oppressed and the preservation of our biological environment from exploitation and pollution. Hardly ever—unless occasionally in matters of military service—is our Christian obedience impeded by others through their recourse to the Old Testament. In fact, we have indulged at times in sympathetic attitudes towards certain Old Testament based concerns and movements, like liberation theology or Jubilee year economics.[16]

Why, then, should most Mennonites still be so ready to claim that the New Testament has superseded the Old? I would

---

opposition to the remaining Anabaptists as far as an eschatological orientation is concerned.

[14]Ollenburger says, "Their separation of Old Testament from New Testament grew out of this commitment [of prior obedience to Christ] and as a result of difficulties which arose when they were not separated." "The Hermeneutics of Obedience," *Essays*, 49.

[15]While this zeal for obedience is humanly attractive and explains the early Anabaptists' stance towards the Old Testament, I agree with my respondent, Ben Ollenburger, that our positive valuation of their obedience does not justify them. Similarly, my call to embrace the whole canon again is based on our identity as Christians rather than a preference rooted in contemporary trends.

[16]This is true even if not all may follow John H. Yoder in interpreting Jesus' call to kingdom ethics as constituting the inauguration of the Jubilee year. See *The Politics of Jesus* (Grand Rapids, MI: Eerdmans Publishing Company, 1972), 26-77.

suggest the following factors: At bottom, one senses an aversion to the Old Testament that has much in common with true Marcionism. Again and again, doubts are expressed about the identification of the God of the Old Testament with the God of the New. This is prompted, above all, by the realism of the Old Testament in which God's activity cannot be disentangled from history, war and judgement. It is perceived that the loving Father of Jesus Christ "would not do such things." Marcion himself was more consistent here, realizing that a rejection of the "lower, evil" God of the Old Testament would require the excision of large parts of the New Testament as well.

None of these objections to the Old Testament would have disturbed the early Anabaptists. They certainly believed in a God who sovereignly ruled the world with power, was involved in all aspects of it and was to be feared as a judge. At the roots of the modern rejection of the Old Testament we must posit at least three developments.

First, individualism was spawned by the Enlightenment and reached its climax in the emphasis of our time on self-realization and individual rights. A New Testament divorced from the Old can, albeit only with violence, be made to serve this individualism, while the Old Testament is totally impervious to it. Second, religion has gradually adapted itself to the private sphere, often seen as the inner haven of the soul in a turbulent outer world. Once again, it is possible, if not legitimate, to privatize the New Testament, but never the Old. Third, this individualizing and privatizing trend merges with the contemporary psychological and New Age tendencies to seek salvation as the ultimate human goal, not in a transcendent reality embracing history and the world (the Kingdom of God), but in an inner tranquillity of the individual self. Once again, the New Testament can be forced to serve this end, but the Old is perceived as so incompatible with this view that it has to be rejected, or at least neutralized.

All such motivations for demoting the Old Testament from an authoritative role in Christian life are, of course, not specifically Mennonite phenomena, but are to be found widely in Western Christianity. The only difference is that Mennonites can establish a formal and superficial continuity between this neo-Marcionite mood and the Anabaptist New Testament orientation.

Not only are the motivations for the modern rejection of the Old Testament totally different from the Anabaptist motivations, as has just been shown; the function of the modern attitude is also very different. While the early Anabaptists de-emphasized the Old Testament so as not to be detained by it from radical Messianic obedience, modern Mennonites (and others) avoid it so as not to allow it to disturb their inner tranquillity. For the Anabaptists, a radical New Testament orientation meant costly obedience and persecution; for moderns it means a more undisturbed, soothing religion of psychological well-being.

Assessing the Losses

Whether one posits that the Old Testament has been superseded salvation-historically by the New, as Yoder claims for the early Anabaptists, or that the two are incompatible from a Neo-Marcionite perspective, one is left with a reduction of the canon.[17]

For the early Anabaptists, this removed an arsenal of theological arguments used by their opponents to blunt radical obedience of the Messianic community (Menno's "church without spot or wrinkle") to its risen Lord. For the post-Enlightenment Neo-Marcionite, Mennonite or other, it removes a constant challenge to the modern search for an individualistic religion of inner tranquillity.

It is only lately and gradually, I believe, that we are beginning to feel the losses also. In the wider church, the possibility of perverting a New Testament detached from the Old has nowhere been demonstrated more clearly and shockingly than in the "German Christians" movement of the Hitler era. It was

---

[17]The body of writings accepted as offering direct authoritative guidance for faith and life, and to which both individuals and the church feel accountable, has been reduced in sheer volume by 77 percent or, in my edition of the Revised Standard Version of the Bible, from 1270 to 293 printed pages. Possibly this quantitative reduction of material for which one is responsible in the first instance is in itself a major factor enticing many to be New Testament (plus Psalms) Christians.

no accident, then, that the interest in biblical theology in the earlier twentieth century took hold first in the Old Testament field.[18]

No such awakening to the losses and dangers inherent in a truncated New Testament canon has, to my knowledge, occurred in the Mennonite church. It is true that individual Mennonite Old Testament scholars receive a respectful if limited hearing in schools, at study conferences and in church-oriented publications. This is especially true if they use the beloved word "covenant" freely; if they "help" us with "problems" like war in the Old Testament or creation versus evolution; and if they isolate certain "Mennonite-compatible" themes like shalom or justice.

Much of the attention given to the study of the Old Testament takes place in the context and mood of "providing background" and "coping with problems." Only a small minority studies the Old Testament with a sense of expectancy, waiting to hear a word from God. All the while, the majority keeps on confidently repeating the Anabaptist dictum that the Old Testament has been superseded by the New.

But, as others have recognized before us, there are losses on the theological battlefield. It is not the subject of this paper to trace the neglect of the Old Testament in the church generally, but to focus on the Anabaptist New Testament orientation and its formal continuation in the Mennonite church of our time. That orientation, as I argued earlier, had its main root in the Anabaptists' desire for a more unimpeded, radical obedience (discipleship) which, in turn, was the prerequisite for the eternal salvation of individuals. Even though the content of this obedience was discerned from the scriptures communally (hermeneutical community) and lived out communally (the emphasis on church discipline), the end (*telos*) of the Christian endeavour was the eternal salvation of the individual.

In this, the Anabaptists were at one with Luther in his quest for a merciful God ("Wie finde ich einen gnädigen Gott?").

---

[18]Though the initial impetus came from Karl Barth's commentary on Romans (1918, 1921), it was taken up most forcefully by Old Testament theologians like Walther Eichrodt, Ludwig Koehler, Wilhelm Vischer and many others. James D. Smart surveys this development in *The Past, Present and Future of Biblical Theology* (Philadelphia, PA: Westminster Press, 1970), 70-74.

For both, the way to salvation was Jesus Christ. The difference lay not in the *telos*, but in the different understanding of Jesus Christ as the way. While both stressed God's grace and human response, or justification and sanctification, Luther accented the former, Anabaptists the latter. As to the end *(telos)*, again they were in substantial agreement, not only with each other but also with the Catholic church of the Middle Ages and of their time, albeit, the Anabaptists pursued this end more radically, with greater eschatological zeal and with less concern both for their own fate in this world and for the fate of this world as such. As a result, Anabaptism could dispense with an explicit theology of the world outside the church, even though it acknowledged in a general way that a measure of God's rule over that world was maintained by divinely ordained magistrates.

This deficiency of a theology with respect to large and significant areas of life can be exemplified in two areas, each of great prominence throughout centuries of Mennonite existence: family and land. Mennonites had large families. Due to their many migrations, family ties became more important than for the more sedentary population that established its identity more through place than through genealogy. There was an explicit Anabaptist-Mennonite theology of the spiritual family, the church. One entered it by baptism upon personal decision, symbolized one's bond to it through communion and submitted to its authority and discipline. But what about the children of Mennonite parents who were either too young to enter the spiritual family or, more problematically, who decided against joining it? Should they be abandoned as strangers or apostates? Or did the biological bond have a theological significance all its own? By way of practice, certain trends developed, such as the tendency to have large families. Was this due to the pragmatism of a farming people that needed workers? Or of a persecuted minority that needed potential converts from within the clan? Or were children a blessing from God, independent of their potential church membership? Only recently has some serious theological thought been given to the children of the second generation,[19] but I know of no theological work on adult children

---

[19]Marlin Jeschke, *Believers Baptism for Children of the Church* (Scottdale, PA: Herald Press, 1983).

remaining outside the church.

Land is as important as are family bonds in Mennonite history and life. From earliest times on Mennonites have sought new land, have developed great land-tending skills and have been sought after as a desirable agricultural population, from the Jura mountains in Switzerland and the Weichsel delta in Prussia, to the Ukrainian steppes, the Paraguayan Chaco and the North American prairies. Nevertheless, a theology of land seems lacking.[20] Migrations appear pragmatic in character; they were motivated by a search for freedom from oppression and for greater prosperity. High quality farming resulted from a struggle for existence and from a belief in the virtue of frugality; it hardly issued from a theological sense of stewardship of the earth. Homeland literature, where it was written at all, bears the stamp of nostalgic reminiscence or of blood and soil ideology, but rarely of a theology of places in the economy of God. While occasionally the Exodus appears as symbol of salvation, the rich land theology of the Old Testament has scarcely been addressed by our ancestors other than in a spiritualized form: we are pilgrims and exiles in this world on the road to a heavenly Canaan.

Why have we not developed a biblical theology of family and of land? Because the New Testament does not give much overt attention to them,[21] while the Old Testament, where these themes are prominent, has been superseded, as we all know. The fact of the matter is that the New Testament builds on the theology of the Old in such areas, setting certain accents differently here and there, but seeing no need to reaffirm what Jesus and the early church could assume. Thus, while the family structure of society is taken for granted in the New Testament,[22]

---

[20]Waldemar Janzen, "The Great Trek: Episode or Paradigm?" *Mennonite Quarterly Review* 51 (April 1977): 127-139 offers a brief sketch of an implicit and minimal (Russian) Mennonite theology of land, especially 135-139.

[21]See my article "Geography of Faith: A Christian Perspective on the Meaning of Places," *Studies in Religion/Sciences Religieuses* 3, no. 2 (1973): 166-182, reprinted in Waldemar Janzen, *Still in the Image: Essays in Biblical Theology and Anthropology* (Newton, KS: Faith and Life Press; Winnipeg, MB: CMBC Publications, 1982), 137-157; and my forthcoming article "Land" in *The Anchor Bible Dictionary* (Garden City, NJ: Doubleday and Company).

[22]Note Jesus' affirmation of the duty to parents (Mark 7:9-13), his provision

God's rich and unlimited grace is joyfully affirmed: God can give mothers and brothers and sisters in the faith to those rejected by their natural families (Matthew 12:46-50), just as God can give a future, that is, an ongoing spiritual family, to those unmarried for the sake of God's calling (Matthew 19:10-12; 1 Corinthians 7:1-7). With respect to land (or wealth), inherent responsibilities are assumed[23] but extended beyond the confines of the "Promised Land" (Acts 1:8).

Family and land are but two illustrations. A fuller listing of areas of life that exist in a theological vacuum for Mennonites would include at least four major groupings:

1. Creation: including land, place, nature, body, medicine
2. Society, political: including government, law/justice, human "rights," liberation
3. Society, economic: including business, work, play
4. Family: including children before baptism, children outside the church

In contrast to our Anabaptist-Mennonite ancestors, however, who were ready to exclude many of these areas of life from an active Christian mandate, we include them in *de facto* fashion, only without an adequate theology. In other words, we have widely accepted the general Christian view of our time that this world is not only means, but also end (*telos*) of God's redemptive work.

Having abandoned the Old Testament as superseded, however, we have gathered up our various concerns for this world either from other Christians or from the secular world around us. We pursue justice largely on the basis of philosophical assumptions of human rights and self-fulfillment. We express concern for politically and economically oppressed groups or peoples under the banner of liberation. We chime in with ecological concerns under the threat to survival. We deny military conquest as legitimizing land claims, but are susceptible to the

---

for his mother (John 19:26-27), the conversion and baptism of a whole household (Acts 10:2, 44-48; 11:14; 16:31; 18:8), and the concern for the family structure in the *Haustafeln*, e.g., Ephesians 5:22-6:9; Colossians 3:18-22.

[23]Note Jesus' concern for the poor, the early church's experiment with community of goods (Acts 4:34-37) and Paul's concern and collection for the impoverished Jerusalem church (1 Corinthians 16:1-4).

unbiblical argument of aboriginal possession. We proclaim the spiritual family but feel instinctively that it cannot and should not displace the bonds of blood altogether. Meanwhile the Old Testament, lying fallow among us, contains rich theological resources for a theology of stewardship of earth and land, of justice, of liberation, and others.

Is it not high time, then, that we reinstate the Old Testament as a full-fledged conversation partner in our ongoing theological discourse?![24] A projection of the manner in which this could happen will be made in the next section of this paper.

The Promise of Canonical Criticism

The model for the theological re-enfranchisement of the Old Testament to be proposed here will draw upon the rediscovery of the methodological and theological significance of the biblical canon, namely, from "canonical criticism." Its most prominent proponents in North America have been Brevard S. Childs and James A. Sanders.[25] Many others, however, have joined the ranks of those searching for ways to overcome the fragmentation of the Bible under the impact of historical-critical scholarship by giving serious attention to the fact that the Bible in its totality emerged and functioned first of all as the authorita-

---

[24]This invitation is based on our claim to be Christians, that is, people created and shaped by the canon, not on any attempt to adjust the canon to our current self-perception.

[25]Of the numerous publications of Childs and Sanders, the following seem most central to their thinking: Brevard S. Childs, *Biblical Theology in Crisis* (Philadelphia, PA: Westminster Press, 1970); *The Book of Exodus: A Critical Theological Commentary* (Philadelphia, PA: Westminster Press, 1974); *Introduction to the Old Testament as Scripture* (London: SCM Press, 1979); *The New Testament as Canon: An Introduction* (Philadelphia, PA: Fortress Press, 1984); *Old Testament Theology in a Canonical Context* (Philadelphia, PA: Fortress Press, 1985). James A. Sanders, *Torah and Canon* (Philadelphia, PA: Fortress Press, 1972); "Hermeneutics," in *Interpreter's Dictionary of the Bible* (Supplementary Volume); *Canon and Community: A Guide to Canonical Criticism* (Philadelphia, PA: Fortress Press, 1984); *From Sacred Story to Sacred Text: Canon as Paradigm* (Philadelphia, PA: Fortress Press, 1987). A fuller listing of works by Childs and Sanders, together with an incisive comparison, can be found in Timothy A. P. Reimer, "Canon as Product or Process?: A Comparative Analysis of the Canonical Hermeneutics of Brevard S. Childs and James A. Sanders" (M.A. thesis, University of Manitoba, 1987).

tive canon of a believing community.[26] It is therefore seen as a body of authoritative writings inseparably linked to a believing community within which it emerged and the identity of which it, in turn, defines.

James A Sanders, taking an anthropological approach (though with a theological interest at heart), sees believing communities of all persuasions engaged in an ongoing process of expressing their changing identity by a commensurate shaping and reshaping of their canon. Sanders certainly does not understand canon as something totally relative and changeable, merely reflecting the self-perception of a community at any given time. Two principles are at work in the canonical functions of texts: the principle of adaptability and the principle of stability.[27]

Sanders looks at the canonical process from a detached vantage point as an analytical observer of a social dynamic found in all groups, even though he himself has a personal interest in the methodological and theological consequences of the academic discipline (as he understands it) of canonical criticism for the Christian church and its canon, the Bible. In principle, the process of canon formation and adaptation could be observed equally well in other religions.

As a matter of fact, I adopted the methodology of Sanders' version of canonical criticism in the earlier sections of this paper when I suggested that the Anabaptists' rejection of the Old Testament was a consequence of their self-understanding as a totally obedient Messianic community. Further, I implied, again in keeping with Sanders, that a different self-understanding of the Mennonite church today calls for a commensurate expansion

---

[26]Walter Brueggemann, Joseph Blenkinsopp, Ronald Clements, Hartmut Gese, Peter Stuhlmacher and Rolf Rendtorff, among many others, use a new understanding of canon, in some form or other, to relate the Testaments to each other. See also such summaries of contemporary trends in this area as John H. Hayes and Frederick C. Prussner, "The Canon and Old Testament Theology," in *Old Testament Theology: Its History and Development* (Atlanta, GA: John Knox Press, 1985), 268-273; George W. Coats, "Old Testament Theology in the Context of the Canon," in Douglas A. Knight and Gene M. Tucker, eds. *The Hebrew Bible and Its Modern Interpreters* (Philadelphia, PA: Fortress Press, 1985), 251-254; and Henning Graf Reventlow, "Das Problem des Kanons," in *Hauptprobleme der biblischen Theologie im 20. Jahrhundert* (Darmstadt: Wissenschaftliche Buchgesellschaft, 1983), 125-137 and "Neuansätze einer biblischen Theologie," ibid., 138-172, with extensive bibliography.

[27]Sanders, *Canon and Community*, 43f., 48ff.

of the canon to include a theologically re-enfranchised Old
Testament. In other words, the Mennonite church has *de facto*
become a community which understands itself as one called to
responsibility for creation, and having a concern for the political-
economic liberation of oppressed groups, and is therefore in need
of a canon embodying this identity.

Such an adaptation of canon to perceived group identity
would, however, be facile and self-serving if left without a
counter-dynamic maintaining the permanence and stability of
canon, and thereby its capacity not only to reflect identity, but
also to critique it on the basis of a truth claim transcending the
church's self-perceptions and needs. While this fact is acknowledged by Sanders, as was mentioned already, greater help
towards this end can be gained, in my opinion, from Brevard S.
Childs.[28]

In a somewhat circular fashion, the church has determined
the canon, and that canon in turn defines the church. In spite
of the lack of unity in the church's delimitation of the canon,
especially with respect to the inclusion or exclusion of the
Apocrypha, there is a *minimal* agreement among all Christians
that at least the books of the Hebrew Bible plus the books of
the New Testament are canon for *all* Christians. Furthermore,
the church has recognized these texts in their *final* form as
canon. Historical-critical analysis may legitimately and helpfully
discern earlier stages of the text and earlier forms of canon, but
these are of interest to the Christian exegete and theologian,
according to Childs, only insofar as they help in elucidating the
final form which alone is authoritative, that is, canon. It is this
final form, then, which must be the object of exegesis and the
basis of theology. Furthermore, as a believer speaking from
within the community of faith, Childs does not treat the emergence of the canon anthropologically, as the community's
formulation of its identity, but theologically, as the community's

---

[28]In spite of considerable divergences between Sanders' and Childs'
understanding of canonical criticism, and a lively debate between them as well
as their adherents and critics, I am convinced that their perspectives to a large
extent support, supplement and correct each other. See Timothy A. P. Reimer's
thesis "Canon as Product or Process?" in which he compares the canonical
hermeneutics of Childs and Sanders.

apperception of God's revealed truth.

Such understanding of the canon seems to me to be completely compatible with the formal and oft-repeated Anabaptist-Mennonite view of the Bible as embracing both Testaments as true Word of God. That the Anabaptists, in actual faith and practice, reduced the canon to the New Testament in order not to be detracted from true Messianic obedience by the Old Testament, seems to me to be the result of a hermeneutical deficiency. They lacked a method of interpretation that would allow them to hear the whole biblical canon as authoritative Word of God for their own time without having a blunting effect on the radical call of Jesus.[29] In this respect, Childs and others have drawn methodological consequences for exegesis and biblical theology from their understanding of canon that can help us hear the Old Testament as God's Word for us without fear that the call of Jesus might be blunted or muted.

The hermeneutic to be outlined in the next section is my own version of contemporary canonical criticism/hermeneutics. It leans heavily on other authors, especially Brevard S. Childs and cautiously, George A. Lindbeck, but does not wish to be seen as a consistent application of any one extant contemporary hermeneutical or methodological school.[30]

Before we proceed to this task, however, it should be said that my invitation to Mennonites to adopt a methodology that can be called in some sense "canonical" is not new. Such invitations have been extended in recent times by at least three

---

[29]The mainline reformers were no more successful in this respect. Luther's internal yardstick of "whatever promotes Christ" ("was Christum dringet") in both Testaments, and the Reformed tendency to read both Testaments on the same level, had their own unsatisfactory consequences. However, they preserved the theological relevance of the Old Testament.

[30]For examples of Childs' own exegetical application of his method, see his *Biblical Theology in Crisis*, 147-219, and his commentary *The Book of Exodus*. See also Reimer, "Canon as Product or Process?" 83-117. For further application of canonical exegesis, see Walter Brueggemann, *Genesis: A Bible Commentary for Teaching and Preaching* (Atlanta, GA: John Knox Press, 1982). See especially his programmatic statement, 2-4. The already classic monograph of George A. Lindbeck, *The Nature of Doctrine: Religion and Theology in a Postliberal Age* (Philadelphia, PA: Westminster Press, 1984), seems to me to provide a broad and compatible theological framework for canonical criticism as I envision it. Its profound and multi-faceted implications need further testing, however, both in my own thinking and in the broader theological world. See especially chapter 6, "Toward a Postliberal Theology."

Mennonite scholars: John H. Yoder,[31] Jacob J. Enz[32] and A. James Reimer.[33] References to their proposals will be made in the further course of this paper.

Proposing a Hermeneutical Model

Before I present a hermeneutical model that again unites the Testaments as theological partners within the canon, I wish to make perfectly clear what my hearers or readers should not expect.

The model to be proposed will not seek to smooth out the historical, literary and theological diversity within the scriptures into a seamless robe on the doctrinal-confessional level. I agree most heartily with A. James Reimer (and George Lindbeck) that "a direct theological reading of the Bible as a whole in the context of the Christian community of faith"[34] will yield the sense of a narrative with an intended unity, a story directly comprehensible to the "naive" Christian reader, and that this "literal" (not "literalistic") sense of the "canon as a whole is the locus of authority for the Christian."[35]

I part company with Reimer (who follows Vander Goot), however, when he imposes an inherent dogmatic structure on this narrative, namely that of "creation-fall-redemption-consummation." I demur even more when Reimer asks us to take especially seriously the interpretive guidance of "summaries, confessional statements, and creeds."[36] It is precisely at this point, I believe, where the history of biblical interpretation was led into one of its major aberrant tendencies. The early church

---

[31]John H. Yoder, "The Authority of the Canon," *Essays,* 265-290.

[32]Jacob J. Enz, "Canon: Creative Biblicism as a Hermeneutical Principle," *Essays,* 165-176.

[33]A. James Reimer, "Theological Framework for the Authority of the Scriptures," *The Conrad Grebel Review* 4 (Spring 1986): 125-140. See also Glenn Brubacher's response in *The Conrad Grebel Review* 4 (Fall 1986): 241-244.

[34]Reimer, "Theological Framework for the Authority of the Scriptures," 136.

[35]Ibid., 137. A similar perspective seems to pervade the work of Lindbeck, *The Nature of Doctrine,* e.g., 120.

[36]Reimer, "Theological Framework for the Authority of the Scriptures," 138.

employed two main instruments to define what was Christian both for its own instruction and for apologetic purposes: the canon and the confessions of faith or creeds. While the canon defined comprehensively the texts genuinely expressive of Christian identity, creeds (like the Apostles' Creed) functioned to summarize canonical teachings or to highlight certain ones as it struggled with heresies.

As long as creeds, and eventually dogmatic systems, remain functional tools for instructional, apologetic, liturgical or other purposes, they are necessary and useful. As soon as they become hermeneutically authoritative, however, that is, control what the canon is allowed to say, they have a reductionist effect on biblical interpretation and a divisive impact on the church.[37] The high point of such a creedal-dogmatic straight-jacketing of scripture was reached in the "High Protestant Scholastic" view of the seventeenth century, well characterized by Yoder as holding

> the assumption that the propositional content of all the canonical writings is in such a way timelessly true and coherent that it is fitting to lift all the significant statements out of their specific setting, whether in narrative, poetry, or epistle, and to reorganize them according to modern [creedal-dogmatic] principles of coherence. . . . and that the coherence of all of the texts recognized as canonical is the coherence of one logical set of propositions in no way contradictory to another.[38]

Perry Yoder has drawn attention to a transformation in the Mennonite confessions of faith through the centuries, from, in my terminology, a canonical to a creedal character.[39] I see a

---

[37]On the last point, see my paper "Maintaining a Spirit of Unity in the Face of Current Diversities," presented at the Consultation of the Council of Mennonite/Brethren in Christ Moderators, Calgary, January 19, 1989, to be published shortly in *The Conrad Grebel Review.* In contrast to the widely held opinion that strong creedal affirmations unify the church, I argue that the opposite is true, that a canonical approach could achieve the end of Christian unity much more effectively. It should also be clear that creeds, where they become "hermeneutically authoritative," do so *de facto*, generally in spite of the protestations of those who promulgate or hold them.

[38]Yoder, "The Authority of the Canon," *Essays*, 268f.

[39]Perry Yoder, "The Role of the Bible in Mennonite Self-Understanding," in *Mennonite Identity: Historical and Contemporary Perspectives*, ed. Calvin Wall Redekop and Samuel J. Steiner (Lanham, MD: University Press of America,

canonical approach to scripture not as helpfully guided by, but
as freeing us from the misguidance of, a hermeneutically authoritative use of creeds and, equally important, of creedal thinking.[40]

It is precisely in the turn from creedal to canonical hermeneutics that I see the greatest hope of overcoming the
Anabaptist-Mennonite rejection of the Old Testament without
jeopardizing the ideal of faithful discipleship which led to that
rejection. But before developing that hope further, I must
mention another road not taken. In those biblical theologies of
our century that have been most sensitive to the theological
needs of the church, the belonging together of the two Testaments has often been sought in the tracing of overarching
themes. The most prominent of these have been the themes of
covenant and of salvation history *(Heilsgeschichte)*. It is inevitable
that such approaches will "leave the Old Testament behind" in
the no longer relevant past in some way or other. It becomes
either the type preparing the ground for the higher New Testament antitype, or the promise fulfilled in the New Testament, or
the Old Covenant superseded by the New. The articles of both
Yoder and Enz are good illustrations of this phenomenon.[41]

This is not to deny that such treatment may be in order
with respect to certain biblical themes; it is merely claimed here
that it is not an adequate hermeneutic for relating the Testaments as such to each other.[42] In fact, the canonical approach to
be presented will not attempt to relate *the* Old Testament to *the*

1988), 69-82; especially 78f. "I propose that the earlier creeds express a
hermeneutical community reflecting on its identity—thus they are longer,
narrative, and seem to systematize a common way of reading the Bible; while the
later creeds grow out of a community reflecting on its theological identity. Put
bluntly, these statements are becoming a witness to beliefs about the Bible or
doctrine, which church members ought to hold," 79.

[40]By creedal thinking I mean the approach to the Bible that expects it to
speak univocally, yielding a seamless robe of propositional truths. Lindbeck's *The
Nature of Doctrine* constitutes a critique of "creedal thinking," that is, of the
"cognitive-propositional theory of religion" (together with the "experiential-
expressive" theory) from the vantage point of his "cultural-linguistic" theory. The
latter subordinates creedal formulations to the "grammar" of the community's
story (based on the canon), which alone is the locus of authority for the believing
community. See e.g., 64, 112ff.

[41]See above, notes 31 and 32.

[42]See below, note 50, and my attempt to sketch such an approach with
respect to Exodus and salvation.

New Testament which, as parts of the Christian canon recede as theologically independent entities divided by a clearly defined boundary line affecting all their themes.[43] Instead, it will be argued that a canonical approach should consider all themes within the boundaries of the whole canon and discern with respect to each theme where the most important biblical treatments affecting it can be found.

With this last statement I have introduced the central feature of my proposed hermeneutical model. In this model, the canon marks out the field within which theological dialogue must move if it is to be, or remain, Christian. It could be compared to a basketball court within which the ball must be bounced; if the ball leaves the court, it is "out of bounds." To pursue our analogy, within this court there are rules and realities governing the ball's movement, but there is no spot within the court where the ball could not at some time legitimately bounce. To say it more plainly, there is no section, book or text in the canon (both Testaments) that should, in principle, be excluded from conveying God's Word to the community for which it is canon, or that should, in principle, be defined as lesser truth, or less God's Word, than another. To return to our analogy, even the weakest player on the court, as long as he/she is tolerated on the team (that is, constitutes a part of the canon) can at some time properly be in control of the ball and can, occasionally, even score a point. That does not mean that he/she ought not at most times play supportively and yield the shots at the basket to the more skilled players. In decoded language, there is room in this canonical approach for ranking one biblical text as a "stronger player," that is, as having a more weighty theological voice than another in most matters. The life and words of Jesus will generally qualify as "strong players."[44] But it does not allow for

---

[43]Hartmut Gese has gone so far as to deny the separate existence of an "Old Testament" prior to a "New Testament," seeing the canonization of the Christian Bible as one continuous canonical process. See his essay "The Biblical View of Scripture," in *Essays on Biblical Theology*, trans. Keith Crim (Minneapolis, MN: Augsburg Press, 1981), 9-33. But already for Luther the boundary line between the Testaments was less significant than the witness to Christ holding them together.

[44]See below, note 50, and my attempt to sketch such weighting with respect to Exodus and salvation.

declaring one part of the canon or an internal norm as having
priority, whether this be the New Testament as such, or the story
of Jesus, or the Sermon on the Mount, or the gospel versus the
law.[45]

Such a view assumes, then, that a contemporary exegete/
biblical theologian in search of the biblical message on any given
topic—such as Christology, liberation, sin and forgiveness,
stewardship of creation, sexuality and marriage, war and
peace—will first take stock of the biblical texts (shorter or
longer) within both Testaments that seem relevant to that topic.
He/she will then proceed to "interface" (Childs' term) these texts,
allowing them to deliver their own distinctive message on that
topic. The assumption is that, in a general way, these contributions will support and supplement each other, as they all
function within the parameters of the canon. For example, they
will all speak within the framework of assuming one sovereign
God, creator of the world and shaper of its history and destiny.
Within such broad common assumptions, however, the intertex-
tual dialogue will be polyphonic rather than homophonic. Texts
will support, challenge, modify or supplement each other. At
points they will appear to be contradictory. Such diversity will
be evident just as much *within* each Testament as *between* the
Testaments. Thus an Old Testament text apparently advocating
war will find itself in just as much tension with other Old
Testament texts advocating peace as with New Testament texts.
On some topics, like family, land or work, the sheer bulk of
material will be found in the Old Testament. Furthermore, we
may well discover that, on many a topic, the combined chorus of
Old Testament texts defines the biblical position, a position to
which the New Testament's contribution consists of little more
than marginal notes, at best adding minor modifications. I
believe this to be the case with respect to a biblical theology of

---

[45]With Childs, "There is no hermeneutical key for unlocking the biblical
message, but the canon provides the arena in which the struggle for understanding takes place." *Old Testament Theology in a Canonical Context*, 15. Childs may
overstate the case a little here. There are certain guidelines according to which
the "struggle for understanding" must be carried on, as he himself has demonstrated often and well. See note 30 and our discussion below.

work, for example.[46] On other topics, the New Testament's volume of contribution to a topic will be more prominent.

Furthermore, in this process of the interfacing of texts an interpreter will find that the texts isolated originally as immediately pertinent will soon lead him/her to yet other texts that initially seemed to lie outside of the subject in question. Ultimately, the pursuit of a single topic would draw in ever wider circles of texts, resulting eventually in a biblical theology snowballed around an initial topical kernel. In this view, it appears of little importance with which text our quest begins. A New Testament starting text would draw other texts into the discussion, possibly first from within its own New Testament book or section (gospels, Pauline letters), then from the rest of the New Testament and eventually from the Old Testament. A beginning point in the Old Testament would expand in analogous fashion to the New Testament.[47]

The chief function of the biblical interpreter is to adjudicate the relative weight of the texts interfaced in discussion of a given topic.[48] Once again, in this model no superior authority is granted *a priori* to any canon within the canon or to any other internal norm. This adjudicating in the dialogue between texts belongs to a second level of dialogue, namely that between interpreters.[49] Rather than positing a set of absolute principles,

---

[46]For a detailed substantiation of this claim, see my paper "The Theology of Work from an Old Testament Perspective," first read at the MCC-sponsored Colloquium on the Theology of Work, Winnipeg, Manitoba, June 15-17, 1988 (Publication anticipated).

[47]For a legitimation of a separate Old Testament theology and, by implication, a New Testament theology as preliminary to a biblical theology, see Childs, "A Canonical Approach to Old Testament Theology," in *Old Testament Theology in a Canonical Context*, 1-19.

[48]In response to several questions raised in the discussion period following the original presentation of this paper, I must plead with my readers to remember that no attempt is made here to present a full exegetical-theological methodology, much less a digest of biblical theology. My task consists of a call for admitting the Old Testament to partnership with the New in the biblical-theological arena, but not to spell out what happens in that arena. It is in the latter process (referred to here, in shorthand, as "interfacing") that aspects of content, of history and of eschatology would come to bear on the relative weight accorded to specific texts. For example, the abrogation of Old Testament food laws would be recognized, not because it happens in the New Testament—Jesus and the apostles probably observed them—but because the era of the admission of the gentiles had begun at Pentecost.

[49]I acknowledge gratefully the warning of my respondent, Ben Ollenburger,

this model calls for a genuine hermeneutical community consisting of all—past and present—who claim the Bible as their canon.[50] As a result, many theological questions will be debated for a long time.[51]

On the other hand, such an approach, though "long-suffering," can lead to closure. The question of slavery is an example. It took centuries of debate, but at this time in the church's history a consensus has been reached. No Christian interpreter can advocate slave-holding as a Christian option today. And let us remind ourselves that this consensus was not achieved on the basis of a New Testament rejecting slavery, as compared to an Old Testament accepting it. Both Testaments accepted this social institution of their time, but both also contained seeds that, in the course of interpretation, could grow into an understanding which rejected slavery.

This illustration also makes clear that the hermeneutical community, often understood by the Anabaptists in synchronic fashion as the presently gathered groups of believers, is here understood to be diachronic, embracing the church of all ages.[52]

---

that the call for interfacing texts from both Testaments may suggest a simplistic biblicism, ready to speak directly to modern issues to the disregard of the tasks of systematic theology. Such a reading is not at all intended here; again, I must draw attention to the limited task of this paper. My concern here, however, remains: that the systematic-theological task include both Testaments.

[50]It should be understood clearly that it is not the object of this discussion to determine which of the texts are more fully the authoritative word of God. All of them were word of God in certain past contexts. The conversation has as its goal to ascertain in what sense, and in what order of priority, these texts should be heard as word of God in *our* context. An example: A mother tells her child in context A: "Be careful!" In context B: "Don't linger so long; get going!" Finding itself in context C, the child needs to ask: "How do I hear mother's words now?"

[51]At the Mennonite scholars' meeting in conjunction with the American Academy of Religion/Society of Biblical Literature sessions in Chicago, November 19, 1988, John H. Yoder encouraged those present to carry on their theologizing on the model of rabbinic discussion, in which there is room for a patient playing out of contradictory opinions. There is much in this invitation that attracts me, but I think the recent models of canonical criticism (like Childs', as well as the one under discussion) hold the same promise, without being burdened by various aspects of rabbinic tradition unhelpful to Christian theology, e.g., its legal(istic) orientation.

[52]In this respect I agree with the spirit of James Reimer's proposal. The hermeneutical community must include the church of the early trinitarian and christological debates, just as it must include—as we have come to realize only recently—the church in the Third World. While canonical criticism takes seriously the Reformation principle of *sola scriptura*, assigning the church's interpretive tradition to a second level of discourse, it does not dismiss that tradition, as the

Decisions reached in more limited communal and temporal contexts, though necessary, must retain a preliminary status.

Conclusion

In conclusion, let us return to the claim made earlier that we are in need of the theological voice of the Old Testament, not only to round out our understanding of all theological areas, but also to provide us with a biblical-theological basis in areas only marginally treated in the New Testament. Often such a deficiency is the result of two contrary assumptions: While the New Testament assumes the ongoing validity of the Old as the Word of God, we assume that the Old has been superseded by the New. To the extent that something is not on the New Testament's theological map, it does not exist for us.

The bi-polar theme, liberation-salvation, offers a primary illustration. The chief paradigm of God's saving action in the Old Testament is, of course, God's liberation of the descendants of Jacob/Israel from Egyptian enslavement as forced labourers. It is a political-economic liberation, although it issues in a reality of faith and hope as well: our God is a God who wants our deliverance from whoever and whatever enslaves us. The ultimate parameters of this faith embrace God's salvation from the cosmic enslavers, "sin, death, and devil" (Luther), toward an eternal "rest" (earlier applied to the land of Canaan, e.g., Deuteronomy 12:9) with God, that is, a "homeland, a better country [than geographical Canaan], that is, a heavenly one" (Hebrews 11:16). The New Testament focuses on this ultimate salvation. What about the liberation of human beings from enslavement here and now, and their need for a homeland? Is that no longer God's will? In Jesus' concern for the sick, the poor and the prisoners there is enough indication that he affirmed earthly liberation as modeled in the Exodus, as well as eternal salvation from the

---

Reformation (including Anabaptism) did in the name of scripture, or as the Enlightenment did in the name of reason. Partnership in dialogue within the court of the canon by all who accept it as canon is the essence of the canonical criticism proposed in this paper.

power of Satan. However, much of this indication is sparse and assumed. Should we not reclaim the full-blown model of the Exodus of Israel from Egypt as a paradigm of God's will for liberation of peoples and groups from political-economic oppression? That is the call of certain brands of liberation theology. While some, from a materialist orientation, go so far as to consider such liberation the real concern of the church, others would like to complete the biblical mandate by adding the concern for (external) liberation to that of (spiritual) salvation.

A canonical reading as advocated here, however, would see such a simple addition of the Old Testament perspective to the New Testament as a shortchanging of theological exegesis. It is interfacing and dialogue between texts, not addition of texts, that is called for. Our needs are not met by adding an Old Testament liberation mandate based on the Exodus to the work of salvation accomplished by Jesus Christ. We need, rather, to reread the Exodus in the light of Jesus Christ. We would then see the Israelites and the Egyptians caught in a common captivity to sin, as the Old Testament also acknowledges. We would recognize the need of both to be saved by the means demonstrated in the suffering servant love of Jesus. We would find a prominent link between Exodus and Jesus in Isaiah 40-55, where a new Exodus from Babylon is promised. To achieve it, God uses both the violent power of the nations (Cyrus) and the (suffering) servant power of God's people. Into this interfacing of texts would soon be drawn texts about God-willed life in exile, for example, Jeremiah 29 or Daniel 1-6. The resultant theology would embrace both liberation and salvation. It would acknowledge God's will for external human freedom and well-being, but also the fact that exile and suffering have their place in a biblical perspective on the God-led path of salvation.

I can do no more here than sketch in the briefest fashion the dynamics and nature of a biblical theology for which a canonical approach holds promise. In particular, I want to conclude with the claim that such an approach should not be felt by us as a "reversion" to "sub-Christian" ways, but rather as a fuller appropriation of the riches of God's truth and grace than a truncated reading of the New Testament can ever offer.

III. Biblical Theology

Mary H. Schertz*

INTERPRETATION AS DISCIPLESHIP: LUKE 24 AS MODEL**

At this point in time, the relationship between a believers' church theology of discipleship and the exegesis of the portrayal of the disciples in the gospels in general, and in Luke-Acts specifically, lacks both description and explanation. Fundamentally, to posit such a relationship implies a relevance between two questions: What does it mean to be a disciple of Jesus Christ? and, What is Luke's view of what it means to be a disciple of Jesus Christ? More precisely, what does Luke's portrayal of the disciples in Luke-Acts reveal about what he thinks it means to be a disciple of Jesus Christ?

While a connection between these two questions may not be significant for all traditions, a believers' church understanding of the biblical witness as source and norm for theology would imply that there ought to be a fairly significant link between them. Together Luke and Acts comprise roughly a quarter of the New Testament. The disciples figure centrally in this literature. If we consider discipleship an important theological concept for believers' church thought and life, and if we take seriously the claim to be biblical in our thinking and living, we can hardly afford to ignore this important resource. Such an understanding at least implies that the burden of proof ought to lie with those who do not posit or who argue against such a necessary relationship.

As logical as the connection may seem, however, the portrayal of the disciples has not been widely used as a source or norm for thinking theologically about what it means to follow

---

*Mary H. Schertz is Assistant Professor of New Testament at Associated Mennonite Biblical Seminaries, Elkhart, Indiana.

**The author would like to thank Margaret Loewen Reimer, Associate Editor, *Mennonite Reporter,* Waterloo, Ontario, and Tom Yoder Neufeld, Assistant Professor of New Testament, Conrad Grebel College, Waterloo, Ontario, for their critical responses to this essay at the Symposium.

Christ. One reason why this has not happened may be the
tension between the ideal and the real. Both lay and professional
thinkers have had a tendency to rank the disciples only a little
lower than Jesus. We have all been influenced to a certain extent
by traditions which have endowed the disciples with sainthood.
This phenomenon has worked against a believers' church
theology of discipleship connected to the New Testament
portrayal of the disciples in two ways.

First, the synoptic disciples at times appear to be something
less than saints. Thus, it has been difficult to relate the biblical
story of the disciples to a theology of discipleship which is
understood as a theology of sainthood. The human ambiguity of
the disciples' record is not a natural source for an idealized
theology.

Secondly, this idealization of the disciples as saints has
resonated negatively with fears that theological reflections
focused on human discipleship might lead to an anthropology
rather than a theology. Such fears are not, of course, unique to
believers' church thinking. In our tradition, however, the
juxtaposition of such fears with an emphasis on discipleship has
had a particular effect. The energy that might have been given to
an examination of discipleship from an exegetical viewpoint has
largely been channelled into considerations of the teachings of
Jesus and ecclesiology. Concentrating on what disciples should
do and on what disciples supposedly can do if they give themselves to the discipline of the believing body, has allowed the
concept of discipleship to flourish in a context of perfectionism
without sacrificing Mennonite modesty or needing to take
seriously the specific witness of the gospels' portrayals of Jesus'
first followers. By so doing, we have avoided some of the
problems of a human-centred theology. On the other hand, we
have missed some important components needed for a mature
understanding of the relationship between the divine and human
known as discipleship.

The purpose of this essay, then, is to begin describing and
explaining the connection between Luke's portrayal of the
disciples and a believers' church theology of discipleship.[1] A

---

[1]While the task of this paper is not the task of defining and describing the

working assumption of the paper is that an examination of the relationship between Jesus and his disciples at the end of Luke's gospel is an inquiry particularly suited to the exploration of the above connection because the way Luke deals with the disciples' failure during Christ's passion reveals his understanding of discipleship in a particular way. A brief survey of pertinent literature and a methodological note, will be followed by an argument that the issue of discipleship emerges in Luke 24 at two narrative levels. These narrative levels are embodied in two relationships. A primary narrative relationship between Jesus and his disciples focuses the issue of discipleship for the reader. In addition, a secondary narrative relationship, established in the prologues of the gospel and Acts between the writer and the reader, provides the contextual stage for Luke's reflections on the dynamics of discipleship. These levels are bonded together with a shared quest for resolution and understanding. At the primary narrative level, the issue of the relationship between Jesus and the disciples, strained by the disciples' failure during the passion, is only partially resolved and understanding between them only partially achieved in Luke 24. At the secondary level, the issue of the relationship between the writer and reader is resolved in the reader's fulsome understanding of what, in Luke's view, discipleship entails. It is in the rich blending of these two narrative levels that Luke's depiction of the disciples offers itself as source and norm for a believers' church theology of discipleship.

Review of Scholarship

Any attempt to describe the discussion either of Luke's view

---

complex relationships between exegesis, biblical theology and systematic theology, several premises about these issues are operative. One such premise is that an exegesis of Luke's portrayal of the disciples is revelatory of Luke's view of discipleship. In that sense, the task of the paper is a task of biblical theology. Another operative premise is that Luke's view of discipleship can be brought to bear directly upon contemporary systematic thinking about discipleship. In this sense, the task of the paper is different from a more intermediate process of biblical theology which involves a systematization of all the biblical material on discipleship. Finally, a third operative premise is that while the relationships between exegetical and theological tasks are not always clear, it is better to explore them through practice than to wait for absolute theoretical lucidity.

of discipleship or of his portrayal of the disciples must begin with an acknowledgement that these particular themes have not received wide scholarly attention over the years. In some respects this deficiency is also true of research on the gospels in general, although the topic has been addressed somewhat more readily in relation to Mark, John and even Matthew.

There are at least two reasons for this inactivity. One is that Luke's depiction of the disciples is generally seen as positive when compared to Mark's description of them. Mark's negativism has been the more problematic, thus exegetically more interesting, and hence has been given greater attention.[2]

A second reason for the inactivity is the way Conzelmann has dominated Lucan studies. In his effort to conceptualize Lucan theology in terms of salvation history, Conzelmann has essentially blurred the distinctions between the character of Jesus and the character of the disciples in what he has designated as the second period of that sacred history. This second period, the ministry of Jesus, is a pivot between the period of Israel and the period of the church. The designation of Jesus' period as pivotal or paradigmatic (and Satan-free) forces Conzelmann to a defense of that period as more ideal than the text warrants. For instance, although he concedes that the Satan-free period ends in Luke 22:3 before the disciples betray and forsake Jesus, Conzelmann misses earlier mistakes and misunderstandings of the disciples which foreshadow their failure.[3] Therefore, the evidence against the disciples gets lost in the idealism. Even those scholars who have argued with Conzelmann on other points have generally not taken issue with him on this matter. Fitzmyer is a case in point. Although Fitzmyer challenges the notion of early Catholicism or ecclesiality in Luke,[4] he essentially affirms Conzelmann's positive

---

[2]Many of the studies of Mark include whole chapters on the role of the disciples. See Vernon K. Robbins, *Jesus the Teacher: A Socio-Rhetorical Interpretation of Mark* (Philadelphia, PA: Fortress Press, 1984) for a major treatment of the disciples in Mark.

[3]Conzelmann describes the time when Jesus was living, the "foundation period of the apostles and eye-witnesses" as "the time of salvation; Satan was far away, it was a time without temptation." Hans Conzelmann, *The Theology of St. Luke*, trans. Geoffrey Buswell (Philadelphia, PA: Fortress Press, 1961), 14-16.

[4]See Joseph A. Fitzmyer, *The Gospel According to Luke I-IX* (Garden City, NJ: Doubleday & Company, 1981), 23-27 for an argument against catholicism in

view of the disciples.

Thus, both the Markan comparison and Conzelmann's salvation history schema have contributed to a consensus that Luke regards the disciples with general approval. Without ascribing cause and effect, this exegetical tendency to see the disciples of Luke-Acts in a positive light is in agreement with the previously described theological tendency to see the disciples as saints.[5] Together, this theological and exegetical consensus has, for the most part, resulted in the desultory interest aroused by most settled questions.

That this consensus has been premature and that nuances were sacrificed in the process is, however, becoming evident. More recently there have been some challenges to this positive view of Luke's description. We will look briefly at two of these challenges.

Robert C. Tannehill essentially argues that the parable of the sower in chapter 8 of Luke's gospel establishes the "norms" against which both the crowds and the disciples are measured. In chapters 9-23 they are found wanting. Persecution, even the threat of persecution, unmasks the potentially short-lived nature of the disciples' faith (rocky soil). Possessions, especially the acquisition of status, are also a potential threat to the disciples' faith (thorny soil).[6]

Tannehill then proceeds to trace the deficiencies of the disciples through the rest of the gospel. The disciples begin well enough, giving the reader the hope that they might be "good soil." They perform the mission (9:1-6) with success (9:10), and participate with Jesus in the feeding of the five thousand (9:13-17). This "success" is temporary, however. Three of the most important disciples sleep through part of the transfiguration (9:32). Then the disciples are characterized as not understanding,

---

Luke-Acts which nevertheless assumes a fairly high view of the "apostles."

[5]Interestingly enough, one might also note that the Western non- interpolations in Luke 24 have an "apologetic" bent, meaning that they tend to represent non-inclusions of material which makes the disciples look bad. Seemingly, Conzelmann and others stand in a long tradition of wanting to see the disciples in a positive light!

[6]Robert C. Tannehill, *The Narrative Unity of Luke-Acts: A Literary Interpretation,* volume 1 (Philadelphia, PA: Fortress Press, 1986), 210, 211.

not perceiving, and being afraid to ask Jesus about those things they don't understand (9:45). Not long after the transfiguration, they begin to argue about who is greatest. From that point on, the narrative describes an increasing discrepancy between Jesus' point of view and the disciples' perspectives. These discrepancies are evident at a variety of occasions: the casting out of demons (9:49, 50); the treatment of villages which do not receive Jesus (9:51ff.); the bringing of the babies to Jesus (18:15ff.); Jesus' prediction of his own suffering (18:34). The disciples' failures are also evident in their dispute over who is the greatest (22:24ff.); their producing two swords in response to Jesus' test (22:35-38); their inability to stay awake through the prayer on Olivet (22:45, 46); the hasty action to slice off the slave's ear (22:50ff.); and finally the denial of Jesus (23:58). According to Tannehill's reading, the disciples are, after their initial successes, consistently deficient.[7]

These deficiencies are, however, completely overcome and the disciples are restored to a proper relationship with Jesus in chapter 24, when he appears to them after the resurrection and teaches them. Through these appearances and instructions, the disciples not only come to understand Jesus but also to worship God with great joy.[8]

In contrast to Tannehill, Jerome Neyrey contends that the text's portrayal of the disciples is more ambiguous.[9] Neyrey notes that the disciples are both commended and condemned, sometimes in practically the same breath. For instance, the positive charges Jesus gives the disciples in chapter 22 are mixed with negative predictions. Thus the rebuke of the disciples' questions about greatness (22:24-27) is juxtaposed with Jesus' note that the disciples are those who have stayed with him and are assigned a kingdom (22:28-30). Likewise, the prediction about Peter's denial (22:31 and 34) encloses a statement that Jesus has prayed for Peter and believes he will repent and strengthen "the brethren" (22:32).

---

[7]Ibid., 273.

[8]Ibid., 293.

[9]Jerome Neyrey, *The Passion According to Luke: A Redaction Study of Luke's Soteriology* (Mahwah, NJ: Paulist Press, 1985), 24.

Neyrey explains this ambiguity with reference to what he sees as the climax of the relationship between Jesus and the disciples: the prayer in the garden. He contends that Luke evaluates the disciples and Jesus in light of values derived from both Stoic philosophy and the Septuagint (LXX). He notes that Luke takes the "grief" that Mark assigns to Jesus and gives it to the disciples. In so doing, Neyrey argues, Luke is indebted to Stoic philosophy, which assigned a negative quality to grief and other such emotions on the grounds that they evidenced a lack of moral fibre. In addition, as Neyrey notes, the LXX also often equates grief with sin. Therefore Jesus, who in contrast to the disciples endures to the end, shows moral courage and emerges as a hero in both systems of value.[10]

Unfortunately, unlike Tannehill, Neyrey does not extend his analysis to chapter 24. Yet, even though he fails to do so and his work tends to be quite uneven, it is the assessment of this writer that Neyrey is somewhat more accurate in his conclusions than Tannehill is in his negative appraisal of the disciples.

Certainly, by the time the reader is informed that the disciples disbelieve the women (24:11), he or she is fully prepared for the disciples' miserable failure. After all, they have, as Tannehill points out, periodically "messed up" by either misunderstanding or simply failing to "go the distance," as, for example, in the sleeping episodes. But Tannehill is overlooking that this portrayal of the disciples' deficiencies is neither as consistent as that of Mark's nor does it "crescendo" as pointedly as Mark's. Up until the passion itself, the disciples continue to do some things right and to receive the approval of Jesus.

In contrast to Mark, Luke portrays the disciples as occasionally failing miserably. It may well be that their periodic failures outweigh their successes. The reader, however, is not led to give up on or reject the disciples as one is in Mark. The distinction needs to be made between episodic failure and consistent failure. In this case, the episodic nature of the disciples' deficiencies in Luke prevents the reader from disassociating from the disciples. Indeed the reader retains an identification with the disciples, albeit an ambiguous one.

---

[10]Ibid., 49-68.

Tannehill overstates the negative assessment of the disciples in chapters 9-23. Consequently, he also exaggerates the restoration of the disciples' relationship with Jesus in chapter 24. There is a kind of resolution—in fact, two resolutions—to the theme of discipleship in Luke's rhetorically significant last chapter. But these resolutions are neither quite so simple nor quite so complete as Tannehill indicates.

A Methodological Note

The contention of this essay is that a specific type of literary analysis may assist the process of the debate about Luke's view of discipleship. The concept of narrative levels, that is, the utilization of different narrative voices, may be illuminative.

As one discovers in introductory English courses, modern writing may evidence a multi-levelled complex of narrative voices with involved ironies operating on this diversity.[11] In ancient literature, these levels are usually fewer and generally less complex. Nevertheless, it is often helpful to distinguish narrative levels insofar as is possible. The exercise is especially pertinent to Lucan studies because this text, unlike the other gospels, specifically defines two narrative levels with two different but related readers or readings.[12]

---

[11]See Susan Sniader Lanser, *The Narrative Act: Point of View in Prose Fiction* (Princeton, NJ: Princeton University Press, 1981), 145, for a diagram of the possible levels of narrative voice in modern fiction. See also her third chapter, 108-148, for an explanation of these possibilities. On page 145 she lists 6 possible narrator-narratee relationships. They are:

1. Historical Author < _____ > Historical Audience
2. Extra-textual Voice < _____ > Extra-textual Audience
3. Public Narrator < _____ > Public Narratee
4. Private Narrator < _____ > Private Narratee
5. Focalizer < _____ > Spectator
6. Character < _____ > Character

In this study, I deal primarily with the third and fourth possibilities. However, I implicitly assume the first, the historical author, Luke, and the sixth, the interaction of the characters. The second possibility, consisting of publisher's "blurbs," is irrelevant and the fifth, the focalizer, is not pertinent to this ancient text which, unlike more modern writing, tends to present a consistent point of view throughout the different narrative levels.

[12]For the purposes of this study, the distinction being examined may profitably be conceptualized as either "readers" or "readings." Whether one designates the difference as the difference between a first and onetime reader

In Luke-Acts there is an explicit reader as well as an implicit reader. A public narrator-narratee relationship is explicitly specified and a private narrator-narratee relationship is implicitly indicated.

The private narratee or implicit reader embedded in the text is similar to those of the other gospels or most other straightforward texts. We assume a first-time reader who is given the information sequentially. This reader does not anticipate the text. The knowledge possessed is the knowledge given in the text up to the point of reading and/or assumed by the narrator as common, cultural information. In other words, the expectations of this reader are assumed to be those commonly created by a basic competency with the linguistic, literary and cultural forms that are present in the social world from which the text emerges.[13]

Luke-Acts, however, is more literarily self-conscious than the other gospels and posits a specific, additional reader. This reader is described in the prologues to the two volumes. From the prologue to Luke, we understand that this reader, Theophilus (God-lover), already knows the events of which the narrative speaks. This reader has been previously "informed," is possibly acquainted with other written and oral accounts and is probably well-educated. What this reader—possibly a specific person but more probably an "Everyman" figure—lacks is a coherent and certain view of the events. At least, that is what the public or explicit narrator promises to provide. If the private narratee receives the information sequentially, this public narratee receives the information synchronically, that is, simultaneously reviewing and anticipating the events of the text in the current reading moment.[14] For the sake of easier discussion, we might designate the first reader, the one who does not anticipate the text, the diachronic reader and the second, the more informed reader, the synchronic reader.[15]

---

and another reader who knows the text well or the difference between a first and second reading by the same reader is largely immaterial.

[13]Lanser, *The Narrative Act*, 138-139.

[14]Ibid., 137-138.

[15]Mikeal C. Parsons, *The Departure of Jesus in Luke-Acts: The Ascension*

Disciples and Readers in Luke 24

In thinking about the theme of discipleship in Luke 24, it is important to keep these two different readers or readings in mind. As previously stated, the contention of this essay is that the issues of discipleship are only partially resolved for the diachronic reader. At the same time they are settled with a fair degree of finality for the synchronic, explicit reader whom Luke designates as "Theophilus."

The Diachronic Reader

For the private or diachronic reader, the resolution of the disciples' relationship with Jesus is foreshadowed but, in the end, withheld or postponed for reasons of narrativity. There is certainly progress toward determining how the disciples will relate to Jesus. The disciples, as narrated characters, move through a succession of four doubts about the reality of the resurrection which are, by one means or another, dissipated. In the end, they move from "disbelieving for joy" to "great joy." The removal of these four doubts is coordinated with a reconciliation process between Jesus and the disciples who betrayed and forsook him at a time when he most needed this understanding, compassion and support.

When the chapter opens, the relationship between Jesus and his disciples is at low ebb. As has been noted, in their last encounters before the passion, the disciples fail Jesus at several points. They operate out of fear rather than freedom when they fail the test of the two swords (22:35-38). They fall asleep when Jesus asks them to pray (22:39-46). In the arrest scene (22:47-53), they displease Jesus by wielding the sword. And, climactically, Peter denies Jesus three times (22:54-60). The last mention of the disciples previous to their appearance in Luke 24 is the bitter scene where Jesus looks at Peter and Peter goes out to

---

Narratives in Context (Sheffield: Sheffield Academic Press, 1987), 19-24, uses the terms "diachronic" and "synchronic" to describe different kinds of critical analyses. The assumption of this study is simpler. In a more common, dictionary understanding, diachronic reading is sequential reading, reading to "get the story," while synchronic reading is an effort to understand the art and vision of a work as a whole.

weep (22:61-62).

The disciples are conspicuously absent in chapter 23. In fact, there are several rather pointed accounts of other people filling the slots left vacant by the disciples. Simon of Cyrene carries the cross for Jesus (23:26). The multitudes and the women of Jerusalem lament Jesus' fate (23:27). It is the thief who understands Jesus (23:42) and it is the centurion who proclaims Jesus' innocence (23:47). Again it is the multitudes who beat their breast and the "acquaintances and the women" who stand at a distance (23:48). Finally, it is Joseph from Arimathea who cares for the body of Jesus and lays it in the tomb (23:50-54). In short, none of the tasks of comfort and care required by Jesus in his extremity are performed by those closest to him.

So it is that, at the beginning of chapter 24, the disciples are both physically absent from the happenings around Jesus and palpably estranged from their Lord. The extent of the alienation is indicated by the fact that they do not believe the women when they return from the tomb and report that it is empty.

It would be wise not to overload the significance of the disciples' disbelief. However, one might wonder if the disciples did not believe the women partly because they were women. In verse 12, which is of course textually insecure,[16] Peter returns to the tomb to see for himself and, more importantly, in verse 24, the disciples on the road to Emmaus report that other (presumably male) disciples went to the tomb to verify the women's story. At any rate, the disciples do not accept the word of the women until it has been recast as a male perception.

It is at this first and greatest moment of doubt, when the disciples judge the most profound news of the gospel story to be "an idle tale," that they manifest just how great the distance is between them and Jesus. If the reader has any question about whether the actions of the disciples in chapter 22 represent failure, or any question whether their absence in chapter 23 does, those questions are answered in verse 11 of chapter 24. The

---

[16]Fitzmyer contends, however, that the inclusion of this verse "merits more than a D in the UBSGNT3 rating." Joseph A. Fitzmyer, *The Gospel According to Luke X-XXIV* (Garden City, NY: Doubleday & Company, 1985), 1547.

disciples, in their doubt of the women, are totally distant and completely estranged from the one they have been following from Galilee.

The second instance of doubt or disbelief centres around the issue of absence and presence. A poignant, visual irony is operative in verse 24ff. In relating events of the recent past to the "stranger" on the road, Cleopas and his friend implicitly confess the disciples' dissatisfaction with the experience of the empty tomb. Conceding that the women were right about the empty tomb, the sentence ends with the plaintive "but him they did not see." What Jesus has told them all along is not enough; the women's report of the empty tomb is not enough; the verification of the women's report by the disciples themselves is not enough. The disciples need to see Jesus in order to believe. Of course, the reader knows that at the very moment the disciples are voicing this need, they are indeed standing face to face with none other than Jesus himself. Their inability to see what is right before their eyes denotes their state of essential doubt and their continuing estrangement from Jesus. This alienation is then confirmed in Jesus' rebuke of them as "foolish" and "slow of heart to believe." It is evident at this point that, in moving from dismissal of the resurrection story to demanding visual proof, the disciples have made some progress toward both faith and reconciliation with Jesus. It is also evident that in their failure to recognize the initiative of grace represented by Jesus' approach, they have some distance to go.

The third instance of doubt follows the confirmation of the empty tomb and of Jesus as a presence. The presence of Jesus has been verified through Jesus' instruction of Cleopas and his friend on the road, through their recognition of the identity of the "stranger" and through the report of the appearance to Simon (27-35). The issue in this third instance of doubt has to do with the kind of presence the risen Christ represents. The appearance of Jesus among the disciples gathered in Jerusalem causes them to be startled and frightened, to sup- pose that they are seeing a ghost (37). Again, their misinterpretation of the kind of presence Jesus represents, their position of essential distrust rather than trust marks the degree of their continued alienation from Jesus. In response to the disciples' lack of faith, Jesus rebukes their questioning and, this time, offers himself for handling in order to reassure them that he is indeed a "flesh and bones" reality (39).

The fourth instance of recorded doubt follows closely upon the third. Even after seeing and handling Jesus, the disciples continue to doubt on the grounds that the resurrection is simply too good to be true. They "disbelieved for joy" (41). At this point, Jesus proves his physical reality by eating a fish and continues to instruct the disciples on understanding his death and resurrection in terms of the scriptures (41b-45). Then, Jesus once more demonstrates his faith in them by commissioning the disciples as "witnesses" (48). By this act Jesus echoes the confidence he has shown in them all along, even while they are predominantly failing him. For example, Jesus assigns the disciples "a kingdom" (22:28-30) even while he rebukes their plays for power (22:24-27). Furthermore, Jesus looks ahead to Peter's continued leadership of the disciples even as he anticipates Peter's betrayal (22:32-33).

Thus, the chapter ends somewhat ambiguously. Certainly the disciples have made progress. They have moved from dismissal of the women's good news as an "idle tale" through doubts about the presence of Jesus, doubts about the kind of presence the risen Christ represents and doubts about trusting their own joy. Furthermore, the disciples were commissioned and, upon their Lord's departure, they returned to Jerusalem "with great joy and were continually in the temple blessing God" (52-53).

However, even though great joy is obviously better than disbelieving for joy, and any kind of joy is better than responding to the gospel as to an idle tale, there is a sense in which this progress is tentative and incomplete. To the attentive and careful diachronic reader this resolution, both of the disciples' doubt and of their estrangement from Jesus, is partial and imperfect for a variety of reasons. While the disciples' minds are "opened to understand scripture," their response to that understanding of scripture is to return to the temple and to praise God. That scene will, for the diachronic reader, offer a certain kind of hope and a certain kind of despair.

In addition to the previous somewhat startling and dubious

association of the words "joy" and "disbelief" (24:41), the scene recalls two things. First, it recalls the birth narratives. As the gospel began in the temple, it ends in the temple. As it began so also it ends with the faithful of Israel. The disciples are expressing things and doing things that have been presented with affirmation earlier in the text.[17]

But the scene also recalls the women who are behaving in appropriately Jewish ways at the beginning of Luke 24, the literary unit under consideration. Like the characters of the birth narratives, these women are also acting as the faithful of Israel when they bring spices to the tomb after carefully observing the Sabbath. Unlike the characters of the birth narrative, however, these women are not commended. They are in fact reproved. The behaviour affirmed in the birth narratives is not appropriate for those who have "come with him from Galilee." Those who have been with Jesus since the ministry in Galilee, those who have heard what Jesus said and who have seen what Jesus did, should not be seeking the living among the dead. At the end of the gospel, those who continue to act in proper Jewish ways are not acting in unfaith but neither are they acting in the fullness of faith. The old religious rituals are not, in and of themselves, totally adequate responses to the new reality.

But perhaps the most striking evidence of final ambiguity is the fact that there is no narrative statement of faith which corresponds with the narrative statement of disbelief. Whereas the narrator has cited the varying degrees of the disciples' disbelief three times (24:11, 25 and 41), he gives no corresponding narrative statement of the disciples' faith. The disciples, in fact, make no verbal response to the resurrection which is not tinged with wonderment and questioning. In short, while it is clear that "great joy" is better than "joyful unbelief," it is also clear that something more is required.

---

[17]In an article, "Narrative Closure and Openness in the Plot of the Third Gospel: The Sense of an Ending in Luke 24:50-53," *Society of Biblical Literature, Seminar Papers* (Atlanta, GA: Scholars Press, 1986), 205-208, Mikeal Parsons claims that Luke 24:50-53 recalls the birth narratives in three ways: Jesus' blessing of the disciples completes the priestly task Zechariah is unable to discharge in 1:23; the return to Jerusalem completes the geographical journey begun by Mary and Joseph in 2:45; the disciples' praising God in the temple mirrors the stances of Simeon and Anna as "the pious people of God."

Because the "great joy" with which the gospel ends is not an unquestioned joy, the issues of discipleship are not completely resolved at the private narrative level. It is not entirely clear whether the relationship between Jesus and the disciples, damaged in the events of the passion, is entirely resolved despite the progress the disciples have made in understanding the scriptures.

Of course, this lack of resolution is confirmed in the beginning of Acts. As the second volume begins, the disciples are still asking the inappropriate question about the restoration of Israel that exposes their lack of understanding about the nature of Jesus' mission (Acts 1:6). At this point, Jesus directly rebukes them for asking the question. He says, "It is not for you to know . . ." (Acts 1:7). Also, the disciples are still being rebuked by the angels for inappropriate behaviour (1:11) in a way that marks their deficiency for the diachronic reader.

The fact that Luke's second volume reiterates the gap between the disciples' actual understanding and the understanding Jesus wants for them reinforces the thesis that Luke's gospel ends inconclusively in relation both to the disciples' faith and to their relationship to Jesus. The reason for this ambiguity can probably best be explained by the demands of narrativity, but may have theological significance as well. Literarily, the fact that the tensions between Jesus and the disciples resurface in the beginning of Acts provides a clue as to why the full resolution of the relationship is postponed in Luke. As D. A. Miller points out, ambiguity is narratable while resolution is not.[18] The partial resolution of the issues of discipleship functions both to close the gospel and to invite the reader into the next volume. On the level of the characters, the first understanding required is that the resurrection is real, that real dead flesh has been transformed into real live flesh (24:39-43). Secondly, the characters must understand the purpose of the passion and resurrection events well enough to fulfill three duties placed upon them by Jesus: to be witnesses of these events (47, 48); to stay in the city and await empowerment rather than dispersing to the countryside (49); and

---

[18]D. A. Miller, *Narrative and Its Discontents: Problems of Closure in the Traditional Novel* (Princeton, NJ: Princeton University Press, 1981), xiii-xiv.

to react to the departure of Jesus with joy and worship rather than sorrow (52). What is required of the characters has to do with a correct understanding of the reality of the resurrection. In that respect the scene resolves and ends the gospel.

However, the disciples' incomplete understanding of what this reality means also functions to sustain the kind of tension that will draw the reader into the next book. In the case of the disciples and their relationship to Jesus, Luke's treatment is dictated by the requirements of his second volume. Luke *has* to do what the other gospels do not need to do: write another volume. He cannot afford to resolve the issue of the disciples either positively like Matthew and John or negatively like Mark because he has to sustain a narrative tension into Acts, at least until some other tension can be created to sustain narratability.

The relationship between Jesus and the disciples is finally resolved with the coming of the Spirit, once a new narrative tension is firmly in place. The tension surrounding the behaviour of the disciples is dramatically resolved after the arrival of the Holy Spirit with the bold declamation of Peter in Acts 2. Peter, the primary agent of denial, has indeed demonstrated his progress toward reconciliation with his Lord by re-assuming his leadership of the disciples in Acts 1, just as Jesus prayed he would do (Luke 22:32). Now, when Peter finally finds his preaching voice and proclaims that it was not possible for Jesus to be held by death (Acts 2:24), an understanding at which he formerly wondered (Luke 24:12) and to which he witnessed in silence (24:34), then the reader knows that the relationship between Jesus and the disciples has been fully restored. Of course, even while the relationship between Peter and Jesus is being resolved, a new narrative tension is being put into place, the tension between the disciples and the hostile crowds.

Thus, we might posit that the resolution of both the disciples' doubts and their relationship with Jesus is foreshadowed in the ending of the gospel but finally postponed until the second chapter of Acts. As noted, this postponement serves a literary purpose. It may also serve a theological purpose: to show how grace is operative in the relationship between Jesus and his followers. Jesus' faith in the disciples consistently anticipates their faith in him. The gospel closes with an important and poignant paradox. The disciples, uncertain as they may be, are commissioned as preachers at the same time as they are instructed to await empowerment. It is the anticipatory faith which Christ has in the disciples as well as the disciples' own partial return to hope and reconciliation that enables them to be the "faithful of Israel" praising God in the temples. These faithful of Israel experience the restoration of their own full service to their Lord with the descent of the Spirit in Acts 2. Meanwhile, they anticipate empowerment and experience grace.

The Synchronic Reader

In contrast to the experience of the diachronic reader, who must await the literary and theological resolution of discipleship in Acts 2, the synchronic reader does find resolution to the issues of discipleship in Luke 24. Thus the synchronic reader understands the issues of discipleship before, and consequently, more fully than the diachronic reader.

While the diachronic reader does not understand until Acts 2 that the resurrection gives the disciples the authority to preach in the name of Jesus, the synchronic reader already understands by the end of Luke's gospel that the resurrection is the authority to preach the story of Jesus as a universal reinterpretation of a Judaic faith not limited to one geographical location or one people.

David L. Tiede has suggested that Luke-Acts is essentially a component in the intra-Jewish hermeneutical debate about "the prevailing question of God's faithfulness to his promises to Israel in the light of its tragic plight and the fate of Jerusalem."[19] Following the destruction of Jerusalem, the Jewish faith was especially vulnerable to the questions of theodicy. The concern, according to Tiede, takes the form of two related questions: If God is a faithful God, why are we destroyed? and, Since God is a faithful God and we are destroyed, what unfaithfulness did we commit to deserve this punishment? Before, during and after the destruction of the temple in 70 CE, the various factions within the Jewish faith had different answers to these questions. The

---

[19]David L. Tiede, *Prophecy and History in Luke-Acts* (Philadelphia, PA: Fortress Press, 1980), 1-15.

Essenes viewed faithfulness in terms of purity, the Pharisees in terms of law and the Zealots in terms of military resistance. Luke's answer in this debate, according to Tiede, was that faithfulness consisted of recognizing Jesus as the ruler of Israel. In that sense, Luke's purpose in writing his two volumes was to preserve the essence of the Septuagintal faith by reinterpreting it in light of the story of Jesus.

The issues in Luke 24 provide a particularly apt arena for verifying Tiede's thesis about Luke's purpose in writing his volumes. In this chapter Luke makes clear that discipleship includes, although it is not limited to, correct interpretation or correct "reading" of the text about Jesus in light of the text of God's acts in Israel's history. As already noted, at the narrative level of a diachronic reading, the risen Christ instructs his estranged and doubtful disciples in an understanding of his suffering, death and resurrection as a fulfillment of scripture. At the narrative level of a synchronic reading, however, Luke demands additional insight into the interconnections between discipleship and correct interpretation/reading.

This additional knowledge has to do with two particular kinds of perception required of disciples, perceptions related to both the social and political dimensions of expanding the vision of Jewish faith beyond its ethnic and geographical boundaries. The first perception necessary to discipleship is a correct identification of the "readers" of the "text" of God's acts among humankind; the second is a correct comprehension of how God acts among humankind.

In this chapter the synchronic reader comes to understand that the readers of the texts about salvation are not limited to those in power;[20] and that the problem with the women is that they do not perceive themselves to be readers of the words and deeds they have witnessed since the ministry in Galilee (24:1-11). The key is the word, "remember" (24:6). In the beginning of the scene, the women neither perceive themselves as readers nor do they consider their own experience with Jesus as text to be read.

---

[20]See Judith Fetterling, "Reading about Reading," in *Gender and Reading: Essays on Readers, Texts and Contexts,* ed. Elizabeth A. Flynn and Patrocinio P. Schweickart (Baltimore, MD: The Johns Hopkins University Press, 1986) 147-154, for a discussion of reading as a metaphor for life and the politics of textuality.

If they had read, and if they had read correctly, they would not have come to the tomb with their spices in the first place. They are essentially at fault for going to the tomb site. They are rebuked for seeking the living among the dead. If they had listened and remembered what Jesus said in Galilee, they would have known that the tomb would not/could not contain Jesus. That the women have been transformed by their experience of epiphany with the two divine beings, that they have learned to read and that they have begun to perceive their own experience as text to be read is evidenced by their "remembering" the words of Jesus and telling "all these things" (24:8, 9) to the disciples.

True disciples are required to read the marginal in the text. This is reenforced for the synchronic readers when they come to realize that the disciples fail to perceive the women as trustworthy interpreters. The disciples find the women's report of the absent body unbelievable not because the possibility of the resurrection is intrinsically unbelievable but because the women's experience is not perceived as text to be read. They do not believe that the female disciples have stories to read. The truth of this assessment is evidenced by the fact that only when Peter and/or some of the "rest" (depending on one's own textual decision at 24:12) have gone to the tomb and seen the empty reality for themselves do the other male disciples begin to perceive the women's story of the empty tomb as a text. As a matter of fact, the patriarchal obtuseness of these male disciples has cost them dearly. If one compares the women's actual experience (24:2-7) with the disciples' report of the women's experience (24:22, 23), the vital component missing is precisely the reminder of Jesus' words in Galilee. Even when the male disciples do begin to perceive the women's story as text, they omit from their reporting, and presumably from their perception or memory, the most "textual" part of the text: the reminder to "read" this new experience in light of the "text" of Jesus' sayings in Galilee. Thus, although at this point the disciples are beginning to trust the women's experience, they still do not recognize the women's cognitive activity, their accurate "reading" of the two texts which has led them to the correct conclusion that Jesus is alive. In other words, the men are ready to begin to believe in the empty tomb, especially since male disciples have corroborated the women's report. But they are not yet ready to do what the women have done. They are not ready to put the two things—the empty tomb and Jesus' Galilean sayings—together in order to arrive at the proper conclusion.

While few, if any, would claim that Luke is a feminist or even that the issue of the disciples' disbelief is primarily an issue of patriarchal oversight, it does seem pertinent to the study of chapter 24 as well as the gospel more generally to note that, once again, Luke is making the point that the words and actions of God are transmitted through the socially marginal as well as the powerful. In Luke's view, the perception of God's actions, the correct interpretation of the good news, is, as often as not, the work of the marginal. Discipleship, according to Luke, involves hearing the good news through the words and actions of the poor, the outcast, the outsider, the women. When the disciples finally come to faith in Acts 2, it is through the Holy Spirit, the teaching of Jesus and their handling of his body and seeing the empty tomb. But the word of the resurrection, the possibility of renewed faith, was first given to them by the marginal. The crisis of joy precipitated by the resurrection transcends all the social boundaries of gender, class and race. Discipleship, in Luke's view, functions on that understanding. That understanding lays new claims upon the marginal them-selves: they must take responsibility to perceive themselves as readers and their experience of God as a text to be read in light of the text of God's past actions. That understanding also lays new claims upon those in power: they must take responsibility to perceive all the people of God as interpreters of God's actions among humankind. In short, that understanding lays new claims of social inclusivity upon the followers of Jesus.

The second perception required of disciples is an under-standing of how God acts in history. While this issue could be described in a variety of ways, even within the chapter under consideration, it is perhaps best focused by the theme of the restoration of Israel. This motif of the redemption of Israel has puzzled a great many scholars. For instance, Tannehill concludes that the lack of fulfillment of the promise emphasized so heavily in the birth narratives is a tragic unfulfillment and is difficult to understand in light of Luke's continued interest in the Jews.[21]

It may, however, be important to understand that the plaintive refrain of Cleopas and his friend functions as a kind of cognitive irony. In that case, one could apply a reconstruction of stable irony to the statement.[22] The operative assumption is that this statement functions something like the mocking of Jesus as the "Christ of God" (23:35) does: to mark a truth for the reader. If so, one might reason along the following lines. First, one rejects the literal meaning of Cleopas' statement (24:21). Cleopas is expressing the disappointment which the disciples feel. They thought Jesus would restore Israel, but the crucifixion has now destroyed that hope. One rejects this literal meaning because one trusts the sincerity of the narrator of the birth annunciations, which include statements of hope in this child as the liberator of Israel.

Rejecting the literal, one casts about for various options to explain the apparent discrepancy between the literal meaning and what one perceives as the author's intentions. Conzelmann's salvation history might be one such answer. The time of Israel is past and the hope itself is inappropriate. Another answer might be Tiede's: what saves Israel, or Judaism as a viable faith in a time of disruption, is a reinterpretation of the faith in light of the Christ myth. In that sense, the gospel itself, which effects this interpretation, or the preached word, essentially the Jesus story in light of the LXX, which is so important in Luke-Acts, becomes the salvation of Israel.

Finally one chooses the answer that seems to be most consonant with what one already knows of the author's intentions and ideology. If Tiede's answer is correct, how does that understanding expand and/or refine Luke's concept of discipleship?

---

[21]Tannehill, *The Narrative Unity of Luke-Acts,* 281.

[22]In *A Rhetoric of Irony* (Chicago, IL: University of Chicago Press, 1974) Wayne C. Booth makes two additional points pertinent to this discussion besides the "four steps of reconstruction," 10-12. The first is that these ironies are intended by the author and are "fixed, in the sense that once a reconstruction of meaning has been made, the reader is not then invited to undermine it with further demolitions and reconstructions," 6. The second is that understanding such an irony is an "astonishing communal achievement . . . the whole thing cannot work at all unless both parties to the exchange have confidence that they are moving together in identical patterns," 13.

While the possible implications of this reconstruction of the
irony are many, one might posit at a minimal level that Luke's
view of discipleship includes an understanding that, at times,
disciples must be open to having their own realities substantially
redefined and redescribed. For the disciples of Jesus, empowered
by the Spirit, that redefinition of reality took the form of moving
boldly into the gentile world. For Luke's readers, the readjust-
ment occasioned by the cognitive irony (resonating of course in
the entire work of Luke-Acts) involved a new recognition that
Israel's understanding of God was preserved in preaching Jesus
Christ to all the nations. Thus, by the end of the gospel, Luke's
synchronic reader comes to understand that discipleship involves
stretching one's mind beyond "normal" social boundaries and
national self-interest.

Implications for a Believers' Church
Theology of Discipleship

As stated previously, it is in the rich resonances between the
two narrative levels described above that Luke's view offers itself
as source and norm for a believers' church theology of discipleship. While it is not the claim of this essay that Luke offers
a comprehensive and systematic theology of discipleship, the
gospel account does provide some criteria for the shape such a
theology might take.

The first criterion this passage suggests is that understanding
and knowing, as categories in which to think about discipleship,
are as important as the more common categories of obeying and
doing. Both of the narrative levels described attest to the
importance of knowing how to interpret correctly the present
acts of God in light of the past acts of God. On both the explicit
and implicit levels, this task of the mind and heart is designated
as an intrinsic task of discipleship. Thus, one criterion for a
believers' church theology of discipleship might be its adequacy
for providing bridging and balancing between such traditional
dichotomies as activism and reflection, doing and thinking, simple
faith and sophisticated interpretation. A believers' church
theology of discipleship needs to concern itself with the task of

interpretation as a category of obedience. The contemporary hermeneutical task is as vital for the ongoing mission of the church as the disciples' correct understanding of the death and resurrection was necessary for the mission of the first church.

The second criterion this passage suggests for a believers' church theology of discipleship is an understanding that the reality of discipleship takes place in a relationship of grace extended through the person of Jesus. Discipleship is not sainthood and it does not take place within a context of perfectionism. Luke's portrayal of the disciples is a highly human one. They are obtuse, demanding, short-sighted and unsupportive at crucial points during the ordeal of the crucifixion and the miracle of resurrection. Yet divine messengers arrive to instruct the women; Jesus appears on the road and in the room to instruct, to let himself be handled, and generally to perform the reality tests the disciples needed. Discipleship thrives and takes its shape in a context of human imperfection and divine initiative. A believers' church theology of discipleship should not be developed in opposition to, but rather as an expression of, the concept of grace.

The third criterion for a believers' church theology of discipleship suggested by this passage is the social inclusivity of discipleship. As the gospel of Luke has made clear all along, the kingdom of God is extended to the poor, the maimed, the blind, the women and children. In the final chapter of the gospel, Luke defines this extension of the kingdom more broadly than he has done heretofore. The thrust of the inclusion is no longer focused on the issue of admittance as such. The insight required is no longer primarily the insight that God also loves such people and, as loved by God, these persons deserve a place among "us." Rather the thrust of the inclusion has now become the necessity of such persons for the vitality of the mission of the church. The good news of the kingdom is also transmitted through the marginal. All disciples are "readers" of the present acts of God in light of the past acts of God. If the marginal do not perceive themselves to be readers and interpreters, if the church dismisses the readings and interpretations offered by the marginal, the good news is lost or diminished. A believers' church theology of discipleship must emphasize the absolute necessity of freeing marginal persons to read and interpret. In this sense it must radically promote and protect the voices of the most marginal of the disciples. What is necessary is ecclesial and hermeneutical solidarity, a binding together of all the disciples in the common task of "reading" past and present acts of God.

Finally, a fourth criterion for a believers' church theology of discipleship has to do with understanding discipleship within a context of worshipful humility as epistemological surprise. This understanding is derived partly from regarding the two ironies operative in the text in light of each other. As noted, the first irony is the visual irony operative in the scene between Jesus and the disciples who do not recognize him on the road to Emmaus. The second is the cognitive irony in Luke's leading his synchronic reader to understand that Israel is restored, in this text and in proclaiming Jesus. These two ironies taken together provide essential clues to a particular understanding of how a disciple worships. In worship a disciple assumes a stance which recognizes the ironic distance between the human perspective and the divine perspective. Moreover, discipleship is a stance which recognizes the divine grace which this distance signifies. In the sense that God draws near to humankind this distance is itself grace. Such a perception involves the simple recognition that we are not God nor are our ways the way of God. As disciples we are not trying to become more like God. Sainthood is not a goal of discipleship, although sainthood is not necessarily an impossibility. The goal of discipleship is an attitude of humility; the task to become comfortably human in relationship with the divine. That those who follow Jesus will both succeed and fail in obedience is, it seems, accepted in Luke's view of discipleship. That those who follow Jesus will both succeed and fail in perceiving God's perspective is, it seems, also accepted in Luke's view of discipleship. That a significant function of the relationship with Jesus characterized by discipleship involves the divine correction of the human perspective is normative in Luke's view. That empowerment by the Spirit allows disciples to accept these corrections with added grace but does not, in itself, eliminate the need for correction seems to be the message of the Cornelius stories in Acts.

Therefore, part of the task of discipleship, or part of the

task of becoming comfortably human in relationship to the divine, is becoming comfortable with a divinely prompted discomfort. As disciples we need to anticipate that our ways of knowing will be challenged by our discipleship as well as by our ways of doing. According to the final chapter of Luke's gospel, at any rate, discipleship has epistemological implications as well as moral ones. Perhaps a believers' church theology of discipleship that is exegetically accountable to Luke's portrayal of the disciples as well as Luke's relationship with "Theophilus" demands a kind of wry anthropology—an understanding that to be human in relation to the divine is to stand in humility and to expect surprises.

Conclusion

In conclusion, this essay has begun to explore the connections between the exegesis of Luke's treatment of the disciples and a believers' church theology of discipleship. An examination of how Luke's two levels of readership function in the conclusion of the gospel discloses four themes which might be useful for such a theology. These themes might be briefly characterized as: understanding or interpretation as a category of discipleship, grace, solidarity and humility. Discipleship involves correctly understanding the present acts of God in relationship to the past acts of God. Discipleship involves accepting as grace the initiative of God extended in the distance between the divine and the human. Discipleship involves standing in solidarity with the marginal as "readers" of God's acts, past and present. Finally, and perhaps cumulatively, discipleship involves humility, not as self-debasement but as taking comfort in one's humanity, a humanity appropriately and worshipfully related to the divine. To take Luke's view of discipleship seriously in the formulation of a believers' church theology of discipleship may be a way to move beyond Mennonite perfectionism, individual and collective, in thinking theologically about what it means to follow Jesus. Taking seriously this gospel's portrayal of Jesus' first followers may indeed have possibilities for a mature understanding of the relationship between the divine and the human known as discipleship.

William Klassen*

THE VOICE OF THE PEOPLE IN THE BIBLICAL STORY OF FAITHFULNESS**

Three distinct aspects of the topic will be considered: first, the voice of the people in the formation of the biblical story; second, their role in the handing down and re-formation of the biblical story; and third, the voice of the people living in a culture committed to equality/democracy and trying to remain faithful to the biblical message. As we respond to biblical calls to faithfulness and remedies for unfaithfulness we are keenly aware that we owe much to the biblical tradition in our commitment to basic human rights, justice and peace.

We must of course, add "and unfaithfulness" to the title since a careful reading of the biblical sources leads to the conclusion that "unfaithfulness" is an integral aspect of the biblical story. For while the calls to faithfulness abound in the biblical story[1] it could well be argued that one of the reasons why the Bible has continued to be read and has transformed lives is because it invites the unfaithful to a God whose love is not dependent upon their faithfulness. Do we not, in part at least, continue to read the Bible precisely because it contains not only great accounts of people who found it possible to obey God but also stories of Abraham/Sarah, Rebekah/Jacob, Moses/Miriam, Ruth/Boaz, Judas/Mary Magdalene, Priscilla/Aquila in whom faithfulness and unfaithfulness seem rather thoroughly blended?

*William Klassen is Principal of St. Pauls United College, Waterloo, Ontario.

**The author would like to thank Jake Elias, Academic Dean and Associate Professor of New Testament, Associated Mennonite Biblical Seminaries, Elkhart, Indiana, and Patricia Shelly, Assistant Professor of Bible and Religion, Bethel College, North Newton, Kansas, for their critical responses to this essay at the Symposium.

[1]See Katharine Doob Sakenfeld, *Faithfulness in Action: Loyalty in Biblical Perspective* (Philadelphia, PA: Fortress Press, 1985) for an excellent introduction to the theme of faithfulness or loyalty, both divine and human, in the Hebrew Bible.

Who is not struck by the fact that all the disciples (except the women) deserted and denied Jesus while he hung on the cross, yet as soon as he could Jesus loved them and commissioned them to be his witnesses? There may just be hope for us as well.

David Schroeder has noted that

> The interpretation of a Scripture passage is not something that can be worked out individually, mechanically, or in separation from the Spirit of God and the community of faith. The Holy Spirit works not only through the individual but also through the community of believers, the church, to give us an understanding of God's will. We must therefore, bring the interpretation of Scripture that we come to in our reading and study to the larger community of faith for its consideration and response. The church, through the work of the Holy Spirit, becomes a discerning community, or, as John Howard Yoder has termed it, the "hermeneutic community." It is not, in the last analysis, the specialized investigations or promulgations of the theologian that carry weight. They may help, but the Spirit of God can work through any individual of the fellowship and through the entire fellowship of faith to lead us to know His will until we can repeat with the early church "it seemed good to the Holy Spirit and to us. . . (Acts 15:28).[2]

It is the thesis of this paper that by and large Schroeder is right. We affirm that the scriptures came into being through the work of the Holy Spirit and the action of the "hermeneutic community." Yet we must take issue with the last sentence of his statement. Now is not the time to downplay "specialized investigations" or the weight they carry. Schroeder's own "specialized investigations" represent a milestone in the study of biblical ethics. For him to say that "they may help" may be modest, but it simply is not adequate. Form criticism and *Gemeindetheologie* have not been separated in Schroeder's work, and it is imperative that they be held together today.

The manner in which this is done is itself a biblical theme. The imaginative study of the Bible by Erich Auerbach concludes that distinctive to the Bible is its rootage among the common people. Whereas Homer, in his writings, introduces only two characters who do not belong to the ruling class, in the Hebrew

---

[2]David Schroeder, *Learning to Know the Bible* (Newton, KS: Faith and Life Press, 1966), 89-90.

Bible class distinctions are absent. "As soon as the people completely emerges, after the Exodus . . . its activity is always discernible, it is often in ferment . . . the origins of prophecy seem to lie in the irrepressible politico-religious spontaneity of the people."[3] Along similar lines Auerbach suggests that, while writers like Petronius and Tacitus "look down from above," "generally almost the entire body of New Testament writings is written from within the emergent growths and directly for everyman." What one finds here is a "revisional interpretation" rooted in Judaism. More importantly it is a manner of portraying reality which is never satisfied with the surface appearance but depicts the "antagonism between sensory appearance and meaning . . . which permeates the whole Christian view of reality."[4]

The emphasis on form criticism has led to the conclusion that any study of a biblical document must consider the role of the community in the formation of that document. The earlier form critical studies tended to minimize the creativity of any one individual.[5]

The point has been made, even though at times overstated, that at the centre of the community which formed the Bible lay not a group of individual geniuses, each expressing his/her individualism by making a contribution to the common life, but rather a new community. How did the voice of the people get heard in this context?

Is it possible to discover how this community theologized? Was it a community which merely transmitted theology that had been defined and constructed by a leader? Was it a community that was committed to a constant redefinition of the significance of God's act in Christ for them? Were they people who had

[3]Erich Auerbach, *Mimesis: The Representation of Reality in Western Literature* (Garden City, NY: Anchor Books, 1957), 18.

[4]Ibid., 41-43. See also Helen Gardner, *The Business of Criticism* (Oxford: Clarendon Press, 1959), especially the section, "The Limits of Literary Criticism," 79-157.

[5]Rudolf Bultmann's disproportionate emphasis in his *Theology of the New Testament,* 2 vols. (New York, NY: Scribners, 1952, 1955) on the pre-Pauline church is indicative of this approach. Although he admits we have very few reliable sources aside from Paul (33) that would help us establish the *Kerygma* of the Hellenistic church, Bultmann devotes pages 33-183 to the *Kerygma* of the earliest church and a scant 30 pages (3-33) to the message of Jesus.

committed themselves to basic "essentials" and who spent a good deal of their time spelling out the significance of this commitment for the concrete details of life? Or were they revisionists, perhaps even architects of new theologies?

We can address only three matters or areas in which the theologizing activity of the community appears evident: theology, christology and ethics.

The Voice of the People and Theology

In some biblical examples of "theologizing," we notice a fundamental revision that took place in how the Jew of the post-exilic period viewed God. We know that at numerous places in the Hebrew Scriptures terms like "man of war" are used to describe Yahweh or Yahweh's actions. When the Septuagint (LXX) translators came upon that expression they consistently translated it not as "the one who promotes" but "as the one who stamps out or destroys war" (the favourite verb is *suntribo*).[6] That is true in Exodus 15:3, in Isaiah 42:13 where we know the Hebrew original and in Judith 9:7; 16:2. Although there are great variations in the translations of the LXX, it appears consistent on one point: very seldom does the Greek text of the Jewish community describe God as a *war God*. When "holy war" is used (true already in the Hebrew) it is generally a war directed against Israel itself (Jeremiah 6:4; 22:7; Micah 3:5). When the first of the seven sons is tortured to death by the Tyrant, his last words are, "Fight a holy (*hieran*) and honourable war (*strateian*) on behalf of goodness (*eusebian*) through which may the Just Providence that watched over our fathers show mercy to his people and vengeance to this accursed tyrant" (4 Maccabees 9:24-25). Here the "war" is for people to remain steadfast in adherence to the Law and to die for it.

In the *Targumim* a similar process is at work. The "sword and bow" (Genesis 48:22; Psalm 44:7) are in fact "prayer and beseeching" (*Targum Onkelos* to Genesis 48:22; *Tanhuma*

---

[6]Used in *Joseph and Asenath*, 10:12 and 12:12, of destroying idols; and in *Testament of Asher*, 7:3, of crushing the head of the dragon in the water.

Beshallah, chapter 9). The "soldier and warrior" and "those who repel attacks at the gate" in Isaiah 3:2 and 28:6 are not warriors in the literal sense but "those who know how to dispute in the battle of the Torah" (*Babylonian Talmud*, Hagigah 14a; *Babylonian Talmud*, Megillah 15b). The sword of the mighty is the Torah (Midrash, Psalm 45:4) and the military leaders of the Bible were changed to "scholars and heads of the Sanhedrin." Even David's "warriors" (2 Samuel 23:8) are none other than manifestations of the might of his spirit "as he took part in the sessions" (of scholars) (*Babylonian Talmud*, Moed Katan 16b). This tendency to see these military images in a non-literal way is prevalent throughout the haggadic literature, although not in the halakhic sources[7].

Could it be that we find here an exceptionally courageous and innovative community which revised drastically its view of God? If so, where did the pressures to do so come from? From a fundamental conviction that if God is indeed a God of War then God also is able to destroy war? Were there influences from Stoics and Cynics or others (Pythagoreans) in the Greco-Roman world?

We will never know the answers to these questions but, in line with the rejection of violence and war found in such documents as the Epistle of Aristeas, we can suggest that there was a community at work in Judaism which was critical of certain canons of speaking about God and which went about revising them.

At any rate the door was opened to the formulation "the God of Peace" used once in pre-Christian literature (*Testament of Dan* 5:2) but adopted in the Epistle to Hebrews (13:20) and by Paul as a revised normative definition of God (Romans 15:33; 16:20; 1 Corinthians 14:33; 2 Corinthians 13:11; Philippians 4:9; 1 Thessalonians 5:23; in 2 Thessalonians 3:16 the "Lord of Peace"). It became possible for Paul to combine the "God of Peace" with one of his most aggressive images when he expressed the conviction or the hope that "the God of Peace will soon

---

[7]See especially Aviezer Ravitsky, "Peace," in *Contemporary Jewish Religious Thought*, ed. Arthur A. Cohen and Paul Mendes-Flohr (New York, NY: Scribners, 1987), 981.

crush Satan under your feet" (Romans 16:20). Singular here is the combination of the violent act which God will carry out and the fact that God is a God of Peace. Instead of crushing war, Satan as host of war will be destroyed. Furthermore, it is remarkable that this battle takes place "under their feet," indicating that in some way the Christians of Rome will be instruments in the eschatological battle.[8] The context indicates that this will happen as they maintain their oneness of spirit and action.

New Testament scholars have not with any diligence or thoroughness investigated the concept of God which appears in the New Testament sources. Indeed a past president of the Society for New Testament Studies once referred to this lack as "The Neglected Factor in New Testament Theology:"

> For more than a generation the majority of New Testament scholars have not only eliminated direct references to God from their works, but also neglected detailed and comprehensive investigation of statements about God. Whereas a number of major works and monographs deal with Christology . . . it is hard to find any comprehensive or penetrating study of the theme "God in the New Testament."[9]

Those who steer clear of such a fundamental task for fear of being branded a Marcionite or of departing in other fundamental ways from basic monotheism should note that within Judaism itself there is considerable freedom to revise fundamental theories about God.

The Voice of the People and Christology

Alongside the work being done by Pauline communities there were the communities of "Q" and of the other gospels, especially Mark, who formed the basis for the others. Here

---

[8]A classic example of what Tom Yoder Neufeld has isolated in *God and Saints at War: The Transformation and Democratization of the Divine Warrior in Isaiah 59, Wisdom of Solomon 5, I Thessalonians 5, and Ephesians 6* (Ph.D. dissertation, Harvard University, 1989).

[9]Nils Dahl, "The Neglected Factor in New Testament Theology," *Reflections* (Yale Divinity School Bulletin) 76 (1978): 14.

community must be seen in its most elementary form, as a people at a certain geographical location gathering in the name of Jesus. It is likely not correct to speak of a "Q" community or of a Markan community but rather of various groups which contributed to these sources for our understanding of Christ. Characteristic of this "group" (as Paul Hoffmann preferred to call them) was its commitment to "homelessness, a radical separation from the family, from caring for property and subsistence, typical already for Jesus' claim regarding discipleship still . . . valid for the Q-group."[10] Whereas "Q" places the stress on homelessness it seems that in Mark already "the separation from one's own 'house' leads to incorporation into a new social structure which is a 'house' again; homelessness is not the unalterable condition of discipleship. So we can speak of a 'community' of Mark, in the sense of settled Christians who are incorporated into social structures."[11]

Today we take for granted that each gospel has its own unique Christology. The question of the amount of freedom exercised by the early Christian communities to select, adapt and revise their picture of Christ has been widely debated but no consensus has emerged. What is uniformly agreed upon is that this decision was made not by councils or wise people but by the community itself.[12] It is widely accepted that the starting process was oral, then as Dibelius asserted, by about the year 45 the first written gospel was produced. It is generally accepted that by the year 60 at the latest, the source "Q" was already in existence. The starting documents are of course lost, but if one grants priority to Mark and assumes that Matthew and Luke use Mark, then any deviation from Mark will need to be explained by peculiar

---

[10]See Dieter Lührmann, "The Gospel of Mark and the Sayings Collection Q," *Journal of Biblical Literature* 108 (Spring 1989): 70. Citing from Paul Hoffmann *Studien zur Theologie der Logienquelle* (Münster: Aschendorff, 1922), 329.

[11]Lührmann, 70.

[12]Gerd Theissen has explored the thesis that "The Jesus movement in the foreshadow of the Kingdom of God brought about a revolution of values, i.e. an assimilation of attitudes and norms of the upper class by little people and outsiders. Aristocratic virtues in association with power, ownership, and education were reformulated so that they were accessible to the common people. The actual revolution through power was awaited from God: In his kingdom the poor, hungry and suffering would come into their own." "Jesusbewegung als charismatische Wertrevolution," *New Testament Studies* 35 (July 1989): 344.

tendencies at work in the circle of the disciples and finalized by other gospel writers.

The discovery of the gospels at Nag Hammadi has forced the question of tradition and gospel upon us with renewed urgency. How do we determine whether a saying of Jesus is genuine or not? What was the church's reaction to the construction of new gospels? Are there perhaps fragments of the sayings of Jesus in these gospels which are in fact more primitive than the ones we have in our canonical gospels? And if the church voted for a plurality of gospels, why limit it to four? Should there not also be a place for a gospel called "The Gospel of Truth," or "The Gospel according to Judas?" Irenaeus said there should be four because there are four winds, but we now know there are quite a few more winds than four!

One of the critical questions about Jesus and the early church deals with his use of violence. In that connection an important attempt to look at the original Jesus and the changes that he has undergone in the interest of the early church was published two decades ago by S.G.F. Brandon.[13] Brandon's thesis is simply that Jesus himself was closely related to the Zealot party and that the "profession of Zealot principles and aims was not incompatible with intimate participation in the mission of Jesus."[14] Even the objection that "Jesus would not have resorted to violence cannot be maintained in the face of the evidence of Jesus arming his disciples and his attack in the temple."[15] This revolutionary picture of Jesus and his intimate involvement with the Zealot party increasingly became a source of embarrassment for the early church so that all of the gospels made a concerted effort to change the revolutionary Jesus into a pacific Christ.

Brandon's book made an important contribution not only because his was the first detailed examination in English of the Zealot connection but also because it drew together various strands of research which force us to take the political atmo-

---

[13]S.G.F. Brandon, *Jesus and the Zealots: A Study of the Political Factor in Primitive Christianity* (Manchester: Manchester University Press, 1967). Note especially the subtitle.

[14]Ibid., 355.

[15]Ibid.

sphere of Jesus' time and his own political commitment seriously. It appeared at a time when third-world theologians were just becoming aware of the radical nature of the gospel in connection with oppression and the limits of political authority.

Since Brandon's work, Hengel's major volume on the Zealots has finally been translated into English.[16] A number of other studies in the past few years, especially by liberation theologians, on the theme of Jesus and violence, demonstrate that the Zealot option is one that cannot summarily be dismissed. Even Perry Yoder allows that "violence or nonviolence, if it is to be compatible with shalom, must be shalom producing, and make sense in the context of a struggle for shalom."[17] The discussion of violence and nonviolence becomes especially difficult when we are told by theologians of the Third World that the "mechanism we use to keep other individuals or groups at arm's length . . . is not precisely hatred, it is violence—at least some initial degree of violence."[18]

What is needed is some precision in the use of the term "violence." In ancient Hebrew the word was *chamas* and the idea was uniformly rejected. Violence is what desperate men who are out of control do. Violence means to violate the other's personhood; that can be done by forcing others to do something by pressure of your will, not theirs. It can lead to taking away the other's life, the most serious form of violence. The concept of "systemic violence," so sharply formulated by Johan Galtung[19] and helpful in our analysis of contemporary society, was not known to the ancients.[20]

---

[16]Martin Hengel, *The Zealots* (Philadelphia, PA: Fortress Press, 1989).

[17]Perry Yoder, *Shalom: The Bible's Word for Salvation, Justice and Peace* (Newton, KS: Faith and Life Press, 1987), 7, although later he indicates that "The Christian way is the way of nonviolence," 143.

[18]Juan Luis Segundo, *The Liberation of Theology* (Maryknoll, NY: Orbis Books, 1975), 159.

[19]See especially Johan Galtung, "Peace Theory: An Introduction," in *World Encyclopedia of Peace*, vol 2, ed. Ervin Laszlo and Johng Youl Yoo (New York, NY: Pergamon Press, 1986), 251-260.

[20]For a peculiarly confused use of the term "violence" see David Dungan, "Jesus and Violence," in *Jesus, the Gospels and the Church*, ed. E. P. Sanders (Macon, GA.: Mercer University Press, 1987) 135-162, especially statements like ". . . the numerous Synoptic accounts portraying Jesus engaged in vigorous aggressive assaults on evil demons, evil persons, and evil institutions? Do they not

But we also need some clarification of the term "Zealot." Some scholars have made much of the fact that Josephus does not use the term, Zealot, to designate a sect before 66 A.D. But the question of Jesus' relation to his own traditions does not hinge on what term Josephus used to describe the "fourth philosophy." Rather from all that we know about zeal as a phenomenon in the first century and about Jesus it would seem that zealotism must have been extremely attractive to Jesus. Such events as the entry into Jerusalem and the confrontation in the temple cannot be fully understood especially in their consequences unless we realize that at the time that Jesus entered Jerusalem a Zealot uprising was in process. His way of "cleansing" the temple was different only in method from the one used several decades later by the Zealots when they ignited the Jewish War against Rome.

More recently the work of Marcus Borg[21] and Richard Horsley[22] has forced us to take more seriously the community in which Jesus lived and the role of that community in forming the cluster of beliefs about Jesus. Although Horsley states categorically that "the standard picture of Jesus the advocate of non-violence . . . is no longer historically credible,"[23] he has, by rejecting the violence of the Zealots, come especially close to recent Mennonite exegetical work in stressing the role of an alternative community. If both are concerned about purity of devotion to the Lord, they also have drastically different ways of promoting that loyalty and of dealing with those who fail to meet the standards to which they have committed themselves. It is especially important that Horsley stressed the renewal of community in the kingdom pronouncements of Jesus.

> Jesus thus insisted that the renewed covenantal community avoid the patriarchal social-economic-political hierarchy that constituted the chain of domination maintaining institutional-

---

exude Jesus' confident hope in God's violence?" 138.

[21]Marcus Borg, *Conflict, Holiness and Politics in the Teachings of Jesus* (Toronto, ON: Edwin Mellen, 1984).

[22]Richard Horsley, *Jesus and the Spiral of Violence* (San Francisco, CA: Harper and Row, 1987).

[23]Ibid., 149.

ized injustice. . . . He both spoke against reversion to patriarchal forms of domination in the local community and he called
for the virtual transformation of the age-old royal-imperial
forms of authoritarian domination only too familiar to Jews
and others in the ancient Near East.[24]

A good case in point is Jesus' rejection of the use of the
term "Father" for the leading teachers in the community.[25]

It is not necessary here to enter into a total assessment of
Horsley's work, only to say that I strongly affirm many of his
conclusions. He underlines the point already made by Brandon
that whatever Jesus said about revolution, his announcement that
the kingdom was here and the guidance he gave his disciples on
how they were to live in community had drastic consequences.
Both his and Brandon's works are so relevant to our topic
because both assume that no matter what Jesus said about
violence, we have access only to what his community handed
down to us. It is furthermore refreshing to find scholars who do
not hesitate confidently to assign to Jesus some of the sayings
the gospels attributed to him. Above all, even "groups like the
people behind Q can survive only when interacting with settled
communities, either founding them or getting support from
them."[26]

Several conclusions can be drawn from this more realistic
way of viewing the life of Jesus when he is seen as reacting to
the Jewish resistance movement. Jesus is not as he is often
presented, the uninvolved observer of political events in his time.
Also there is a difference in the way he and the Zealots sought
to bring about social change. If it is true that Jesus really tried
to arm his disciples, then the real change in strategy came only
in the Garden of Gethsemane, perhaps a few hours before his
arrest.

However, Horsley's work suffers from a lack of utilization
of Jewish literature of the time. Our evidence that Jesus faced a
clear choice between the violent way and the nonviolent way

---

[24]Ibid., 244.

[25]See Horsley who, citing Bultmann, states that "even the most sceptical and
cautious of form critics thought that Matthew 23:8-9 could be 'dominical,'" 240.

[26]Lührmann, "The Gospel of Mark and the Sayings Collection Q," 71.

comes from Josephus, but even more from such sources as the *Assumption of Moses* and the Psalms of Solomon. Furthermore, the prominence which the person of Phineas enjoys in first-century Jewish sources[27] reflects the popularity that Zealot heros enjoyed among the people of that time. It is a considerable surprise to find how popular Phineas was not only in the Hebrew Scriptures but also in the literature of Judaism, including among such moderate figures as Philo and Josephus.

We illustrate the point in only one literary source, the Wisdom of Jesus ben Sira, where the Greek text in the closing benediction reads as follows: "May God grant us a joyful heart,/ and in our time send Israel lasting peace." And the Hebrew text adds: "May his faithfulness stand by Simon and may he preserve for him the covenant of Phineas which will not be broken for him or his posterity as long as the heaven stands." The addition of Phineas here, as elsewhere in a number of Jewish texts of the time, shows that he is a popular folk hero, undoubtedly familiar to Jesus. Is his absence in the New Testament attributable to mere chance or are we permitted to conclude that Phineas does not appear on the pages of the New Testament because Jesus led the way for his community to reject the Zealot Phineas as a prototype for himself and his followers? The voice of the people is not blindly followed. Jesus has the courage to reject certain widely accepted role models and lift up others instead.[28]

Brandon ascribes creativity to the early church at the point of defining Jesus' way of meeting violence, a way which could be quite unique in history. Even if the early church after the fall of Jerusalem saw the mistake made by the Zealots, one would need to ask if that in itself would have caused them to revise the idea of a revolutionary Jesus—one who even asked his disciples to arm and one who, according to Brandon, used violence in cleansing the Temple—into a pacific Christ. Can the view of Jesus be so easily transformed? Is it not the rule that apostles of

---

[27]In the article cited in note 28 I deal with all biblical and extra-biblical references to Phineas known to me. They include extensive attention paid him in Talmudic materials as well as Pseudo-Philo, Josephus, Philo. He is ignored by the New Testament and by the writers at Qumran.

[28]See my essay, "Jesus and Phineas: A Rejected Role Model," in *Society of Biblical Literature: Seminar Papers* (Atlanta, GA: Scholars Press, 1986), 490-500.

nonviolence are often accused of violence and that, in fact, they are transformed by later generations into apostles of violence?

Is this not what we are seeing today when the theologians of revolution cannot quite get rid of Jesus and instead make him into a revolutionary figure who is not afraid to use violence when he confronts the establishment? In view of the consistent rejection in the history of the church of a pacific Christ one wonders whether the forces in the first century were really strong enough to transform a violent Jesus into a nonviolent Christ.

The importance of form criticism in such a study cannot be overestimated. It has cast a great deal of light on oral tradition but as a tool it can also be used to destroy Brandon's arguments thoroughly. For in reading his book it becomes clear that he can use the form critical approach where it consistently supports his thesis, but where it does not he must rely on other methods of research. Furthermore his approach to Christology is severely limited because he does not avail himself of the material in the Epistles when, according to sound form-critical methods these sources would also need to be taken seriously in a discussion of the early Christian conceptions of the role of Jesus. He asserts that

> the representation of him (Jesus) as living aloof or insulated from the political realities of first century Judea, which the evangelists fabricated for their own particular apologetic needs, confirmed and sanctioned an evaluation that became doctrinally imperative. However, it is well to remember that Christian tradition has preserved, in the Apocalypse of John, the memory of another, and doubtless more primitive, conception of Christ—of the terrible rider on the white horse whose eyes are like a flame of fire.[29]

This one excursion which Brandon makes into epistolary literature to arrive at a primitive conception of Christ introduces a host of problems. Who is to decide whether the portrait of the rider on the white horse is really more primitive than the ones portrayed in the gospels or in 1 Peter. And what indeed is the meaning of this symbolism in the book of Revelation?[30]

---

[29]S.G.F. Brandon, *Jesus and the Zealots,* 320.

[30]If anything, one would expect a more violent concept of Christ in the book

The truth probably lies somewhere between the extremes. The gospel material can lead us only to the conclusion that the church worked in the direction of adapting the dominical sayings to their own situation, clarifying the meanings for their particular situation with a degree of freedom and also a considerable commitment of faithfulness to "the words of the Lord." Even in the transmission of the sayings of Jesus they saw themselves as a hermeneutical community whose responsibility it was not only to repeat but also to interpret who Jesus was and what he said. They drew no rigid distinction between interpretation and transmission of material. Therefore, we cannot help but conclude that history and theology are present in the Gospel of Mark as they are in the Gospel of John and that in fact the very structure of the gospel is an integral part of the theologizing of the early Christian community.

As an example of the incredible freedom of the early Christian communities to reformulate theology, that is, their basic beliefs about God, I have cited above the simple New Testament formula: "the God of Peace." Its only other appearance is in the *Testament of Dan*. For the most part scholars who have noticed the singularity of this expression have dismissed it as a "Jewish liturgical formula." Few have seen it for what it is: an imaginative redefinition of God in a community where it was all too easy to visualize God as a God of War.

Space does not permit us to explore a case in which theology and Christology flow together uniquely to formulate a *novum* in history: Ephesians 2:11-22. Here the theme of people-hood is central but so is Christology. And the fundamental affirmation made by the author that the divisions of history on which communities thrive have been overcome by Christ who destroyed the enmity and brought reconciliation and peace could have served the church well. That this passage ends on the note of the temple and the divine presence of God among God's people strikes us as particularly relevant since it undoubtedly was written after the temple in Jerusalem was in ruins. If Christianity over the centuries had found its locus here it might have been

---

of Revelation to be tamed down by the year 100 rather than to have it re-emerge.

able to avoid the terrible scourge of anti-Semitism and perhaps also the curse of individualism which have so plagued the church.

The Voice of the People and Ethical Norms

Oscar Cullmann, in a brief discussion of Paul's ethical position, states that

> the working of the Holy Spirit shows itself in the testing, that is in the capacity of forming the correct Christian ethical judgement at each given moment and specifically of forming it in connection with the knowledge of the redemptive process, in which, indeed, the Holy Spirit is a decisive figure.[31]

Cullmann sees this testing as the key to all New Testament ethics. He appeals to Romans 12:2 and Philippians 1:9; 2:13 and concludes,

> certainty of moral judgement in the concrete case is in the last analysis the one great fruit that the Holy Spirit, this factor in redemptive history, produces in the individual.[32]

In the Christian community this testing is joined with the process of spontaneous inspiration. Hence Paul warns the Thessalonians not to quench the Spirit, not to despise prophesying "but test all things and hold fast to that which is good" (1 Thessalonians 5:19).

Considerable attention has been given to the phenomenon of testing in recent literature, particularly in ethical literature. C.F.D Moule saw "the organ of perception through which the Holy Spirit may be expected to speak with distinctively Christian moral guidance as the Christian worshipping congregation listening critically."[33] The words "Christian worshipping congregation" probably meant something different to him than worship in

---

[31] Oscar Cullmann, *Christ and Time,* rev. ed. (London: SCM Press, 1962), 228.

[32] Ibid.

[33] C.F.D. Moule, "The New Testament and Moral Decisions," *Expository Times* (September 1963): 372.

the primitive church. Both Cullmann and Moule, however, fail to see that the testing to which Paul refers involves far more than simply the knowledge of the individual to find the path on which to walk. For Paul expresses the confidence that each of them has been filled with all knowledge to take the right way and also that they have become equipped to admonish one another (Romans 15:14, where the New English Bible unfortunately weakens the original *nouthetein*).

Much more is at stake here than merely giving advice to one another. The testing and knowledge of the divine will have their true place only in the congregation and in union with other members of the body of Christ. After all, the congregation constitutes an all-inclusive fellowship of life and love. In it each one serves the neighbour and each one is responsible for the neighbour. Just as one member of the body has a solidarity in both joy and suffering with the whole so the individual is in all thinking, testing and knowledge always a member of the body of Christ. All that happens to the individual in the Spirit and in Christ at the same time takes place in the church. Thus it is not insignificant, as Wolfgang Schrage has shown, that the admonitions to test (with the sole exception of Philemon 6) always appear in the plural.[34] It is the congregation that is to test what is the will of God (Romans 12:2). It is Paul's prayer that the Philippians as a group "may see their love grow ever richer and richer in knowledge and insight of every kind, and may thus bring the gift of true discrimination" (Philippians 1:9-10a). It is also for the Colossians as a group that he prays that they may receive from God "all wisdom and spiritual understanding for full insight into His will" (Colossians 1:9, 4:12).

Individuals are included in this mandate for testing insofar as they are members of the church. The dangers of knowledge are overcome precisely in the fact that the one who arrives at knowledge does so as a member of the body, in union with the fellow Christian and in responsibility for the neighbour. Hans Jonas has shown that the Pauline view, in which the value of the

---

[34]Wolfgang Schrage, *Die konkreten Einzelgebote in der paulinischen Paraenese* (Gütersloh: Verlagshaus Gerd Mohn, 1961), 174. See also his *Ethics of the New Testament*, trans. David E. Green (Philadelphia, PA: Fortress Press, 1987).

individual charisma is constitutive for the whole congregation, is quite different from the anarchistic individualism and the claim to absolutism found among the gnostic pneumatics.

Quite expressly Paul articulates how deeply he feels about their unity of thought and action. There is a certain stereotyped character in his admonitions to the congregations to "have equal regard for one another" (Romans 12:16) that "you may agree with one another after the manner of Christ Jesus, so that with one mind and one voice you may praise the God and Father of our Lord Jesus Christ" (Romans 15:5) or his appeal "in the name of our Lord Jesus Christ: agree among yourselves and avoid divisions; be firmly joined in unity of mind and thought" (1 Corinthians 1:10) or "agree with one another" (2 Corinthians 13:11) or "fill up my cup of happiness by thinking and feeling alike, with the same love for one another, the same turn of mind and a common care for unity" (Philippians 2:2; see also Philippians 4:2). Here clearly the common search for the right way is included.

Almost certainly when in Philippians 2:2 he writes about "having the same love" he does not refer the similarity of love to the measure of strength of love but rather to its direction and nature. And the noun *phronesis,* as Bultmann has noted, means "one's attitude in which thinking and willing are one."[35]

In many of these places, particularly in Romans 12:16, Paul may be addressing himself to the self-sufficiency of the pneumatics and is trying to prevent an attitude from developing which would assume that a person is clever in his/her own right and does not need anyone else. Thus the members of the Roman church are urged to remain open to the criticism and insight of other members of the congregation. Paul directs himself to those who have confidence in their own abilities to make choices and assume that they have the right to do as they feel is right. Thus the correct way can be determined only by listening to one another and finding ways of conversing with one another, but not in the self-satisfied isolation of an individualism apart from the congregation. To walk in the Spirit means not to go it alone or

---

[35]Rudolf Bultmann, *Theology of the New Testament,* 214.

to take one's own path but rather to take one's place among the ranks of those who are marching in the same direction and toward the same goal. Those who live in the Spirit must also march according to the parade rules given by the Spirit (Galatians 5:25). This verb *stoichein* clearly has a normative element in it. The one who marches in the parade or in the army can do so only when close attention is paid to the one marching in front, behind and beside.

This respect for others under certain circumstances is carried so far that Paul makes it the summit of his appeal in 1 Corinthians 11. The last link in the chain of Paul's argument is that "there is no such custom among us or in any of the congregations of God's people" (verse 16). To the same congregation he asks bluntly, "Did the word of God originate with you? Or are you the only people to whom it came?" (1 Corinthians 14:36)

It needs to be emphasized, however, that Paul never insisted that the majority voice was the voice of God.[36] In Second Temple Judaism a synod of duly authorized rabbis could make a decision on a specific instance and this decision could only be invalidated through another meeting which had more authority and more members. At Qumran also the plenary assembly could make specific decisions. It was only in later Judaism that the leading personalities tended to impose their will upon the assembly. For the early Christians the norm to be sought is defined in Romans 15:5 as *kata christon Jesoun*. In the application of this norm, however, the majority has no right to manipulate or coerce the individual. Even in the very smallest fellowship, a type of the larger fellowship, namely marriage, neither partner is to withhold the self from the other except through mutual agreement (1 Corinthians 7). The fact that Paul here deviates from Jewish teaching, in which the agreement of the woman was not essential for sexual intercourse,[37] shows that

---

[36]At the same time he apparently does not hesitate to prescribe a vote to assure a repentant sinner of love and forgiveness, or at least so I read 2 Corinthians 2:5-11. In addition the writer of Luke-Acts (Acts 14:23; 15:22) leaves the impression that selection of leaders proceeded with the participation of those led.

[37]See Paul Billerbeck, *Die Briefe des Neuen Testaments und die Offenbarung Johannis* (München: C.H. Beck, 1954), 367-368 for material on 1 Corinthians 7:1-

Paul values regard for women and the meaning and responsibility of the individual in the fellowship very highly. The weak are not to be coerced and their decision is to be genuine without any compulsion of conscience.

Nevertheless no individual has a private or independent existence; one is not allowed to form one's life alone. Paul sees the congregation always as a totality and as a unity. "All of you are one in Christ Jesus" (Galatians 3:28; see also 1 Corinthians 12:13). Specifically the sin of the individual Christian is no private matter which can be regulated with God alone and which is of no concern to other members in the church. That which the individual member does is part of the responsibility of the total congregation. For example, it is the congregation which is responsible for the case of fornication (1 Corinthians 5:1). Responsibility for each other, however, does not extend to the point of control. It is only later that Ignatius in one letter (Polycarp 5:2) assumes that a marriage must receive the consent of the bishop.

Further evidence of this corporate assumption of responsibility for each other (2 Thessalonians 3:11) would seem to indicate a control over the life of the individual. In fact it is only a warning that when certain Christians decide not to work and idle away their time, the total community is affected. Paul makes a direct appeal to these people but he does so in the context of a total appeal to the congregation there. The same thing holds true of the question of the courts of law (1 Corinthians 6:1). The fact that this happens is seen as a point of criticism for the total fellowship.

The end goal is clearly stated at a number of points. In Paul's basic appeal in Romans 12:2 he calls for a renewed mind which searches more intensely for the will of God in the context of communal existence within the church. This involves not only moral behaviour but also moral knowledge and is never an individual ethical phenomenon. The goal of this knowledge is, according to Colossians 1:9, "that your manner of life may be worthy of the Lord and entirely pleasing" (see also 1 Corinthians

2; also Leonard Swidler, *Women in Judaism* (Metuchen, NJ: Scarecrow Press, 1976), 126-130.

10:33). Thus Paul maintains that every act which is recognized as necessary through the full knowledge of the divine will is at the same time tied to the *areskei* of the Christian church as much as it is to worthiness before the Lord. Although Paul does not give to the church the right to approve everything, he does say that all actions must be taken with the church in mind and with reference to the church.

While church members each have a gift they do not each have a different ethic. Yet this sober insight into the limits of the individual and the variety of gifts makes absolutization or isolation of the individual impossible. The individual and the congregation belong together. This has extensive consequences for the knowledge of that which God has commanded. Precisely the differences of gifts and responsibility make it difficult for us to keep the fellow believer in mind. Implied also is the necessity of listening to the other when trying to find out what is to be done in a specific moment.

In addition to the general admonition for all members of the church to seek after *epignosis* and to test the divine will, a special gift is given to individual charismatics. Through the Spirit one has the gift of wise speech (*logos sophias*) while another, by the power of the same Spirit, can put the deepest knowledge (*logos gnoseos*) into words (1 Corinthians 12:8). Commentators have had great difficulty with the interpretation of these two expressions. Lietzmann assumed that Paul spoke here without any precise logical differentiation; Bultmann also saw no precise difference, either in form or content, in these two expressions. Others have seen the word of knowledge and the word of wisdom as forms of *didache* to be distinguished from revelation and prophecy. But Bultmann has correctly observed that on the basis of 1 Corinthians 13:2 and 14:6 this is impossible.

Weiss sees the "word of knowledge" as closer to the idea of revelation and mystery (1 Corinthians 13:2; 14:6). Consequently he understands the word of knowledge as the penetration into the higher mystical knowledge whereas the "word of wisdom" he sees closer to the area of *didache* (1 Corinthians 6:5; Romans 16:19; Colossians 1:9; 3:16; 4:5 where *sophia* emphasizes more of the capability of making practical moral judgements which is also closer to the LXX usage). Although 1 Corinthians 2:6 would cause us to hesitate to make any confident distinctions, Weiss seems to have greater justification for his distinction. It is significant that neither knowledge nor *sophia* are here seen as charismatic gifts but as *the word* of knowledge and *the word* of wisdom. Only as knowledge and wisdom are actualized in a word and proclaimed to the church do *sophia* and *gnosis* become charismatic gifts and obtain their value. This corresponds to the observation made above that all charismatic gifts are directed toward the church and must serve the goal of edification.

Thus there exist in the congregation individual charismatics who have to a special degree the function of speaking wisdom and knowledge, who give to the total congregation clarification and knowledge, direction and prodding in their moral questions and problems, indicating what God wants done here and now. Herein it also becomes clear that any privatization of moral knowledge is impossible and that the Pauline ethic is no private ethic but a congregational ethic.

This does not mean that in the congregation some gifts are not more common than others. It seems, for example, that the apostles are most highly regarded, perhaps because their number is limited, the prophets are second and then the teachers. All three of these seem to use the gift of wise speech and seek to put the deepest knowledge into words (1 Corinthians 12:8). Nevertheless, Paul puts a special premium on prophecy and puts it next to love when he says, "Above all aim at prophecy" (1 Corinthians 14:1, 5). The prophets, clearly both female (Acts 2:18; Joel 2:28, 29; Acts 21:9; 1 Corinthians 11:5; 14:24) and male seem to have been a well-defined circle of persons with a specific gift from the Spirit, even though all are urged to seek the gift (1 Corinthians 14:1, 5, 39; note the crescendo to verse 39, *dseloute to propheteuein*).

The specific mark of prophetic speech is that it has a concrete actual character which seeks to draw out and make the apostolic admonitions concrete. To some extent it is also instructional (1 Corinthians 14:31, especially verse 6). But its specific nature does not consist in teaching, in the preservation, transmission and exposition of tradition but rather in knowledge, formulation and proclamation directed toward specific situations giving new admonitions and directions to these situations.

Through the gift of prophecy the congregation receives a prophetic proclamation of what obedient service would be as the divine word is proclaimed to a specific situation in that particular hour. Thus its proclamation has less to do with the transmission of gospel truth than with being an actual call for commitment to a particular course of action.

It is not so important then that the word of the prophet be transmitted but rather that it be heard.[38] The prophesying is limited to the times when the congregation meets. There is an illegitimate (1 Thessalonians 5:19) but also a legitimate (1 Corinthians 14:30) silencing of the prophet. Prophecy has to do with a word daily casting light upon the way of the church and not with directions which are given once and for all. Actual direction in leadership is given case by case and anew for each concrete situation. It is essential that specific situations are addressed intelligently through Spirit-given knowledge. Hence the congregation must clearly understand what is being said.

Any prophecy which the individual keeps for him/herself or has received independently of the congregation is inconceivable for Paul, just as having private knowledge is impossible. Here again he separates himself radically from Gnosticism which emphasizes the use of private gifts for the individual. Nevertheless, Paul seems to allow that *gnosis* is different from prophecy at this point: *gnosis* has its basis in the individual while prophecy is always directed toward sharing with the congregation.

Thus there is a difference between the gift for prophecy and any appeal to purely personal insights or leadings given by the Spirit. The correct attitude toward prophetic instruction is neither disobedience nor blind obedience but rather obedience which is free, voluntary, intelligent and at all times critically testing. It is the function of the church as a totality to test these prophecies (1 Thessalonians 5:21; 1 Corinthians 14:29). There is also the special gift of distinguishing between spirits (1 Corinthians 12:10). In no case is it assumed that the prophetic *pneuma* is beyond discussion and an uncontrollable entity.

No outer criteria are given in the New Testament on how the genuine and the false prophets can be distinguished except

---

[38]See Wolfgang Schrage, *Die konkreten Einzelgebote in der paulinischen Paraenese,* 183.

as we have them in 2 John and in the *Didache*. The testing takes place not only with reference to specific courses of action but also according to the analogy of faith (Romans 12:6), and cannot avoid the basic question whether the Spirits that are being tested proclaim that Jesus Christ has come in the flesh and that he is Lord (1 John 4: 1 Corinthians 12:3).

What appears evident is that theologizing, both in its fundamental sense as conceptualizing God and divine activities in relation to the world in which the early Christians lived and in the specific ethical course of action, was closely related to community life. The main purpose for the gathering of the community was to engage in this kind of theologizing. The apostolic concern focused on conversation among the various members of the church. It was focused in the desire that all the gifts which the Spirit had so richly given to the churches would be exercised. Both the gifts of service and the gifts of the word were to be given free expression in the church with adequate provision made for testing and evaluating that which was said and done.

The early church was then in the most fundamental sense a hermeneutical community in which the apostolic message was repeatedly tested and checked out over against other understandings of Christ's significance to the world. This hermeneutical community lived in creative tension between the upbuilding of its own inner life and the proclamation of the message to the outside. The events of Christ's life and his significance were constantly reinterpreted as the early Christians met the pagan mentality, as they debated the issues with the Jews and as, in their own meetings, they sought for ways in which they could be faithful to God's will as it had been revealed in Jesus Christ. If they saw themselves along the lines of a Roman *societas* then the goal of unity was basic, for once they lost their unity they lost their existence. Roman societies based their right to exist on their unanimity.[39]

---

[39]See J. Paul Sampley, *Pauline Partnership in Christ: Christian Community and Commitment in Light of Roman Law* (Philadelphia, PA: Fortress Press, 1980).

Conclusion

It is time now to review the quote with which we began this essay. It does not stress enough our need for "specialized investigations" carried out by scholars trained in the classical disciplines, called by Christ to work in the church and in the academy and to raise the critical issues that need to be considered. Must we be prepared to yield to just anyone what we can learn from David Schroeder about New Testament sexuality and ethical household codes and treat the opinions of Ms. Laywoman or Mr. Layman equal to Schroeder's?

It is not possible to address the question assigned to me: To what extent do we as Mennonite conferences today live up to the standard set for us in the scriptures? In my judgement we err most in the way we proceed to try to find the will of God. We do not have faith in our local congregations and do not believe that all theology must have a relational and pastoral dimension.

We must, under the guidance of our communities and the Holy Spirit, have the courage to point out areas in which writers of Holy Scripture have been unfaithful in their handing on of God's word to us. Three examples suggest where that may be the case.

First, Titus 1:12 proclaims that "Cretans are always liars, evil brutes, lazy gluttons." Let me state quite clearly and publicly, I do not believe that. Nor do I believe for a moment that those lines are divinely inspired, coming as they do from an ancient poet;[40] nor that the handing down of those words throughout the centuries as part of the so-called "good news" has served God's redemptive purposes. How would you feel if you were a pastor in Crete charged with having to interpret this to Cretans? What we have here is a classic case of stereotyping and discrimination.

Second, the writer to Timothy, in supporting his argument

---

[40]*Greek Anthology*, trans. W.R. Paton, Book VII, Epigram 275 (London: William Heinemann, 1970), 151. The problems this passage has created for scholars can be seen in the essays by Rendel Harris in *Expositor* II (1906): 305-317; III (1907): 332-337; IV (1912): 348-353; V (1915): 29-35. See also Otto Eissfeldt, "Kreter und Araber," *Theologische Literaturzeitung* 72 (April 1947): 207-212.

that women are to be silent in church, argues that Adam was formed before Eve, then adds:

> And Adam was not the one deceived; it was the woman who was deceived and became a sinner. But women will be saved through childbirth, if they continue in faith, love and holiness with propriety (2:11-15).

Certain options present themselves when we encounter a text like this. We can stickhandle our way around it and in some way try to reconcile it with Genesis, with Romans 5 and 1 Corinthians 11 and 14. Or one can (and *I* must) see this author as someone who was never liberated by Christ from the male chauvinism which attributes the fall of humankind to women and wants them to bear the whole burden of human sin. Are we allowed to treat this author as someone who has never seen the glorious freedom of Jesus who travelled with women, discussed Torah with them, allowed them to touch him and kiss him in public and accepted them as broken creatures but, above all, commissioned them to proclaim the good news in the kingdom alongside men, being equal in every respect to them? Could it not be that he has never heard Paul proclaim that in Christ there is neither male nor female (Galatians 3:28)? In short, to use Jim Sanders' terminology, he operates within a different canonical frame of reference.

We need only look about us and see what enormous harm this one writer has done in the church with his falsehoods. Are we not forced to conclude that he is an unfaithful carrier of the traditions of Jesus? We must have the courage to say so if women are ever to experience the church and its institutions as a community in which they can exercise the gifts of the Holy Spirit and be equally represented on the faculties of universities, to say nothing of our biblical seminaries or Bible colleges where one would expect them to be far ahead on such matters of equal opportunity.

Third, there is the matter of patriarchy. Unfortunately, for many people feminism now has a tarnished reputation. One of my daughters, who is studying theology, occasionally sends me material to read, which she fears her father might miss. When she learned that I was writing an article on "love in the New

Testament" she sent me Rita Nakashima Brock's book *Journeys by Heart: A Christology of Erotic Power.*[41] At first the title itself did not capture me. Yet as I read the book I became increasingly intrigued by Brock's thesis and was struck by the accuracy of her conclusions. First she undertakes a serious theological review of where we are in theology and asks whether we still believe that "By your fruits you shall know them." If so, it is clear that patriarchal theology has damaged the church beyond recognition. Above all she reminded me that relational theology, beginning with God's overture of love towards us, is the only theology which can be defended from scripture; clearly, the heart, as she defines it, should be seen as the scene of erotic power. Her strong affirmation of a relational church, a community which she calls a "Christa community," is worthy of attention. With Schüssler-Fiorenza she sees

> the focal point of early Christian self-understanding not as a holy book or a cultic rite, not mystic experience and magic invocation, but a set of relationships: the experience of God's presence among one another and through one another.[42]

Brock's focus is to turn patriarchy inside out and to "examine the broken heart of male dominance".[43] One of the reasons we are so weak in the church today may be that we have failed to listen to the oppressed amongst us—our own people who have been wounded by and redeemed from manipulative sexual patterns or the abuse of power. It is even sadder that we allow ourselves to adopt motions, denuded as they usually are of pastoral warmth, before a majority of our congregations have had an occasion to discuss the issues involved. For we have no right to say, "it seemed good to the Holy Spirit and us" until we have carried the pain and rejoiced in the freedom of those whom Christ has set free.

The imperfect practice of democracy is better, by which I mean only a surer way to protect the weak, than the kind of

---

[41]Rita Nakashima Brock, *Journeys by Heart: A Christology of Erotic Power* (New York, NY: Crossroad, 1988).

[42]Ibid., 115.

[43]Ibid., xvi.

mixed-up polity which now governs our Mennonite family, a polity in which a small group manipulates the rest of us into positions that may reflect their views but have little to do with the glorious gospel Jesus brought where the highest values were not food and drink (and we may add, sex) but "justice and peace and joy in the Holy Spirit" (Romans 14:17). Perhaps the order in which those are placed is not haphazard. At any rate they all belong together and they are undoubtedly the three greatest gifts of the Spirit for community living. As Paul said: "True, it has an air of wisdom, (we return to the *logon sophias*) with its fake piety, its self-mortification, and its severity to the body; but it is of no use at all in combatting sensuality" (Colossians 2:23). Michael Welker has said

> The forgiveness of sins is the process that creates the requisite conditions for the unity of human beings with God where those conditions do not exist. On the basis of forgiveness of sins, the unity of Christ . . . comes into effect. Human beings who are freed from sin and the self-destruction to which it leads do not merely passively participate through the Spirit in that event which brings fullness of life to this earth. In the Spirit they are full of God's power.[44]

Paul Hanson has pointed out the central element of compassion in the ministry of Jesus and in his formation of the Kingdom. As a result of Jesus' work

> those who by human standards were denied the benefits of the community were drawn into the true community of shalom, including the blind, the deaf and the dumb. . . . Throughout the history of community spanned by the Bible, a remarkably consistent pattern recurs at those points where the community experiences God's presence intimately and intensely, a pattern in which the primal response of worship is followed by the desire to embody the qualities recognized in God's redemptive initiative on behalf of humans, the qualities of righteousness (justice) which looks out for the rights of all people and a compassion that draws into the protection of the community of shalom those excluded by human standards.[45]

---

[44]Michael Welker, "The Holy Spirit," *Theology Today* 46 (January 1989): 19-20.

[45]Paul Hanson, *The People Called: The Growth of Community in the Bible* (San Francisco, CA: Harper and Row, 1986), 425. The way in which Katherine

Where such a community is in the process of becoming, the voice of the people becomes the voice of God. The outsiders who come to participate in their common life conclude: "God is certainly among you" (1 Corinthians 14:25).

The question of faithfulness is without doubt the one question upon which all hinges (1 Corinthians 4:2). But it is also one of those ultimate questions which is not decided in the first instance by our self-scrutiny; certainly it does not matter in the least whether any human court judges. The judge is the Lord and ultimately we all rest our case on the Lord. When that One brings to light what darkness hides, then each one will receive from God his/her praise (*epainos*) (1 Corinthians 4:3-5).[46]

Doob Sakenfeld works with the concept of "authority in community" could be useful to Mennonites, especially if we could rid ourselves of the concern to find out "who is right." "Feminist Biblical Interpretation," *Theology Today* 46 (July 1989): 154-168, esp. 165-168.

[46]Not as the New English Bible, "such praise as he deserves," nor as Jerusalem Bible, "for each one to have whatever praise he deserves from God." The King James Version and Revised Standard Version have it more correct, although it is surprising how often when I have asked people to read this verse in class they commit a deeply ingrained human error and read: "each will receive his condemnation." Luther had it right, but *Die gute Nachricht* version (1982) brought in the element of merit. The Greek is unequivocal, which simply provides evidence that rational translators have difficulty comprehending the miracle of the gospel and turning it into language we can understand.

IV. Contemporary Theology

A. James Reimer*

HOW MODERN SHOULD THEOLOGY BE? THE NATURE AND AGENDA OF CONTEMPORARY THEOLOGY**

One of the difficulties in speaking about "the modern" is the variety of ways the term is used in contemporary discussions. It cannot be assumed that the term means the same for scientists, sociologists, historians, philosophers, poets and theologians. What is "modern" for many signifies whatever is current: the latest idea, invention, movement or event. How modern in this sense should theology be? It ought obviously to be as current as possible, at least if it hopes to communicate something appropriate to the age in which one lives. This is not, it appears, what the organizers of this conference had in mind, however, when they framed the question: "How modern should theology be?" The term, modern, here is used more technically to refer to a certain historical epoch with particular assumptions about freedom (individual autonomy), reason (technical and analytical rationality) and history (the chronological sequence of time from past to present to future). In this essay I will concentrate on the agenda(s) of contemporary theology in light of the "historical" understanding of the term, modern, answering only indirectly the question of how modern contemporary theology should be.

In some literary circles the modern figure (referring to writers such as James Joyce, D.H. Lawrence, T.S. Eliot and Virginia Woolf) is someone who "is acutely conscious of the contemporary scene, but . . . does not accept its values." In the words of literary critic Stephen Spender, it is the modern person to whom "it seems that the world of unprecedented phenomena

---

*A. James Reimer is Associate Professor of Religious Studies and Theology at Conrad Grebel College in Waterloo, Ontario.

**The author would like to thank Helmut Harder, Professor of Theology, Canadian Mennonite Bible College, Winnipeg, Manitoba, and Don Stoesz, a doctoral student in theology, McGill University, Montreal, Quebec, for their critical responses to this essay at the Symposium.

has cut us off from the life of the past, and in doing so from traditional consciousness."[1] For the nineteenth-century philosopher Friedrich Nietzsche and his twentieth-century interpreter Martin Heidegger—the two thinkers the late Canadian philosopher George Grant considers to be moderns *par excellence*—the modern age begins with the loss of God as an eternal horizon for all human endeavour and experience.[2] In a similar vein sociologists frequently talk about the modern in terms of secularity, disenchantment, individualism and the loss of social cohesion provided in the past by the great religious traditions.

Grant, greatly influenced by Nietzsche and Heidegger, views moderns as those who have accepted the liberal assumption of freedom from all external restraints (or limits) that lies behind the rise of modern technology. Technology in Grant's thought presupposes a view of nature as devoid of value and at our own disposal, humans as free to dispose of nature the way they see fit, reason as a means of controlling nature and history as cumulative progress. Liberalism is for him that "set of beliefs which proceed from the central assumption that . . . [the human] essence is . . . [human] freedom and therefore that what chiefly concerns . . . [humans] in this life is to shape the world as we want it."[3] Although Grant thinks Heidegger, following Nietzsche, has correctly described the "oblivion of the eternal" which characterizes the modern age, he objects to Heidegger's happy acquiescence, and believes that we are finally not fitted for this modern view of reality. After much reflection he concludes that the classical way of looking at things (including the views of both Jesus and Plato) is more adequate than our own. Grant avows that despite the deprived nature of our technological language, it is possible through imagining, remembering, desiring, thinking and contemplating to experience, momentarily at least (presum-

---

[1] Stephen Spender, *The Struggle of the Modern* (Berkeley, CA: University of California Press, 1965), 78.

[2] For an examination of the late Canadian philosopher George Grant's understanding of the modern, especially in relation to Nietzsche and Heidegger, see my "Do George Grant and Martin Heidegger Share a Common Conservatism?" in *The Chesterton Review: George Grant Special Issue* XI (May 1985): 183-198.

[3] George Grant, *Technology and Empire* (Toronto, ON: House of Anansi, 1969), 114, note 3.

ably as individuals), the eternal verities which transcend our and every historical period.[4] The Eternal, he thinks, can take care of itself and break through even our age. In fact, nature is already revolting against human control and domination. In doing so the inadequacy of the modern historicist and anthropocentric project is unmasked. Grant considers himself both a Christian and a Platonist. It is here where he parts company with Heidegger and Nietzsche.

Behind the philosophical analysis of Nietzsche, Heidegger, Grant and others, is the assumption that the great watershed in western intellectual history is the Enlightenment: that constellation of factors accompanying the rise of modern science, reason, freedom and time as history (in contrast to the classical conception of time as enfolded within eternity).[5] It was the German theologian Ernst Troeltsch (1865-1923) who identified these intellectual currents of the Enlightenment rather than the theological and ecclesiastical motifs of the Reformation as the true birth of the modern world.[6] While there may be room to debate this basic assumption—there may be reason, for example, to argue that the modern as it emerged with the seventeenth and eighteenth centuries is not as novel as these philosophers have made it out to be—it is this understanding of the modern which shapes my own thinking on the subject of "How modern should theology be?" I believe with Grant that the Enlightenment and its effects has virtually cut us off from a reverence for the past and that the Eternal enframes the temporal. In affirming this I

---

[4]See Grant, *Time as History* (Toronto, ON: Canadian Broadcasting Corporation, 1974).

[5]We should also note other important thinkers in this development, such as a view of modern science as represented by the inductive-empirical method of observing nature put forward by Francis Bacon (1561-1626), the turn to the rational human subject as the only ground for certainty as espoused by the philosopher Rene Descartes (1596-1650), the protest against all heteronomy (external authority) in favour of autonomous reason most forcefully present in the thought of Immanuel Kant (1724-1804), modern views of historical and evolutionary time beginning with G.W.F. Hegel (1770-1831). Together these figures, among others, and the influential intellectual currents they represent, including their social, economic, political and religious consequences, mark off the seventeenth and eighteenth centuries (often referred to as the Enlightenment) as a crucial turning point in western history and as the birth of the modern world.

[6]See Claude Welch, *Protestant Thought in the Nineteenth Century*, volume 2: 1870-1914 (New Haven, CT: Yale University Press, 1985), 277.

am in effect saying that ancient Christianity, as portrayed in the biblical text and understood in classical theology, continues to be more adequate to human existence and self-understanding than theologies based on historicist perceptions of reality.

What has become increasingly transparent in the twentieth century—more so than it was for Troeltsch—is that the so-called "modern paradigm" is losing its explanatory, symbolic and moral power in light of the crises that are facing contemporaries. This has given rise to talk about the "post-modern" world; a world where the Enlightenment assumptions about science, reason, freedom and history are no longer uncritically accepted, in fact are frequently seen to be part of the problem, leading to our present *aporias* ("dead ends"). The question, "How modern should theology be?" when put in this light, takes on entirely new dimensions.

Theology, in my opinion, does not have the freedom to be or not to be "modern," or "non-modern" for that matter, as if its practitioners sit above the historical flow of things making such choices. It has been shaped by modern scientific, rational and historical assumptions. We participate in the age of which we are a part. The fact is that new paradigms can not arbitrarily be created or chosen; they emerge gradually replacing older paradigms that have lost their power. The urgent question for theology, therefore, is whether, on one level, it is willing to release itself from some of the assumptions of the previous historical (the modern) epoch and open itself to the emergence of a new paradigm. It dare not absolutize any historical moment: either the pre-modern, the modern or now apparently the post-modern. On a more important level, however, the question for theology is whether it has the capacity to receive an Eternal Word from outside, yet within, a given paradigm and then to address the challenges of a post-modern world with this histori-cally-cloaked Eternal Word.

While there is growing consensus that the previous para-digm is finished, or at least seriously inadequate, and that something has to be done to save this planet, for example, there are competing analyses of the problem and its solution. The dilemma which seems to characterize the emerging paradigm is a sense of urgency that some kind of common front, including shared values, will be necessary if we are to find global solutions to the various crises facing us, realizing all the while that the contemporary global scene is defined by an increasing fragmentation of life and loss of corporate identity (the apparent impossibility of a common front).[7] It is to these competing motifs and analyses of the crises in current theology that I want to turn my attention in this essay.

There appear to be at least three conflicting theological agendas arising out of different diagnoses of the present global situation in contemporary theology: the total triumph of modern technology (including its threat to our planet) and the need for a new metaphysically or transcendentally based ethic in a disenchanted universe; increasing economic disparity and political oppression and the struggle for social justice; and growing diversity, pluralism, fragmentation and loss of social cohesion with the accompanying concern for identity, tolerance, dialogue and ecumenicity. A proliferation of theological literature is appearing in each of these three areas, and individual theologians, schools and even denominations frequently identify with one or other of these camps. One could, with some justification, characterize these three fronts as neo-conservative, left-wing and liberal causes, respectively.

My own theological work has taken me into all three spheres of theological concern. In the remainder of this essay I will consider in greater detail the first of these (the technological), then comment briefly on the second (social justice) and third (inter-Christian and interreligious discourse) theological agendas in light of the first. I suggest that all three are legitimate theological concerns challenging us to serious reflection in the

---

[7]For an overview of the nature of scientific paradigms as applied to theology, and the various paradigm shifts in theology throughout history, including the most recent one, see Hans Küng, "Paradigm Change in the History of Theology and the Church: An Attempt at Periodization," *The Conrad Grebel Review* 3 (Winter 1985): 19-20. Küng, basically following Thomas S. Kuhn's view of paradigm and paradigm shifts in the natural sciences, defines paradigm and paradigm shifts as the "values, techniques, and so on shared by the members of a given community." Ibid., 20. He identifies six basic paradigms in the history of Christian theology: primitive Christian apocalyptic, early Christian Hellenistic, medieval Roman Catholic, Protestant Reformation, modern enlightenment and contemporary. What characterizes the contemporary post-enlightenment paradigm is its diversity (its profusion of theologies).

light of the three articles of the *Credo*. (Incidentally, I understand *Credo* not as alternative to Canon but as personal and corporate appropriation and confession of Canon; as affirmation of the mysteries of faith which are as well (perhaps even better) chanted, sung, poeticized, even painted as logically argued and rationally analyzed.)

The Technological Crisis and the Search for Transcendence

Technology raises questions for us as Christians concerning the nature of God's transcendence and relationship to the created order (nature), issues especially appropriate for consideration under the first article of the Creed: belief in God as Creator and Sustainer (or Ground). There is growing literature on the nuclear, environmental and bio-medical dangers resulting from the global triumph of technical rationality. As I read this material I detect quite a different diagnosis of the current situation, a different critique of modern assumptions, and different solutions, than I find in literature where the overriding concern is emancipation and social justice, for instance. Rather than attempting a comprehensive survey of this literature I want to concentrate on the thought of one particularly significant contemporary Jewish philosopher of technology, Hans Jonas, and draw some conclusions for theology. The reason I choose Jonas is not only because of his profound insights into the contemporary technological situation but also because I am fascinated with his critique of all eschatological-utopian thinking and his philosophical attempt as a non-Christian to articulate a responsible ethic for our age.

Jonas was born in Germany in 1903, fled Nazi Germany to England in 1933, spent the years 1935 to 1948 in Palestine, taught at McGill University (Montreal) and Carleton University (Ottawa) during the years 1949 to 1954, and since 1955 has been associated with the New School of Social Research in New York. He describes himself as having gone through three academic stages: a pre-war preoccupation with existentialist philosophy and ancient gnosticism, a post-war turn of interest to the natural sciences and the philosophy of organicism (he found himself sympathetic to Whiteheadian process philosophy but in the end could not go along with it); and, in the last part of his career, a concern with practical philosophy or ethics, growing out of his fear of what was happening to our planet because of modern technology.[8]

Before his emigration to England in 1933 he studied with the philosopher Martin Heidegger and the Protestant theologian Rudolf Bultmann. While he pays great compliments to Heidegger as a teacher, he observes that Heidegger failed to connect his philosophy of Being to the physical and organic ground of Being, to nature itself. The German philosophers did not take the natural sciences seriously, he notes.[9] It was this growing conviction—that our own being, our very transcendence over nature, our freedom and our morality (*Sittlichkeit*) are themselves grounded in nature—that becomes a dominant theme in Jonas' second and third stages. It becomes especially crucial for his very influential environmentally concerned work in the area of ethics and technology. The almost inevitable cumulative effects of our daily peacetime use and application of technology, he comes to realize, is a much greater threat to us and our future than the danger of a nuclear disaster.[10] In his essay, "Technik, Freiheit und Pflicht (Technique, Freedom and Responsibility)," an address delivered in Frankfurt, October 11, 1987, on the occasion of his receiving the German Book Publishers Peace Prize, he masterfully elaborates on how we as humans have become *the* danger to

---

[8]Jonas, "Wissenschaft als persönliches Erlebnis," in *Wissenschaft als persönliches Erlebnis* (Göttingen: Vandenhoeck & Ruprecht, 1987).

[9]Ibid., 19ff.

[10]Ibid., 28. See also Jonas, *The Imperative of Responsibility: In Search of an Ethics for the Technological Age* (Chicago, IL: University of Chicago Press, 1984), where he says, "My main fear rather relates to the apocalypse threatening from the nature of the unintended dynamics of technical civilization as such, inherent in its structure, whereto it drifts willy-nilly and with exponential acceleration: the apocalypse of the 'too much,' with exhaustion, pollution, desolation of the planet. Here the credible extrapolations are frightening and the calculable time spans shrink at a frenzied pace. Here averting the disaster asks for a revocation of the whole lifestyle, even of the very principle of the advanced industrial societies, and will hurt an endless number of interests (the habit interests of all!). It thus will be much more difficult than the prevention of nuclear destruction, which after all is possible without decisive interference with the general conditions of our technological existence," 202.

nature.[11] Technique is the product of our own human freedom and this freedom now calls us to responsibility. Our responsibility is to limit, to set boundaries to our own freedom, premised on the notion that "Life is a good or a 'value in itself.'"[12] It is a collective duty and therefore a political one. Jonas, himself a fugitive from modern tyranny, is fully aware of the great temptation of fascism for the twentieth century, and thinks the challenge is to walk the precarious line between preserving fundamental rights and freedoms and limiting, coercively if necessary, those individual freedoms that threaten the survival of human and nonhuman nature. There are no clear blueprints for the future—the technological reality in which we live is much too complex—and there is no possibility of stepping out of it. There can be no more talk of utopia (such thinking being itself partly responsible for the threat facing us) or of an earthly paradise, but only of a world which continues to be habitable (*Weiterwohnlichkeit der Welt*). "This means, that we will probably for our whole future have to live in the shadow of the threat of calamity."[13]

In 1976, in a remarkably personal essay, "Im Kampf um die Möglichkeit des Glaubens" (The Struggle for the Possibility of Faith), Jonas reflects on personal memories of his teacher Rudolf Bultmann and on some of the philosophical aspects of the latter's work.[14] Jonas, together with Hannah Arendt, both Jewish students of Heidegger, attended Bultmann's New Testament seminar in 1924. What is particularly significant about his essay for our purposes—there are some highly interesting details about his personal relationship with Bultmann as a Jew prior to emigration in 1933 and immediately after the war which we cannot go into—is Jonas' critical evaluation, as a non-Christian, of Bultmann's perception of the scientific worldview and the possibility of belief in the modern world. While he agrees with

[11]Jonas, "Technik, Freiheit und Pflicht," in *Wissenschaft als persönliches Erlebnis*, 32-46.

[12]Ibid., 40.

[13]Ibid.

[14]Jonas, "Im Kampf um die Möglichkeit des Glaubens," in *Wissenschaft als persönliches Erlebnis*, 47-75.

Bultmann that the Enlightenment has put religion on the defensive, he thinks Bultmann concedes too much to modern science when the latter says that "In any case modern science does not believe that the process of nature can be broken through by supernatural powers. . . ."[15] Science, says Jonas, holds only to a methodological precept, not a metaphysical one. Bultmann solves the problem by arguing that God does not break into natural processes in any external sense but that behind all immanent-external necessity stands inner-transcendent personal and divine freedom.[16]

It is at this point where Jonas offers his own unique contribution to the debate about the possibility of metaphysics in the modern world. The example he uses is free human agency that does not violate the canons of modern science and history. Jonas shows how every time humans act there is, in effect, a nonphysical (one might say metaphysical) intervention in the physical realm. Every time we as human beings act with conscious decision in the face of a number of alternatives the physical course of events is altered, caused to move in a direction that it would not have moved had no such nonphysical intervention taken place.[17] Jonas provides us with a philosophical defense of metaphysical freedom; a freedom that is rooted in the physical realm of nature but is nevertheless distinct from it, transcends it and intervenes in it. Applied to theology this would mean for the believer, according to Jonas, that what can be attributed to human action surely cannot be denied of God; that is, God surely also has the capacity to intervene in a nonphysical way with the physical world while preserving the integrity of that physical world.[18]

One of the agendas for contemporary theology in the face of the rationalistic, historicist and technological legacy of the Enlightenment is to reflect on how transcendence might be understood in the post-modern context. Jonas' example of free human action as a form of non-physical intervention in the

---

[15]Ibid., 54.
[16]Ibid., 60-61.
[17]Ibid., 64.
[18]Ibid., 63-64.

course of the physical world, can provide theology with a phenomenological analogy for understanding divine transcendence, freedom and intervention in nature and in history.

Having introduced some of the main themes of Jonas' life and thought, I turn now to his more sustained treatment of the novel nature of modern technology and the need for a new metaphysically-based ethic of responsibility, as he offers it in his book *The Imperative of Responsibility*.[19] I concentrate on three significant aspects of his argument which have important implications for the contemporary theological agenda: his view of the modern versus the classical worldview, his proposal for an ethic of responsibility that is grounded in Being itself and his critique of all eschatological-utopian thinking.

Classical versus Modern Ontology

To read Jonas carefully is to find that he is torn between the classical and the modern view of reality. He feels we are trapped in the modern and need to take responsibility in the modern sense but his proposal draws on important classical motifs. The classical world viewed nature as essentially immutable and "given once for all." Human control was insignificant in the face of "abiding nature." Responsibility for nature was not a prominent theme. Nature could take care of itself. Ethics was defined in terms of the good, the virtuous; what was good for human beings in the present would be good for them in the future. The ancients thought "vertically (in terms of the eternal)" not "horizontally (the prolongation of the temporal)." In classical ethics "The drive is upward, not forward, toward being, not into becoming" (125).

This has changed in the modern period. What dominates modern existence is dynamism, that is, historical change. Our ontology is not one of eternity but of time. At the basis of this novelty is a new view of nature and human action. Nature, including "the whole biosphere of the planet," has become vulnerable to the intervention of human science and technology. It can no longer take care of itself. Nature can no longer carry

---

[19]Subsequent page references to this book will appear in the text.

the freight of human exploitation. It thus has acquired a "moral claim on us." The irony is that this novel situation comes exactly at the point where nature has become disenchanted, reduced "to the indifference of necessity" and "divested . . . of any dignity of ends," a result of "the dominant, scientific view of Nature." Nature has become desacralized, stuff at our disposal. According to Jonas, "the very same movement which puts us in possession of the powers that have now to be regulated by norms—the movement of modern knowledge called science—has by a necessary complementarity eroded the foundations from which norms could be derived, it has destroyed the very idea of norm as such" (22).

An Ethic of Responsibility

The challenge Jonas faces is to establish a modern (or post-modern) ethic which is grounded in norms outside of human willing; that is, outside the historical dynamism which has created the technological threat in the first place. He does this by developing a view of nature which is neither supernaturalistic (what he considers to be traditional religious dualism) or naturalistic (modern evolutionary and deterministic materialism). His basic moral axiom is "Act so that the effects of your action are compatible with the permanence of genuine human life" (11), or to put it differently, "Never must the existence or the essence of . . . [humanity] as a whole be made a stake in the hazards of action" (37). This contradicts an eschatological or utopian-progressivist ethic which considers "everything past as a stepping-stone to the future" (16) and insists on continually improving "what has already been achieved, in other words, for *progress*, which at its most ambitious aims at bringing about an earthly paradise" (36).

Implicit in this call for a non-utopian ethic is the need for ontology, the idea of humanity as such, an "ought" which stands above all present or future particular human beings; the idea that there ought to be human beings generically speaking. In other words, ". . . it follows that the principle of an 'ethic of futurity' does not itself lie within ethics as a doctrine of action . . . but within metaphysics as a doctrine of being, of which the idea of . . . [humanity] is a part" (44). This, however, runs headlong against one of the central dogmas of our time: that there is no metaphysical truth; that being is neutral, value free; that one cannot derive an "ought" from an "is." This, nevertheless, is precisely what Jonas sets out to argue persuasively for in this book: "the metaphysical *grounds* of obligation" (44-45); that "value, or the 'good'" is intrinsic to Being itself. We cannot here go into the details of Jonas' sophisticated attempt to show how nature in its most primitive form has a *telos* in the Aristotelian sense, an "aiming" or "directional" quality. According to Jonas, "already in the 'simplest' true *organism* . . . horizons of selfhood, world and time . . . are silhouetted in a premental form" (75). This "purposiveness" within nature itself is the basis for value, the ought, the good. Human beings, themselves rooted in nature, stand out from nature and, unlike the rest of nature, have the metaphysical freedom to say yes or no to nature. This is the source of human obligation. Human nature is obligated to say yes to nature and to limit its own arbitrary will and inclinations; obligated by the good of Being itself. Our duty to say "No to Not-Being," caring for the future of all nature is a type of "metaphysical responsibility," based not on self-interest or utilitarian calculation but on the goodness of Being as such.

A Non-Eschatological Basis for Justice

At times Jonas appears to lament the loss of the Eternal found in traditional religions and in Platonic thought. It may be, he reflects, that sometime in the future "Plato's way" will once again become "eligible." In fact, "we must leave it open whether it may not be more adequate to the truth of being than ours." He even admits that "the abolition of transcendence may have been the most colossal mistake in history. . . ." Nevertheless, for the moment we cannot extricate ourselves from our situation; "responsibility for what has been set aside and is kept moving by ourselves, takes precedence before everything else" (129). The novel view of nature and human action characterizing the modern era requires a novel ethic of responsibility if Being is to survive. This means, however, that one of the central aspects of the modern will have to be rejected: eschatological and utopian thinking as found particularly in Marxist and neo-Marxist thought.

Although Jonas is highly sceptical of the possibilities of limiting human freedom in the "capitalistic-liberal-democratic complex" (147) and considers the publically controlled economy of Marxist countries as offering greater hope in this regard, he is sharply critical of the Promethean dream of an earthly paradise (a classless society) and of faith in the omnipotence of technology as a means to material well-being present in Socialism (155). Contraction rather than the expansion of productivity will be necessary. This contradicts eschatological thinking. Our hope lies in recovering "absolute *presence* in itself—no past, no future, no promise, no succession, whether better or worse, not a prefiguration of anything, but rather timeless shining in itself. *That* is the 'utopia' beyond every 'not yet,' scattered moments of eternity in the flux of time. . . . The basic error of the ontology of 'not yet' and its eschatological hope is repudiated by the plain truth—ground for neither jubilation nor dejection—that genuine man is always already there and was there throughout known history: in his heights and his depths, his greatness and wretchedness, his bliss and torment, his justice and his guilt—in short, in all the *ambiguity* that is inseparable from his humanity" (200). What is required for our world to survive, to be able to bear the burden of human activity, is "to *unhook the demands of justice, charity and reason from the bait of utopia*" (201).

Theological Implications

My intent here is not to give a thoroughgoing and much needed biblically and theologically based response to technology. Carl Mitcham and Jim Grote have made a valiant attempt to begin such a project in their anthology, *Theology and Technology*.[20] My purpose is rather to show how in contemporary theology there are a variety of preoccupations. Three examples are technology, social justice and inter-Christian and inter-religious dialogue. Each of these have their distinctive agendas

---

[20]Carl Mitcham and Jim Grote, eds. *Theology and Technology: Essays in Christian Analysis and Exegesis* (New York, NY: University Press of America, 1984).

and their respective diagnoses of the modern situation. Their
theological answers differ remarkably from and frequently conflict
with each other.

I have spent considerable time examining Jonas' philosophical analysis of technology and its challenges for modern ethics
because I believe it raises crucial questions for contemporary
theology, including Mennonite theology. I want to reflect briefly
on three of these: our view of history, our view of God and
nature and our view of human action.

History

Jonas' critique of eschatological and utopian thought,
including the whole genre of "already/not-yet" thinking needs to
be taken seriously. In Jonas' mind this kind of thinking simply
legitimates the forward directionality and progressivism that lies
behind the modern misconception that true humanity lies in the
future; that there is no authentically experienced humanity in the
present; that every past and present event and moment is simply
a stepping-stone for that which is still to come. This poses a
valid challenge to all the future-oriented theologies that have
become so prevalent in recent decades, including various forms
of political, liberation and hope theologies.

All Christian theologies which emphasize the importance of
history (becoming) over ontology (being) are vulnerable to
Jonas's critique. This applies even to the *Heilsgeschichte* (Salvation history) tradition. George Grant, according to Joan E.
O'Donovan, identifies the *Heilsgeschichte* approach with liberal
historicism: "Grant sees liberal historicism and *Heilsgeschichte* as
sharing above all a common understanding of time as a finite,
irreversible process in which individual events have ultimate and
unique importance. They both portray events as actions, springing
from the will of a universal agent (God or Mankind), of which
individual agents are instruments, to carry out a plan, purpose,
or program for the world. . . . Both *Heilsgeschichte* and liberal
historicism recognize history as the realm of a sovereign will to
whom all things are possible, because the end of history springs

from it, so that evil (negativity) is not finally necessary."[21]

There is no doubt that eschatology is central to a Christian view of history. Modern secularized eschatologies like Marxism are profoundly indebted to the Judeo-Christian tradition in this regard. The danger arises at the point where this eschatological vision is no longer embraced by an eternal divine reality, contains no eternal content and is defined exclusively in terms of the chronological movement from past to present to future. For moderns it is virtually impossible to think of eschatology in anything but historicist terms. For the classical Christian, however, history and all historical willing took on relative meaning before an eternal truth: the eternal reality of God and God's historical revelation in Christ mediated by the Holy Spirit. Another way of expressing this would be to say that Christian truth is both *foundational* (it grounds the tradition and the created order) and *eschatological* (it is incomplete and awaits final redemption).

I partially agree with O'Donovan's gentle chiding of Grant for his almost total avoidance of eschatology in favour of tradition as foundation. O'Donovan argues that

> The Truth . . . has a double presence among us: Christ is present in the unified testimony of the Spirit and of Scripture. And in his double presence, the Truth is present as present and future as well as past: his presence is *eschatological* rather than *foundational*. He is the Truth of the End pre-eminently, and the Beginning under the sway of the End. The revelation of Christ in Scripture is foundational in only one sense: it is the foundation of an ongoing community of believers, a temporal community of faith, hope and charity.[22]

For O'Donovan past, present and future are placed within the embrace of eternal truth. The eschatological end is more than historical culmination. It is proleptically present in the beginning. I would, however, put more emphasis on the foundational nature of the truth of Christ (as in some sense distinct from eschatology) than O'Donovan appears to be doing here. The truth of

---

[21]Joan E. O'Donovan, *George Grant and the Twilight of Justice* (Toronto, ON: University of Toronto Press, 1984), 159.

[22]Ibid., 169-170.

Christ is both eschatological and foundational; that is, foundational not only to tradition but to the created order itself. The Anabaptists' notion of "the Christ of all Creation" or "the Gospel of all Creatures" would be worth exploring in this regard.[23]

God and Nature

A second challenge Jonas' analysis throws at Christian theology concerns our view of God and nature. Classical ontology, Jonas argues, viewed nature as eternal and abiding, not vulnerable to human historical action. This has changed. Nature after Francis Bacon has been divested of value, disenchanted; it has become stuff to be controlled and exploited for human purposes. Jonas' solution is to "re-enchant" nature (although he does not use this term), to show how there is a purposive quality within even lower forms of nature—the root that becomes genuine subjectivity in higher nature (human beings)—that provides us with an ontological basis for obligation; that is, Being has value in itself and it falls on us as humans to preserve Being. What is the challenge here for Christian theology? I believe we, particularly Protestants, need to reexamine our understanding of nature and its relation to the divine. Protestants traditionally, and I would include Mennonites here, have tended to emphasize God as acting agent over (if not to the exclusion of) God as ground of being. God is understood primarily as "personal willing," the One who acts; human beings are seen as those who are called to will God's will, to fulfill divine purposes within history. In Mennonite theology, this frequently takes the form of emphasizing moral and ethical obedience (discipleship) as the determining factor for Christian theology.

There is no denying that fundamental to the Old and New

---

[23]See Walter Klaassen, ed. *Anabaptism in Outline* (Scottdale, PA: Herald Press, 41-70, esp. 50. There is in some early Anabaptists the basis for developing a natural theology; related to the concept of the "gospel of Christ" and "the whole of the Scriptures" being already manifest in creation and in the work and suffering of creatures. According to Klaassen, "The idea is basically that knowledge of God comes to man first through the created world which prepares the way for the gospel of Christ. But it is also more than that; the suffering of Christ was seen to be already inherent in the processes of nature which require suffering and death that there may be life. Again, it is the idea of 'the Lamb slain from the foundation of the world.'" Ibid., 42.

Testament is the concept of God as One who acts within history and calls God's chosen people to obedient action. However, there are also other more feminine metaphors for God as the ground, sustainer and bearer of life and nature which are closer to the ontological imagery that Jonas calls for. The environmental crisis facing us, brought about by arbitrary historical willing, now demands of us to retrieve these what I would call "sacramental" or "ontological" metaphors for describing the relation of God to nature; the notion that God is graciously present within the natural order; God grounds, sustains and bears nature. In short, the continuities between lower and higher forms of nature (including of course humanity itself) need to be retrieved. Here it seems to me Protestants can learn something from the Catholic notion of *analogia entis* (the analogy of Being), in which all being in some sense participates in the being of God. In the Thomistic tradition God is defined as "Being Itself" (*ipsum esse*); to the extent that anything has being it is contingent upon and participates in God, the Ground of Being. The danger in this more ontological tradition is that the personality of God tends to be lost in the face of an abstract notion of Being; that sin, evil and the fallenness of the created order—the radical discontinuity between God and the world—are not emphasized strongly enough; and that the concern for religious and moral conversion is weakened. This is why the ontological tradition needs to be combined with the Barthian dialectical tradition of *analogia fide* (analogy of faith) and *analogia Christi* (analogy of Christ). Both of these theological traditions—the analogical and the dialectical—are important for Christian theology today.

Human Action

The main point Jonas makes as far as responsible ethics in our technological age is concerned, and I fully agree with him here, is that norm(s) for ethics must have an objective basis outside of historical action itself. Jonas as a philosopher makes the case for this objective ground being the "value, or the 'good'" that is intrinsic to Being itself. Christians can learn from Jonas' revivification of nature. No longer can we afford to think of nature as dead stuff. We need in our theology to retrieve the value that is intrinsic to nature, including human nature, all the while recognizing that for us the source of obligation is ultimately not nature itself (nature is not self-sufficient) but God as the creator and sustainer of nature. For the Christian, this objective ground is God in God's threefold being: Creator, Christ, Spirit. Ethics, in short, is anchored in the three-fold divine reality and revelation. The demands of historical justice are rooted in God's own justice and righteousness, not necessarily in what liberal democracies, social democracies or Marxists label justice. This is where Jonas makes what is perhaps his most provocative statement for contemporary theology: What is required for our world to survive, to be able to bear the burden of human activity, is to *"unhook the demands of justice, charity and reason from the bait of utopia"* (201).

Exploitation, Oppression and the Struggle for Social Justice

This brings me to what I consider to be the second major stream of thought in contemporary theology: a preoccupation with questions of economic disparity between rich and poor, political oppression and the struggle for social justice. By devoting the amount of space I have to technology and its challenges for modern theology, I am suggesting that this is where the most pressing agenda for modern and post-modern theology lies. I believe this to be the case, although I fully support the urgent need for theology to engage itself with questions of social, political and economic justice. It seems to me, however, and here I agree with Jonas, that our fight for justice will need to be reconceived in less historicist language than is frequently the case if we are to survive as human beings and remain faithful as Christian believers. Our view of justice will need to be framed within a more classical understanding of eternal justice and righteousness.

My treatment of this particular theological agenda will be considerably shorter than the first. I will again restrict myself primarily to looking at one representative, Gregory Baum and his theology as reflected in his recently published collection of essays *Theology and Society.*[24] Like Jonas, Baum grew up as a Jew in Germany. He emigrated to England, then to Canada during World War I as a 16-year old boy. Here he converted to Catholic Christianity and became a priest. In the 1970s his theology, which had been deeply influenced by what he calls the "soft liberation" theology of Vatican II (in contrast to the "hard liberation" of the more radical theology he now espouses, in which reality is viewed as conflictual rather than harmonious) and by the liberating insights of modern psychology, underwent a remarkable shift to the left. This change came about largely through his studies of sociology and social philosophy at the New School for Social Research, New York City, the academic home of Hans Jonas and other German intellectuals.

In the past two decades Baum has become, without a doubt, the best-known Canadian theologian, giving voice to social criticism in a wide range of journals and books, most consistently in his own periodical *The Ecumenist.* Evident throughout his writings are the influences of critical social theory and recent left-wing movements within the Roman Catholic Church, notably in Latin America, Canada and the United States; movements that are committed to Christian solidarity with the poor and the struggle for social justice around the world.

Underlying all his recent work is the assumption which he takes from Latin American liberation theology that ideas must

> be evaluated by their effect on people's lives. The ultimate norm of truth . . . is the transformation and emancipation of the human family. If a scholar, a social scientist, a thinker, a theologian is not committed to the emancipation of human-kind, the knowledge which he or she generates will, no matter how brilliant the mind and how convincing the arguments, lead to the alienation of people (121).

The passion for theology as a transforming power comes through on every page of this volume, which is divided into three parts: the first dealing with social teaching as it is evolving in the

---

[24]Gregory Baum, *Theology and Society* (Mahwah, NJ: Paulist Press, 1987). The page numbers that appear within the body of the text in the following section of the paper refer to this book. See also Baum's recent CBC Massey Lectures published as *Compassion and Solidarity: The Church for Others* (Montreal, PQ: CBC Enterprises, 1987).

Catholic church; the second concerned with theology and various movements of emancipation around the globe; and the third treating a variety of critical social issues facing the church.

Baum traces what he considers to be a remarkable shift to the left by a "significant minority" in the Catholic church in many parts of the world since the early 1970s. What is emerging in the Catholic Church of Canada, he says, is a "minority deeply marked by a new religious experience, Christians for whom faith and justice are inextricably intertwined, who read scripture and ecclesiastical doctrine in a new light, who discover in them the transformative power of Jesus Christ, and who for this reason find themselves in solidarity with the poor and marginalized" (21).

Baum considers Pope John II's call for "the priority of labour over capitol," "the solidarity *of* and *with* the poor," to be a clear indication that the church at the highest level has adopted a more radical form of social analysis and has in effect, blessed liberation theology. This new social gospel is, however, to be clearly distinguished from Marxist and Neo-Marxist critical theory. For one thing, its call for solidarity grows out of theological and ethical thought (44) in the context of "religious experience, tradition and community" (225). It is a call for social justice that is based on a "transformist" Christology which assumes that "Divine Revelation illumines and transforms the world" (91, 92). The transcendence of God is important but not in the individualistic and pietistic sense. Transcendence rather functions theologically as a source and inspiration for social criticism; ". . . and encounter with the transcendent" means "being overwhelmed by the divine call to justice, being turned inside out by the revelation of a new light on reality. . . ." (126).

The most fascinating aspect of Baum's book, especially pertinent for our consideration here, is his conversation with the great classical social thinkers on two issues related to the Enlightenment: modern science and technology. Baum is fully aware of the dangers of historical reductionism and the negative side of the Enlightenment: the triumph of positivism or instrumental rationality, the total mechanization of life and the consequent loss of precisely that freedom which the modern era intended to secure. The basic Enlightenment commitment to emancipation, Baum thinks, needs to be affirmed but under the rubric of the Christian view of salvation: "Without the Christian doctrine of salvation, the emancipatory struggles against domination appear as a Promethean project, as humans saving themselves" (139). Salvation includes emancipation, but it is an emancipation grounded in what Christians believe to be God's revelation in Christ: "that God enlightens and empowers people . . . to become the subject of their history" (139).

What is significant about Baum's social vision is his much more optimistic (than Jonas') view of modern technology in the struggle for social justice. He is harshly critical of Jacques Ellul and neo-conservative sociologists like Peter Berger for being overly pessimistic and deterministic in their analysis of modern technology. Although Ellul and Berger differ in important ways, they have, Baum believes, a misplaced diagnosis of the modern problem. Each of them erroneously identifies the primary form of contemporary degradation as being technocracy and bureaucracy, and laments the concomitant loss of transcendence. They see socialist alternatives as simply increasing technocracy and bureaucracy, and end up with little more than offering solutions for isolated individuals or small mediating groups (211, 297).

In contrast, Baum sees the dominant form of alienation in the modern world as being economic and political rather than technological. He credits critical theorist Jürgen Habermas with convincing him that technocratic theories of alienation are exaggerated and disregard certain humanizing trends in modern society (166). Baum urges Christians to remain suspicious of a technocratic theory of alienation because of its inherent determinism; that is, of not recognizing the genuine freedom of human beings to continue the struggle. It also relativizes the condition of the poor and the marginalized. Baum's greater optimism concerning technology and its possibilities is in keeping with Pope John Paul II's own stance. Modern technological development is not to be despised in itself but affirmed as a gift from God if it is to be properly understood and used. Such a positive view of technology, however, is conditional upon the acceptance of the priority of labour and workers over capital and large corporations, protecting worker's jobs, decentralizing capital, struggling for greater worker management and community ownership and preserving the environment (54, 80-81, 93, 100). In short, technology's positive potential for human emancipation ought to be recognized and its negative consequences repudiated.

While Baum would probably agree with most of what Jonas says about the danger of technology to our environment, and while he would most certainly agree that we must limit our freedom to shape and control nature, and to develop a responsible ethic if we are to survive, there is a different spirit at work in Baum's theology, as also in most left-wing political and liberation theologies. The primary devotion is to historical and social justice; everything else is defined with reference to this passion. Fundamental to the emancipatory project is a commitment to historical becoming, to prophetic-eschatological thinking, and a suspicion of metaphysical and ontological language as espoused by Jonas. Baum's softer interpretation of technology and the modern scientific enterprise generally is a natural part of his struggle for historical freedom. The question is whether it is possible to combine Jonas' quest for an ethic based on ontology (Being) and Baum's struggle for social justice in the context of history (Becoming). This is the urgent challenge for contemporary theology within the emerging paradigm. In my view both are absolutely essential and urgent.

Longtime friend of Baum's, another German intellectual emigré, Rudolf Siebert, is keenly aware of the danger which is present in political and liberation theologies, of reducing theology to historical action. In his own work he combines metaphysics and the historical struggle for social justice through a Hegelian synthesis. Siebert, professor of sociology and religion at the University of Western Michigan, directs the annual course "Future of Religion" at the Inter-University Centre of Postgraduate Studies, Dubrovnik, Yugoslavia. Scholars from socialist and non-socialist countries gather there to talk about the nature and future of religion in the modern/post-modern world. In a recent book, *The Critical Theory of Religion: The Frankfurt School*, Siebert examines the critical thought of various members of the Frankfurt School of Critical Theory, particularly its most recent member, Jürgen Habermas. He also analyzes German political theologians Johann Baptist Metz, Helmut Peukert and Edmund

Arens.[25] Siebert himself, like Baum, is a strong advocate of political and liberation theology. He finds that many political and liberation theologians are too optimistic and deal unsatisfactorily with the "theodicy" problem (God and the problem of evil). He criticizes them for tending to reduce theology to communicative praxis and for not dealing adequately with sin, evil and suffering.

Siebert's own solution is to call these critical philosophers and political theologians back to Hegel, who he considers to be the last great Christian philosopher to attempt a bridging of the classical and modern world. Siebert feels that much more can be rescued from traditional religious-metaphysical systems of meaning than these thinkers, especially Habermas, assume. For Hegel the transcendent and objective reality of God, the Absolute, still remained the central starting point. Human intersubjectivity was still grounded beyond itself, mirroring the communicative intersubjectivity within the Absolute itself (God as trinity). Human suffering and death were still seen as reflecting the tragedy within God. The crucifixion and resurrection of Jesus took on meaning only in relation to God's own crucifixion and resurrection. Human action and historical justice were grounded in absolute divine justice.

For those of us in a strong biblically-oriented and confessional-theological tradition, Siebert's Hegelian starting point sounds strange; too philosophical. Why not go back in an unmediated way to the biblical narrative itself? The point is that there is no unmediated access to the ancient texts. We read the biblical story from within the modern and now emerging postmodern context. Hegel is one of the giant transitional figures between the pre-modern and modern eras who attempted to bridge the two worlds. Central to his whole enterprise was a trinitarian philosophical-theological schema. In my own theological work I also have tried to retrieve some form of classical trinitarian theology as an onto-metaphysical framework for ethics in the contemporary world; as a way of combining concerns like those of Jonas and Baum.

---

[25]Rudolf J. Siebert, *The Critical Theory of Religion: The Frankfurt School* (New York, NY: Mouton Publishers, 1985). For a review of this book see my "Hegel's Contemporary Relevance," *The Ecumenist* 26 (July-August 1988): 75-78.

Pluralism and the Concern for Interreligious
and Inter-Christian Discourse

A third agenda item for theology today, one that appears to
be producing more theological literature currently than the other
two combined, particularly in North America, is religious
pluralism and the search for both identity and unity while
respecting genuine diversity.[26] What is interesting about this
stream of theology is that, in contrast to the technological and
the social justice agendas, it perceives the most obvious fact of
the modern world to be diversity and pluralism. For some this
is seen negatively as fragmentation and the loss of cohesion. For
others it is viewed positively as an opportunity for developing
greater tolerance and understanding others' points of view,
thereby enriching one's own. Nevertheless, what we have here is
quite a different diagnosis of the contemporary situation than
that given by the first two groups. The first school of theology—that concerned with technology and its threat to our
world—sees the world becoming ever more the same, overrun by
the technological monolith, with diversity being merely a surface
phenomenon. The second group—that devoted to the cause of
social justice—tends to divide the world into the oppressor and
the oppressed, and to suspect that the "liberal" concern with
pluralism and interreligious dialogue is a North American
concern that ideologically avoids the most pressing issue of our
time.

This is not the place to examine in detail the daily increasing volume of literature on this subject by David Tracy, Hans
Küng, John Hick, George Lindbeck and many others. What I
find intriguing about this genre, however, is what appears to be
a renaissance of interest in the doctrines of religious communities as a way of identifying oneself and one's differences
from and commonalities with other groups. Liberal theology
appears suddenly to have rediscovered the importance of the

---

[26]A Mennonite example of this preoccupation with diversity and identity is
the recent book edited by Calvin Wall Redekop and Samuel J. Steiner, *Mennonite
Identity: Historical and Contemporary Perspectives* (Lanham, MD: University Press
of America, 1988).

dogmatic and creedal tradition after its long eclipse in the Post-Protestant-Scholastic period. "Church doctrines," says Lindbeck, "are communally authoritative teachings regarding beliefs and practices that are considered essential to the identity or welfare of the group in question." There is no such thing as a creedless Christian community. "A religious body cannot exist as a recognizably distinctive collectivity unless it has some beliefs and/or practices by which it can be identified."[27]

Not only are doctrinal categories seen as a useful way of organizing Christian belief; they are also a way of accommodating interreligious understanding. This is what William A. Christian sets out to do in his recent philosophical study, *Doctrines of Religious Communities*: "If we think of religion as a kind of human activity about which something can be learned, and survey the scene from that point of view, a striking fact is the existence of a number of massive and enduring communities with non-overlapping memberships, each with its own body of doctrines." William Christian divides the doctrines of religious communities into *primary doctrines* ("for example . . . their teachings about the constitution of the world in general and about human nature in particular") and *doctrines about doctrines* ("principles and rules to govern the formation and development of its body of doctrines").[28] He concentrates on the latter, showing how there are some governing principles that are common to the various religious communities.

There is, however, something quite new about the way doctrines are treated here, different from the traditional dogmatic tradition. This is particularly evident in Lindbeck's understanding of doctrines as self-sufficient intrasystematic "cultural-linguistic" models (borrowing heavily from the late Wittgenstein's notion of "language-games") in contrast to what he calls the "classical cognitivism" of traditional orthodoxy, where doctrines represent propositional truths and "experiential-expressivism" where a common, universal "experiential core" among all religions is

---

[27]George Lindbeck, *The Nature of Doctrine: Religion and Theology in a Postliberal Age* (Philadelphia, PA: The Westminster Press, 1984), 74.

[28]William A. Christian, Sr., *Doctrines of Religious Communities: A Philosophical Study* (New Haven, CT: Yale University Press, 1987), 1-2.

assumed. In Lindbeck's "cultural-linguistic" approach, "religions are thought of primarily as different idioms for construing reality, expressing experience and ordering life."[29] No common propositional or experiential framework is assumed. Even within a single religious community, doctrines in the "cultural-linguistic" model cannot be assumed to correspond to a common foundational experience or cognitive truth.

It is not my intent to evaluate the adequacy of this new retrieval of doctrinal thinking within contemporary "liberal" (or perhaps more accurately, "post-liberal") theology; it is rather to point out that doctrinal language is being given a lot of attention but in a significantly new way. One critical question I would raise about this post-liberal doctrinal thinking is the following: Is the "cultural-linguistic" model, which in my view inevitably leads to a religious relativism (that is, there can be no universal truth claims that transcend any particular cultural-linguistic-doctrinal complex) adequate to meet the challenges of our age? I think not. There is a growing sense that the ethical issues raised by the technological and the social justice agendas of contemporary theology are universal and global ones which require a united front. The ethical urgencies raised by the technological crisis, for instance, call for a non-relativistic metaphysics and ontology.

It is this conviction that has inspired my own interest in classical theology. I would like to conclude by suggesting, as I have in a number of articles in the past few years,[30] that for Christians, including Mennonites, classical trinitarian and christological doctrinal categories are richer in potential for interpreting God, human and nonhuman nature and historical action than are other alternatives. These doctrines are more than "regulatory rules" for Christian communities; they are archetypal truths, "metaphors of ultimacy."[31] J. Denny Weaver misunder-

---

[29]Lindbeck, *The Nature of Doctrine*, 47-48.

[30]See, for example, my "Mennonite Theological Self-Understanding, the Crisis of Modern Anthropocentricity, and the Challenge of the Third Millennium," in *Mennonite Identity*, ed. Calvin Wall Redekop & Samuel J. Steiner, 13-38; and "Toward Christian Theology from a Diversity of Mennonite Perspectives," *The Conrad Grebel Review* 6 (Spring 1988): 147-159.

[31]Don S. Browning, in his brilliant book *Religious Thought and the Modern Psychologies: A Critical Conversation in the Theology of Culture* (Philadelphia, PA:

stands me when he caricatures my proposal as follows: "Mennonite theology would look like classic Protestantism with some
additional points lower down in the outline for a few doctrines
or practices—such as adult baptism, feetwashing, pacifism,
community—to exist alongside but not central to classic theology
shared by all Christian traditions."[32] What I do hold is that
central to the Christian faith is an affirmation of the
threefoldness of God and the twofoldness of Christ, as classically
formulated in the creeds and that this holds for all Christians,
including Anabaptists and Mennonites. Further, I hold, as I try
to show at some length in my article on "The Doctrine of God"
in the forthcoming fifth volume of *Mennonite Encyclopedia*, that
in the sixteenth century most Anabaptists accepted the standard
trinitarian creedal pattern but interpreted the trinity itself with
a heightened ethical consciousness, bringing in ethical concerns
not at the end of a list but right at the start in their interpretation of the first article of the creed. The point I try to emphasize, however, is that Christian theology, including Anabaptist-Mennonite theology, dare not start with ethics (that is,
with human action) but must begin and end with God in God's
threefoldness: Creator, Christ, Spirit.

All three of the agenda items I have discussed in this essay
will no doubt receive even greater attention in contemporary
theology in the future than they have up to now. All three are
legitimate concerns and need serious reflection by Christian
theology in the context of the Christian community. I would
suggest that these three very different streams of contemporary
theology could be fruitfully brought together and thought of in
terms of the threefoldness of God. The issues raised by modern
technology might fruitfully be reflected upon in light of a
Christian doctrine of creation, a doctrine that has unfortunately

---

Fortress Press, 1987), convincingly shows how all the modern psychologies,
whether they like to admit this or not, have theories of moral obligation that grow
out of certain "deep metaphors" or "metaphors of ultimacy," behind which lie
distinctive ontological, metaphysical or cosmological worldviews. I view Christian
doctrines similarly as deep metaphors of ultimacy; they are more than rules in a
particular language game.

[32]"Mennonites: Theology, Peace, and Identity, J. Denny Weaver responds to
A. James Reimer and Thomas Finger," *The Conrad Grebel Review* 7 (Winter
1989): 73.

not received nearly the attention it deserves by Mennonites. The second—that of dealing with economic and political oppression and the need for social justice—could appropriately be considered under Christology; a Christology, however, that receives its true meaning only as a trinitarian Christology not a Jesus-monism. A doctrine of the Holy Spirit offers provocative possibilities for the third set of issues—religious pluralism and interreligious understanding—for the work of the Holy Spirit defies easily-definable human-religious and denominational boundaries while remaining the very Spirit of Christ and of God.

Lydia Harder*

DISCIPLESHIP REEXAMINED: WOMEN IN THE HERMENEUTICAL COMMUNITY**

Twenty-five years ago a group of students graduating from Canadian Mennonite Bible College argued about the wording of the theme for their graduation service. David Schroeder's classes in biblical theology were probably the strongest influence in the choice of the two main concepts we were considering: freedom and obedience. The discussion centred on the way these concepts relate. Should the theme read "Freed to Obey" or "Obey to be Free?" I was one of the students who argued first one way and then another, not convinced that the tension between the two concepts could be wholly resolved. Theological study had told me that according to my Anabaptist heritage, obedience was central to discipleship. Moreover, I had begun to experience something of the freedom God gives to those who follow. Yet I had a vague intuition that obedience and freedom could not be put together as easily as our class was trying to do with either choice of wording.

Today I am struggling with the same tension, but the issue has become larger than a mere question over proper wording of a graduation theme. This tension, as I see it now, is deeply rooted in the experience of many women in our churches and society who obey but do not find freedom; who serve but do not discover abundant life. It finds expression in the ambiguity women feel as they ask how they can authentically and freely communicate their experience within the hermeneutical communities where their voices have been marginalized.

*Lydia Harder is a doctoral student in theology at the Toronto School of Theology, Toronto, Ontario.

**The author would like to thank Carol Penner, a doctoral student in theology at the Toronto School of Theology, Toronto, Ontario, and Perry Yoder, Associate Professor of Old Testament, Associated Mennonite Biblical Seminaries, Elkhart, Indiana, for their critical responses to this essay at the Symposium.

On Method

To address the central issues of women in the hermeneutical community, I will look closely at a process of biblical interpretation which takes into account both the context of the reader as well as the content of the biblical texts.[1] The motif of discipleship will be the central guide in bringing these two foci together.[2] My concern throughout this study will be to understand how women can responsibly and freely participate in biblical interpretation within the church. In this I am partly emulating a process I have learned from my Anabaptist forebears. As expressed by Walter Klaassen, Anabaptists claim that the "text can be properly understood only when disciples are gathered together to discover what the Word has to say to their needs and concerns."[3] This emphasis on the body of disciples as the primary "clue-generating community"[4] for biblical interpretation is important for the church since it makes women and their experience integral to the theological process.

Yet it is not really Anabaptist theology but rather feminist theology that has helped me to understand more clearly how important the relationship between theory and practice actually

---

[1]See my article "Hermeneutic Community: A Feminist Challenge," in *Perspectives on Feminist Hermeneutics,* ed. Gayle Gerber Koontz (Elkhart, IN: Institute of Mennonite Studies, 1987), 46-55. There I propose that both Mennonite and feminist hermeneutics acknowledge two poles in the interpretive process. By linking past faith-knowledge to present faith-experience in the hermeneutical community, Mennonites have tended to recognize the contributions of both text and interpreter in determining the meaning of a text for contemporary life. I suggest that a feminist hermeneutic challenges us to more clearly define the shape of the hermeneutical community. It challenges us to look more closely at the tradition that provides our pre-understanding, as well as the institutions and language that affect the communication process among the members. This paper takes the next step in analyzing this process.

[2]Harold S. Bender's focus on discipleship as essential to Anabaptism has had considerable influence on Mennonite theological writings and preaching. For him discipleship expressed the inseparability of belief and practice, faith and life. See "The Anabaptist Theology of Discipleship," *Concern,* no. 18 (July 1971).

[3]Walter Klaassen, "Anabaptist Hermeneutics: Presuppositions, Principles and Practice," in *Essays in Biblical Interpretation: Anabaptist-Mennonite Perspectives*, ed. Willard Swartley (Elkhart, IN: Institute of Mennonite Studies, 1984), 10. See also the essay by John H. Yoder, "The Hermeneutics of the Anabaptists," ibid., 11-28.

[4]Willard Swartley uses this expression in his concluding article "Afterword: Continuity and Change in Anabaptist-Mennonite Interpretation," ibid., 327.

is.[5] Here I have come to see how extensively theology has concerned itself with abstract truth at the expense of seriously examining the practical function of concepts in the faith community. Hence it is necessary to integrate the theoretical and the practical import of discipleship. We must ask what discipleship has meant for both women and men as they participated in the life of the church. How has it affected the way they communicate their experiences and understandings of the Bible within the congregation?

In the first part of the paper I will make some preliminary observations about the relationship between the community *tradition* of discipleship and the community *practice* of biblical interpretation within Mennonite congregations.[6] In the second part I will concentrate on developing an understanding of discipleship as presented in the gospel of Mark. I have chosen Mark, the gospel of the "way" of discipleship, because I want to begin with concrete *stories* of discipleship.[7] Although the *teachings* on discipleship in Matthew and Luke, especially as presented in the Sermon on the Mount, have been more influential in Mennonite writings, it is significant to begin with a reexamination of the context of Jesus' actions and life. In this way, I am emphasizing the dynamic nature of discipleship which all too easily becomes static as teachings become rules. Because Mark knows of the "paradigmatic discipleship of women"[8] this gospel becomes particularly crucial in examining what discipleship meant for both women and men in the early church.

---

[5]A key book on this subject is *Feminist Interpretation of the Bible,* ed. Letty Russell (Philadelphia, PA: Westminster Press, 1985). See particularly the article by Katharine Doob Sakenfeld, "Feminist Uses of Biblical Materials," 55-64, for an understanding of how women have countered the way the Bible is used to justify their traditional place in Western culture. The focus on the *function* of the text, on how the texts have been *used* not only for salvation but also for oppression, is central for both liberation and feminist scholars.

[6]When we think concretely there must be a specificity about our observations. In this preliminary sketch I am basing my observations on my own and other women's experience of life and theology in Mennonite congregations in Canada in the past few decades.

[7]In his book, *Mark: The Way for All Nations* (Scottdale, PA: Herald Press, 1979), Willard Swartley has recognized the theme of the "way" in Mark. He has, however, not studied the stories of women in relation to this theme.

[8]Elizabeth Schüssler Fiorenza, *In Memory of Her* (New York, NY: Crossroad Press, 1984), 50.

One final comment on method. An important aspect of theological method is choosing conversation partners with whom to discuss and test ideas. Both my Mennonite heritage and feminist theology have influenced the questions I am asking and the approach I am taking.[9] In addition to consulting biblical scholars of both literary and historical-critical persuasions as I tested and refined my inductive reading of Mark, I also engaged in dialogue with several intentional "hermeneutical communities" formed for the purpose of giving shape to this paper. This included not only several meetings with a group of Mennonite scholars and pastors, but also numerous discussions with women who are part of Mennonite congregations. Both aspects of this approach have helped focus my questions and observations about understanding women in the hermeneutical community.

The purpose of this paper is not to outline a conclusive definition of discipleship or of the hermeneutical community, but rather to analyze the process itself. This study seeks to examine the way we search for truth as part of the ongoing journey of life. It is to challenge past formulations by giving a central place to women's reality.

The Historical Context

The ambivalence and tension that Mennonite women feel as they begin to participate more directly in scholarly theological study no doubt has many causes.[10] It is clear that part of this ambivalence arises out of their perception and understanding of

---

[9]It is important to recognize a pluralism in feminist theology and to avoid reducing the contribution of the individual writers to several stereotypical characterizations. However, a number of elements can be identified which are shared by a large group of feminist writers. Margaret A. Farley has named the underlying principle for a feminist hermeneutic "the conviction that women are fully human and are to be valued as such." "Feminist Consciousness and Interpretation of Scripture," in *Feminist Interpretations of the Bible*, 44. This includes the related principles of equitable sharing and mutuality between women and men.

[10]Gayle Gerber Koontz points out the ambivalence which women, who first attended the Anabaptist-Mennonite consultation to draw together Mennonite women scholars to discuss Bible and theology at Associated Mennonite Biblical Seminaries in Elkhart, Indiana (Summer 1986), had about their work. See "Preface," in *Perspectives on Feminist Hermeneutics*.

faith as taught and practised by their congregations. Included are both the theological tradition and the pattern of social interactions within the community.

Emphasis on the hermeneutical community has been of particular importance for Mennonite women. By implication all members of the congregation are responsible for discerning the meaning of the Bible for both their personal and their communal lives. Neither hierarchical authority, nor specialized theologians are to be the final judges of the Bible's meaning. There is no privilege of the powerful. Accountability is to the whole community of faithful followers. The congregation discovers the guidance of the Spirit through mutual dialogue and counsel.

Practically, this means that women in the Mennonite church have been given freedom to participate in Bible study. Women have faithfully attended adult education classes, Bible schools and Bible colleges. However, not until recently have women become adult education teachers, pastors, writers or theology professors. Their understanding and experience were included only indirectly in the theological heritage which formed the life of the church. Books on Mennonite history and Anabaptist theology were silent about women's participation in the faith heritage. There were almost no female writers of books on Mennonite theology and mission. Issues that especially concerned women, such as family violence and pornography, were not addressed as part of the Mennonite understanding of peacemaking. Other issues such as abortion, marriage and divorce were usually discussed only by men. The boards of congregations and church conferences were usually male-dominated even though women were actively involved in the life of the church. Women's voices were often heard only by other women in women's Bible study groups or in auxiliary organizations in the church.

The silence of women in biblical interpretation has been supported by another aspect of the theological tradition.[11]

---

[11]Di Brandt has recognized the contradiction between the Mennonite emphasis on the "priesthood of all believers" and the silence of women in the church. She points out that the language of submission and obedience and "brotherhood" speak of arbitrary privilege and power of one group of people over another. See "The Silence of Women Is a Goal of Pornography," *Mennonite*

Discipleship, understood primarily as obedience, service and self-denial, supported the silent role of women. These features of discipleship conformed so closely to the characteristics of women as defined by society that their role was not questioned. A committed disciple was to obey the will of God, that is, to live a life of service and self-denial. This implied being humble, giving up power and going the way of the cross. Love, nonresistance, cross-bearing and separation from the world were all part of being disciples. These expectations also coincided with the role of women in a patriarchal society.[12] Ideal mothers were to love and give unceasingly of themselves. Women who stayed in the home were protected from the world and its evil as these have traditionally been defined. Nonresistance, love and cross-bearing describe the way women were expected to respond to the demands of men who are "the head of the home." Thus the ethic of discipleship has affirmed the status quo for women in a patriarchal society.

This emphasis has affected how women have come to understand themselves. They have developed a personal-domestic as opposed to a communal-public self-understanding. This has grave implications for the formation and articulation of a church theology.[13] In its relationship and institutional structures the church has not challenged the patriarchal separation of the personal-domestic and the communal-public realm according to gender. Women therefore applied the texts to their domestic life and learned to serve the aims of the mission organizations of the

---

Reporter, 24 June 1985, 11.

[12]Barbara Hilkert Andolsen outlines how feminist ethicists are struggling with the traditional understanding of "agape" as self-giving love and sacrifice in the context of women's experience. See "Agape in Feminist Ethics," *Journal of Religious Ethics* 9 (Spring 1981). For an example of a Mennonite woman's struggle with the dilemma of self-denial interpreted as self-sacrifice, see Tina Hartzler, "Choosing to Be Honest Rather Than Good," *Festival Quarterly* 13 (Summer 1986): 7-9.

[13]Elizabeth Schüssler Fiorenza has pointed out the implications of maintaining this duality between the domestic sphere and the public sphere: "Wherever the 'private sphere' of the patriarchal house is sharply delineated from that of the public order of the state, women are more dependent and exploited; while in those societies in which the boundaries between the household and the public domain are not so sharply drawn, women's positions and roles are more equal to those of men." *In Memory of Her*, 86.

church.[14] Men were given responsibility for shaping a "public theology" which directed the church in its social and political functions.

As a result women have learned that talk of servant-leadership did not apply to them. It was not considered the duty or obligation of women to initiate theological conversation in public places. This view has been reinforced by texts from the epistles which stressed silence and obedience. Discipleship was "internalized" to mean submission and support for the structures of the church.

Women have struggled with the roles assigned to them and with an understanding of discipleship that supports unquestioned obedience to this teaching. They were, however, not able to highlight this in conferences or articulate it in Mennonite writings. Even today feminist theologians struggle to be taken seriously because the issues they speak to are considered marginal.

For men the notion of discipleship functioned very different-ly. Service, self denial and nonresistance challenged the status quo of male roles in the larger society. The demands of discipleship in the complexities of the economic, political and social realm were considered to be primary agenda for theology. Much has been written by men about the issues they face as they attempt to live according to an ethic of servanthood in the community and in public life. It is in this way that the issues related to the use of power in social and political life have been made central to Mennonite theology.

As women have entered public life in their vocations, changes are also coming about in the life of the congregation. Women are no longer content to be on the periphery of the hermeneutical community. Therefore central theological formulations are being reexamined in order to include women's experience. Areas of life that society and the church have so often separated along gender lines—the personal and the social, the intellectual and the emotional, the domestic and the communal—

---

[14]I have been told on a number of occasions that I was lucky I could study theology purely for pleasure. The implication clearly was that I did not need to be responsible for the theology of the church but could study for personal enjoyment and enrichment.

public—now must be integrated. One way to begin this process is by exploring the biblical text with an openness to reinterpreting important theological formulations so that they can become freeing for all people. Serious engagement with the early Christian faith will invite us to hear again the call to discipleship. For Mennonite women this renewed listening to the text is fundamental as they seek to enter more fully into the hermeneutical community.

Women and the Biblical Story

Since discipleship is clearly an important theme in Mark, a study of this early gospel can guide us to a deeper understanding of what following Jesus meant for the early church.[15] The focus in this section of the essay will be on the women who followed Jesus. We will endeavour a careful reading of the text and ask whether there are not aspects of discipleship that are often missed when the focus is only on the Twelve.

Women as Followers

Before focusing on the women's response to Jesus we must first examine whether Mark includes women when he refers to the disciples of Jesus.[16] Many commentators have simply equated

---

[15]There are many studies of the disciples in Mark. See for example, Ernest Best, *Disciples and Discipleship* (Edinburgh: T. & T. Clark Ltd., 1986) and Willard Swartley, *Mark: The Way for All Nations*. Some important studies that provide a corrective to the above by focusing more directly on the women disciples in Mark are: Elizabeth Struthers Malbon, "Fallible Followers: Women and Men in the Gospel of Mark," *Semeia* 28 (1983): 29-48; Elizabeth Schüssler Fiorenza, *In Memory of Her*, 316-323 and Winsome Munro, "Women Disciples in Mark?" *Catholic Biblical Quarterly* 44 (April 1982): 225-41.

[16]This question can be studied from various historical and literary perspectives. Historical questions would include the following: Were there in fact women among the immediate associates of Jesus? Were women considered disciples by the early Christian community of which Mark was a part? Does Mark, as a redactor, accept women as disciples? Do the women represent a specific group in the early church? I will try to understand how women fit into the theology of discipleship in Mark's narrative account. Historical and more complex literary questions form a necessary background to our subject, which the limits of this paper will not allow me to explore as thoroughly as is necessary. Nor can I speak of how discipleship is described in the other gospels.

the disciples with the Twelve.[17] Though the term, discipleship, may be used generically to include all persons who follow Jesus, the particular texts used to define its characteristics are about male disciples. We must therefore look carefully at the way Mark speaks of the disciples. Whom does he include and whom does he exclude? Why does he choose certain people and not others in the way he tells the story?

Mark uses the word "disciple" forty-two times to speak of the associates of Jesus and makes specific reference to the Twelve in eleven verses. The word "apostle" is used once.[18] There are a number of different texts which focus on three members, or even one member of the disciple circle, namely Peter. Although "disciple" seems to be a favourite word of Mark's, it is not completely clear how inclusive the term is. Moreover, it is not evident how the disciples are set apart from the crowd, even though the disciples and those with Jesus are distinguished from his opponents, particularly the scribes and pharisees.

Elizabeth Struthers Malbon suggests that a better understanding of discipleship would include all who meet the demands of following Jesus.[19] The word "follow" is used in the calling of Simon and Andrew as well as Levi. It is used in a number of places in the sense of journeying "on the way" with Jesus.[20] Jesus uses the term when he challenges the crowd and his disciples to deny themselves, take up the cross and "follow" him (8:34). Peter speaks of having left all to "follow" Jesus (10: 28), and Bartimaeus "followed" Jesus on the way (10:52). It is interesting that in the passion narrative the term is used specifically of women. There it speaks of Mary Magdalene, Mary the mother of Jesus, and Salome, who, "when he was in Galilee, followed him, and ministered to him . . ." (15:41). Mark writes the women into the story only at the end even though he points out that they were present from the beginning. An important question for us to

---

[17]Ernest Best prefers to see the Twelve as normally signifying the wider group of followers rather than seeing Mark place a deliberate emphasis on the Twelve as the only disciples. He understands Mark as deliberately widening the tradition with its focus on the Twelve. See Best, *Disciples and Discipleship*, 103.

[18]Ibid., 133.

[19]Malbon, "Fallible Followers," 30

[20]Best, *Disciples and Discipleship*, 5.

examine is: how do the stories of women in the rest of the gospel relate to discipleship?

Mark gives another clue to understanding discipleship by the way in which he pictures the relationship between the larger group of followers and the Twelve. Some commentators would use a diagram of two concentric circles to describe this relationship with the innermost core closest to Jesus being Peter, James and John, the next group being the Twelve and the largest circle including all the other disciples, perhaps even the crowd. Women are excluded from the inner circle, unless the women in chapter 15 would be taken as a parallel inner circle.[21]

Perhaps the relationship between the larger and smaller groups of disciples is best seen in the role each fills in Mark's story. Some functions are common to both groups.[22] Both groups travelled with Jesus in Galilee and on the way to Jerusalem. Both received private teaching. Jesus rebuked both for their failure to understand. Jesus called on all to deny themselves, take up the cross and follow. However, several passages suggest a role for the smaller groups which is not explicitly stated for all the disciples. In the appointment of the Twelve we read that they were chosen by Jesus to be with him and "to be sent out to preach and have authority to cast out demons" (3:13). This is followed in a later chapter with the sending out of the Twelve two by two with authority over the unclean spirits (6:7). They preached, cast out demons and anointed with oil many who were sick (6:13). It is in this context that we have the only use of "apostle." "The apostles returned to Jesus and told him all that they had done and taught" (6:30).

A more specific role is also associated with the groups of two or three. Peter and Andrew were called to become "fishers of men." Peter, James and John were witnesses to the raising of Jairus' daughter and to the transfiguration. These three were also asked to be with Jesus in his prayer at Gethsemane. The women were witnesses of the death and received a specific command-

---

[21]Both Schüssler Fiorenza, *In Memory of Her*, 320, and Munro, "Women Disciples in Mark?" 231, understand this inner circle in terms of commitment and leadership and would include the women in Mark 15 as a parallel inner circle to the male leaders.

[22]See Best, *Disciples and Discipleship*, 103.

ment to ". . . go, tell his disciples and Peter that he is going before you to Galilee . . ." (16:7).

This would suggest that in Mark the smaller groupings are the ones called to specific responsibilities or tasks. They are not insiders who alone receive esoteric teaching so that they will understand Jesus more clearly. This teaching is open to all followers—to all who have "ears that can hear." All followers must exemplify their response to Jesus in their actions. However, Mark gives particular functions of public leadership to the smaller groupings of persons who are responsible for participating in the mission of Jesus. In his portrayal of the smaller groupings Mark emphasizes the specific challenges and responsibilities associated with an open acknowledgement of commitment to Jesus and his mission.

In Mark's story then, women remained hidden in the crowd much longer than male followers of Jesus. Although Mark includes stories of women who responded to Jesus, they fade back into the crowd and are not openly part of the circle of disciples around Jesus and they do not directly participate in the mission of Jesus. Nevertheless it is clear that Mark considered the women followers of Jesus and included them in his use of the word "disciple."

Mark in Historical Perspective

In his narrative Mark most often associates women with the crowd or with the larger grouping of unnamed followers. The primary actors are male. Women are clearly present in his gospel in no less than sixteen contexts, but they do not become the primary characters of the story. They are generally pictured as silent; and their direct conversation is seldom recorded. In a number of places they exemplify self-denying service. They are named and specifically identified with the disciple-circle only in the passion narratives. Until then they are presented "as minor characters who make brief cameo appearances and then disappear. . . ."[23] Prior to chapter 15, verse 40, Mark mentions no

---

[23]David Rhoads and Donald Michie, *Mark as Story* (Philadelphia, PA: Fortress Press, 1982), 129, includes women within the group of characters called the "little people."

woman by name except Herodias (who clearly is not one of the disciples) and Mary, the mother of Jesus. A number of commentators have pointed out that in contrast to the Twelve, women exemplified the servant role of true discipleship. The socially accepted role of women and the understanding of true discipleship seemed to coincide fairly well. To be considered disciples of Jesus, women needed to accept the role that society placed on them and remain hidden in the crowd, quietly carrying out their role of supportive servants.

Munro is convinced that this "anonymity and relative invisibility of women in Mark is due in part to the androcentric bias of his culture which viewed women only in terms of their relations to men. . . ."[24] There are, however, hints that this patriarchal picture is not completely accepted by the writer of Mark. He begins to correct his androcentric bias by stressing stories that show Jesus' solidarity with the social and religious outcasts of society. The controversy dialogues and sayings in Mark indirectly challenge patriarchal structures.[25] Furthermore, the stories in which women appear do not picture them solely in stereotypical roles. There is a move here to place women into the public realm. A critical impulse that denies male centrality in God's kingdom can be seen in Mark's mention of the "many women" who already followed from the beginning and in the important part women play in the resurrection accounts.[26] In order to understand the importance of these changes we must look more closely at specific women portrayed in the Gospel of Mark.

Mark's View of Discipleship for Women

Even though Mark does not tell his stories from the point of view of women, insight into the issues that they faced can be

---

[24]Munro, "Women Disciples in Mark?" 226. Androcentrism implies that the texts are "reflective of the experience, opinion, or control of the individual male writer but not of women's historical reality and experience." Schüssler Fiorenza, *In Memory of Her*, 108.

[25]See Schüssler Fiorenza, *In Memory of Her*, 143-144.

[26]Here I differ from Munro who sees a redactional silencing in Mark in which women's prominent role is obscured. See Munro, "Women Disciples in Mark?" 234-236.

gained by paying attention to the stories where women appear. It is especially important to note the places of tension in these stories. Women who had internalized the values of their society would have felt some of the same tensions regarding their role as did the male writer. An important clue, therefore, is to be found in the actions or words of women which created anxiety in the other actors in the stories. Throughout the Markan narrative, we note that when the mystery of the kingdom has implications for their own lives the disciples protest or do not understand or are afraid.[27] Hints of misunderstanding or fear are also important clues in understanding the struggle of women disciples. Furthermore, Jesus' response to the women may provide a clue to the particular challenge laid before them. His praise of a woman's action would point to an aspect of following that is new and important. A closer look at the key stories in which women play a role will highlight the visions and struggles of women followers of Jesus.

Mark 3:31-35. In this short episode Jesus responds to the request of his mother and brothers to see him by placing obedience to God over against the usual primacy of natural blood relationships. Doing God's will creates a new social reality which is to substitute for the requirements usually associated with close family ties. The inclusion of the word "sisters" suggests that the group sitting around Jesus included women who had become part of a new community committed to doing God's will; women who were followers of Jesus. Implicit in this pericope is the idea that family relationships do not confer status or special treatment on disciples of Jesus. The assumption that women understand their place primarily in terms of their household status is shattered in this passage. Women, as well as men, are challenged to follow wherever Jesus leads.

Mark 5:25-34. The struggle of the woman healed of the flow of blood is described by words such as fear and trembling. She attempts to receive healing unobtrusively by touching the garments of Jesus. She is well aware that because she is unclean she is an outsider. Did she struggle with a deep sense of

---

[27]Swartley points out that in Mark fear and amazement function as the opposite of understanding. See *Mark: The Way for All Nations,* 200.

unworthiness and therefore try to reach the healing power of Jesus in a quiet, undemanding way? Her faith is strong and she receives the desired healing. But Jesus takes her a step further. He challenges her to tell the whole truth in a public place in front of the crowd gathered around him. The healing miracle gave her the courage to speak up. Jesus affirms her by calling her "daughter" and telling her to go in peace.

Mark 7:24-30. In this story we have the rare phenomenon of direct conversation by a woman. (The only other such occasions are in chapter 6 with Herodias and in chapter 16 where words are spoken by the women going to the empty tomb.) The dialogue between Jesus and the woman clearly centres on accepted social and religious divisions between Jews and gentiles. The woman challenges Jesus to go beyond these accepted divisions and heal her daughter. It is noteworthy that for "this saying" she can go her way, knowing that the demon will have left her daughter. Her challenge to Jesus was understood by him as a sign of her faith. We can assume that it was not easy for the woman to go beyond the accepted social customs in order to try to reach the Jewish rabbi with her concern.[28]

Mark 10:13-16. This story does not specifically mention women but it is generally assumed that women were among those bringing children to Jesus. The rebuke of the disciples based on an accepted social division between children and adults brings forth both Jesus' indignation and his beautiful words, "Let the children come to me." Jesus affirms those who recognize his acceptance of the little ones.

Mark 14:1-11. In this story a woman anoints the head of Jesus. By this "prophetic sign-action" Jesus is named and recognized as the Anointed One, the Messiah, the Christ.[29] This passage begins the stories on the passion of Christ just as in a parallel way the narrative of Peter's confession introduces the

---

[28]Sharon Ringe has interpreted this story as told in Matthew and Mark by focusing particularly on the gifts and ministry that the woman gives to Jesus. She says, e.g., "Her gift was not the submission or obedience seen as appropriate for women in her society, but rather the gift of sharp insight—the particular insight of the poor and outcasts. . . . Her gift was also the gift of courage. . . ." See "A Gentile Women's Story," in *Feminist Interpretation of the Bible,* 71-72.

[29]Schüssler Fiorenza, *In Memory of Her,* xiv.

section on the prediction of the suffering of Jesus. However, here the confession is not made in words but in action. In comparison to some of the other gospel narratives, this woman is pictured as anointing the head, not the feet of Jesus. A hint of boldness arises here which suggests a deep love for Jesus. This is the story of a disciple of Jesus who has understood his Messiahship and is ready to proclaim this insight with her actions. By placing the story of Judas' decision to betray Jesus into the same context the writer of Mark emphasizes the contrast between these two disciples.

We can only guess what this action meant for the woman by noting the criticism she received for it. The money should have been given to the poor. She has broken accepted religious patterns with her action. Jesus, however, commends her and prophesies that her action will be proclaimed wherever the good news is preached throughout the world.

Mark 15:40-47. Here the emphasis is on the women who witnessed the death and burial of Jesus. The women are named and yet are part of a much larger group that has been following Jesus to Jerusalem. Their role until this point had been to "minister" to Jesus, something that fits in well with the accepted role of women. But here they suddenly enter front stage as primary witnesses to Jesus' death, burial and resurrection. They watched from afar, probably because of a very real fear they had for their lives.[30]

Mark 16:1-8. This story begins by repeating the names of the women. Again anointing is mentioned, thus connecting this story with the one in chapter 14. The direct speech indicates the women's worry—the very practical matter of rolling away the large stone. The story emphasizes the largeness of the stone and the weakness of the women. The women see the young man dressed in a white robe who tells them that Jesus has risen. They receive the command to go and tell his disciples and Peter that he is going before them to Galilee. The women are entrusted

---

[30]Luise Schottroff has uncovered the historical evidence in the writings of Josephus and Tacitus which points to the danger of death for women who mourned the death of one who was crucified. "Maria Magdalena und die Frauen am Grabe Jesu," *Evangelische Theologie* 42 (January/February 1982): 5-6.

with the message for the other disciples. It is important to note how their feelings are described. They are amazed when they see the empty tomb and the young man. This amazement changes to trembling and astonishment when they are given the command to proclaim the resurrection. According to this ending of Mark they do not say anything to anyone because they are afraid. The story ends with the silence, fear and disobedience of the women.

Discipleship Reexamined: Summary Reflections

What then does the call to discipleship mean for women? The women in Mark are generally pictured as part of the larger group of "little people" who have little status in society and often come to Jesus for healing.[31] Their behaviour demonstrates faith and service. This coincides with the orientation to family and home for women in a patriarchal society. However, our brief survey of the main stories reveals that women too struggle with their response to Jesus and that this response requires breaking out of pre-established roles.

In Mark's telling of the story, several clues indicate that the issue for women was whether to become visible, whether to step out from the crowd in order to gain healing or express love. It was not easy to take the initiative for overcoming social barriers in order to gain access to Jesus, whether these stemmed from the Jew-gentile, adult-child or clean-unclean dichotomies. Renouncing the self meant a willingness to speak in public both about one's uncleanness and about one's healing (as the woman with the flow of blood did); it meant courageously and persistently challenging the barriers which denied them access to Jesus (as the mothers of the children or the gentile woman did). Following Jesus may also have meant that women gave up the security and status of their place in the family social unit to be included in a new social grouping of those who do the will of God. Being

---

[31]David Rhoads and Donald Michie, who coined this phrase for the women in Mark's narrative, have also characterized them as "flat" characters with several consistent traits unlike the Twelve who are "round" characters with conflicting traits. See, *Mark as Story*, 122-136.

obedient to God could mean risking arrest and death.

The last few stories in Mark bring new aspects of women's experience into the open. Women are shown not only as those who need healing but also as those who become responsible. Rhoads and Michie point out that the women and the other "little people" begin to fulfill the roles expected of the Twelve who fail Jesus at the end.[32] The woman who anointed Jesus becomes a model of discipleship in her love and understanding of Jesus. The women who witness the death and burial demonstrate a courage which the other disciples lack. It becomes clearer that, for both women and for men, following Jesus may mean risking or sacrificing money, reputation and even life.

Malbon interprets the focus on the women in the final chapters as a reversal of the historically conditioned expectations which the implied readers would have had of women.[33] The reversal of outsider and insider permeates Mark's gospel and is clearly stated in Mark 10:31: "many that are first will be last, and the last first." The historical reality of women's discipleship overturns the expectations of the implied reader who expects little from women.

In this context the ending of Mark is particularly crucial. The story ends in ambiguity. The women are challenged to become the proclaimers of the good news of the resurrection. They are asked to accept the responsibility of being the first witnesses to the other disciples and to Peter. But Mark ends the story telling of their failure.[34]

The early church as well as biblical commentators have been uneasy with this ending. The other gospel writers affirm that the

---

[32]Ibid., 132-133.

[33]Malbon, "Fallible Followers," 41-42.

[34]I am accepting the ending in v. 8 as the ending by the original author. The added endings give us the viewpoint of the early church. It is interesting that Elizabeth Schüssler Fiorenza, as well as most male commentators, do not want to recognize this flight of the women as disobedience to the command of the angel. See *In Memory of Her*, 322. This does not fit the picture of the women as paradigms of true discipleship. However, if women are to be seen as responsible agents in history, they must also be seen as those who are tempted and sometimes fail. I would concur with Thomas Boomershine and Gilbert Bartholomew, who feel that the dominant tone of the ending is negative. It brings to the fore the "powerful conflict between responsibility and fear. . . ." See "Mark 16:8 and the Apostolic Commission," *Journal of Biblical Literature* 100 (Summer 1981): 237.

women did tell the story, though the disciples did not believe them and thought it was "an idle tale." Several later additions to Mark's gospel also support this version. First Corinthians is the only record which cites the proclamation of the resurrection going through Peter and the Twelve without mention of the women. Church history confirms that both men and women have continued to struggle with the role of women as proclaimers of the good news.

The ambiguity of the ending of Mark's gospel remains if we stay with the question of the author's intention. No clear indication of his purpose is given.[35] However, the unclear ending leaves the decision with the reader who must supply the ending. The narrator asks the reader to evaluate and respond to the silence of the women. Will the women overcome their feelings of weakness and fear? Will they accept the command to proclaim the good news? Will they become full and responsible partners with the other disciples in spite of initial failure?

By bringing the silent women into the foreground, Mark is suggesting a direction in which God is leading the early Christians in their understanding of discipleship. Malbon summarizes the twofold message: "anyone can be a follower, no one finds it easy."[36] I suggest in addition that the women in Mark leave us with the challenge to become free from the social barriers that bind us. In turn we are empowered to step out from the crowd and become involved in Christ's mission. Discipleship means accepting responsibility for the gospel message and following Jesus into the world.

This understanding of discipleship opens our eyes to new characteristics of the Jesus whom we are challenged to follow. The emphasis is now on the leadership of Jesus in his courage to act even at the point of greatest vulnerability. We are struck

---

[35]Malbon suggests that the significance of the women's silence is found "in the outward movement of the text from author to reader." See "Fallible Followers," 45. As the narrator's story ends and reaches the point of silence, the hearer/reader's story begins. It is time for the reader to act and speak, thus continuing the line of followers. Swartley points out that the Gospel shows us the direction of discipleship but does not close the challenge. It is left open for them and for us to finish the mission begun by Jesus, the Christ, the Son of God. *Mark: The Way for All Nations*, 198.

[36]Malbon, "Fallible Followers," 26.

with the boldness of Jesus as he questions the institutional structures which attempt to define and limit his relationships to people (Mark 2; 11:27-33; 12:13-40). We understand in a new way those stories in which Jesus is not able to do any great work because nothing is expected of the carpenter from Nazareth (Mark 6:1 6). We recognize the leadership of Jesus in his questioning of the traditions and in his breaking out of established social and religious norms (Mark 7). We gain courage by noting Jesus' answer to those who questioned his authority (Mark 11: 27-33). We identify with aspects of Jesus' struggle in Gethsemane realizing that the human temptation is to avoid the responsibility and pain of doing God's will (Mark 14:32-42). The way of the cross is understood as a way of courageous suffering which arises out of inner strength and leads to freedom from that which limits doing God's will.

The emphasis in this definition of discipleship is placed on the need to be freed from those institutions and social expectations which limit full participation in the mission of Jesus. The challenge is to step out of the crowd and be willing to confess publicly the need for healing as well as the joy of full acceptance. A disciple is empowered and freed to obey the call into mission.

The Tension within Discipleship

To fully understand the dimension of discipleship that comes to the fore with the women in Mark we must briefly compare their experiences with the stories of the Twelve. These are focused particularly well for us in the narratives following Peter's confession. In chapter 8 Peter is rebuked for having in mind the things of human value rather than the things of God. One must be willing to give up even one's life for the sake of Jesus and the gospel. In chapter 9 Jesus follows up on the discussion of who will be the greatest by taking a child and placing it in the midst of the Twelve. Following Jesus means being willing to be last of all and servant of all. Chapter 10 emphasizes giving up riches in order to enter the kingdom as well as leaving relatives and lands for the sake of the gospel. It also includes the story of James and John who wanted to sit at the right and left of Jesus in glory. This is followed by the teaching of a new way of leadership which does not lord it over others but which willingly serves as Jesus did.

The emphasis in these passages is on following Jesus who gives up his "power," "prestige" and "position" to follow the way of the cross.[37] Jesus is the one who chooses a life of servanthood and ministry. He does not exercise his prerogative to rule by lording it over others but willingly suffers and dies for the sake of the people whom he loves. He chooses to associate with sinners and outcasts, he identifies with the "little ones" and willingly serves, giving his life for the sake of those undeserving of his love. He becomes an outsider so that outsiders may become insiders in the kingdom of God.

If we compare this understanding of discipleship with that gained from the women disciples we note that there is a certain tension between the two understandings of what following Jesus means. One focuses particularly on what discipleship means when one perceives oneself or is perceived as being powerless; the other focuses on what it means when one is seen or sees oneself as having or deserving power, prestige or status.[38] If one is already in the position of a servant, a "little one," the need is to become empowered, to break through the structures which bind to gain healing and take responsibility for the gospel message. However, if one is in a position of power and leadership the need is to become a servant, to willingly give up power which may limit or dominate the other. The paradox in Mark's understanding of discipleship warns us against an oversimplified understanding which is not related to the social reality of life.

Conclusion

How does this study of discipleship set a direction for a reexamination of how women and men are involved in the

---

[37]Swartley uses these three terms to summarize the emphasis of these passages. *Mark: The Way for All Nations*, 140.

[38]Sandra Schneiders, "Evangelical Equality: Religious Consecration, Mission and Witness," *Spirituality Today* 38 (Winter 1986): 298-300, speaks of the superior/inferior paradigm for human relations which is prevalent even in our notions of equality. She points out that in looking at Jesus we can see both the refusal to dominate as well as the refusal to be dominated. Discipleship may then mean the refusal to accept both the under or the over position in the accepted social hierarchy.

hermeneutical community? What new questions does it raise for our consideration?

Firstly, this study points to the complexity of the theological notion of discipleship. If we try to understand what following Jesus means in particular social and religious contexts instead of only in an abstract general way, we will be able to see more clearly both the opportunities and temptations that face us as Christians in the twentieth century. We will better understand what it may mean to follow Jesus in the communities in which we are often labelled according to our position in the hierarchical ladder of status and prestige. We will be able to identify how we have internalized false understandings. The theology of discipleship will then challenge our too easy acceptance of the roles that society assigns to us. It asks us to bring together theory and experience, the theological formulation and its concrete function in the community.

Secondly, if this analysis of the biblical notion of discipleship has any validity at all, it implies that we must consciously restructure our hermeneutical communities. We must begin to take women as well as other "little people" seriously in how we plan our discussions and interactions, whether in the congregation or in the academy. We must look for the silent people in our biblical discussions and theological writings and find ways to empower them so that they too can participate in shaping the theology of the church. We must be sensitive to the way our key theological formulations sometimes function to make persons outsiders to the hermeneutical process. We must make discipleship an inclusive word rather than one that renders some persons outsiders.

Finally, this study also challenges us to reflect on the reasons why certain emphases have become more important than others in the teaching, preaching and theological writings of Mennonites. Why has discipleship as obedience to institutions and structures become internalized for many persons even though Anabaptism began with a challenge to many institutions of its day? Why have we so easily identified with the male rather than the female disciples?[39] What threatened the church so that

---

[39]Though we cannot directly equate or correlate the experiences of women

obedience rather than empowerment became primary in its understandings? Why did the church accept the easy dualism between private and public, personal and social, female and male? Who benefits from these divisions?

Discipleship can function to exclude, marginalize and silence persons in our hermeneutical communities. The paradoxical relationship between freedom and obedience, service and empowerment can remind us that as we listen to each other we will hear again the call to discipleship from the One who invited all to follow in the "way."

---

disciples as portrayed by Mark with women's role in the hermeneutical community today, we can draw parallels because of the patriarchal nature of both societies. However, other factors such as class and race must also be considered in the way that we identify with both female and male disciples. Though women, as female, may identify themselves as marginalized, as scholars they share the advantages of the male elite and often also belong to the privileged who have financial power. Men, as male, may identify themselves as the privileged but as Mennonite scholars in the ecumenical scene, they may see themselves as marginalized. In particular social situations we may need to identify with both women and men as presented in Mark.

V. Theological Ethics

Duane K. Friesen*

A CRITICAL ANALYSIS OF NARRATIVE ETHICS**

One of the most important and influential paradigms of contemporary ethical thought is narrative ethics, otherwise known as virtue ethics. The most prominent spokesperson for this approach is Stanley Hauerwas. Narrative ethics is a particularly promising way of thinking about Christian ethics, and is especially helpful in illuminating Anabaptist-Mennonite theology and ethics. Hauerwas views himself in continuity with the work of John Howard Yoder, a prominent Mennonite ethicist, even though Yoder has not described his own work in these terms.[1]

In this paper I will describe and analyze the work of Stanley Hauerwas by juxtaposing his ethic with two other competing ethical paradigms, natural law ethics and liberal democratic ethics. Other paradigms, for example, liberation ethics, could be considered, but I emphasize the dialogue of narrative ethics with natural law and liberal democracy because that is the particular agenda of Hauerwas. My main objective in this essay is to identify and analyze three crucial problems raised about narrative ethics by a natural law ethic and by democratic liberalism. They are: the epistemological question, or what determines the truthfulness of a narrative; the charge of sectarianism, or what the emphasis on the centrality of the church in narrative ethics means for the church's relationship to the world; and the allegation that an ethic of virtue does not adequately guide decisions, that is, the issue of the connection between an ethic

---

*Duane K. Friesen is Professor of Bible and Religion at Bethel College, North Newton, Kansas.

**The author would like to thank John Friesen, Associate Professor of Church History, Canadian Mennonite Bible College, Winnipeg, Manitoba and Ted Grimsrud, Pastor, Eugene Mennonite Church, Eugene, Oregon, for their critical responses to this essay at the Symposium.

[1]For another non-Mennonite ethicist promoting the narrative approach in combination with Anabaptist ethics, see James Wm. McClendon, Jr., *Ethics: Systematic Theology,* vol. I (Nashville, TN: Abingdon Press, 1986).

of virtue and an ethic of obligation or concrete action. I will seek to address these criticisms from Hauerwas' perspective, elaborating my own perspective where I think his position is inadequate. Finally, I will conclude by reflecting on two implications a narrative ethic has for an Anabaptist-Mennonite ethic.

Three Paradigms

Natural Law

I am using "natural law" in a broad sense to cover a variety of positions, all of which have the following central characteristics: a universal moral law exists, which is a moral standard that applies to all human beings irrespective of their particular historical or cultural circumstances; this universal moral law can be known by all rational beings capable of transcending particular cultural or historical biases; and this universal moral standard can be used as a norm by which to judge the behaviour of human beings—whether it be positive law, the general structure of society or institutional behaviour of the state, such as the conduct of war. The U.S. Roman Catholic Bishops' statement in *The Challenge of Peace* is a good example of natural law ethics. The Bishops say:

> The wider civil community, although it does not share the same vision of faith, is equally bound by certain key moral principles. For all men and women find in the depth of their consciences a law written on the human heart by God. From this law reason draws moral norms.[2]

Though natural law positions have varied considerably, for the most part they share the three common assumptions stated above. In Thomas Aquinas the natural law is the eternal law of God built into the nature of things and known by human reason. Some have grounded natural law in the Bible by referring to either the Decalogue as God's law of nature or the "law written on the heart" as stated by the apostle Paul in the Letter to the

[2]National Conference of Catholic Bishops, *The Challenge of Peace, God's Promise and Our Response: A Pastoral Letter on War and Peace* (Washington, D.C.: United States Catholic Conference, 1983), par. 17.

Romans. Luther and Calvin both continued the natural law tradition by utilizing the biblical texts we have mentioned.

With the Enlightenment a variety of forms of thinking about natural law developed. Locke grounded morality in fixed and permanent moral truths. Kant sought to ground all religion in ethics by basing ethics on those universal moral principles which all rational beings can will to be a universal law. In the contemporary arena, the equivalent of a natural law theory is developed by John Rawls who asks us to consider which general principles of justice we, as persons operating out of rational self-interest and as those in an "original" position of not knowing what position we will have in society, would choose. For persons such as W.D. Ross a natural law ethic is elaborated through a series of *prima facie* duties—duties such as telling the truth or not harming others—which rational beings intuitively utilize to judge the rightness or wrongness of action. Other contemporary philosophers, such as Roderick Firth, have defended a natural law approach through the "ideal observer" theory. Firth says that when fully rational human beings put themselves in the position of an ideal observer who is objective, dispassionate and omniscient, they are able to judge the rightness or wrongness of an action so that all humans in this position could agree on what constitutes right action.

In much of contemporary Christian social ethics some form of natural law thinking has been assumed. Whereas both Reinhold Niebuhr and Paul Ramsey, for example, believed that the concept of Christian love was central to Christian ethics, for both, love was adapted to a standard that could apply to the behaviour of all human beings.

For Niebuhr love modified his concept of justice, but never in such a way that justice could not be a universal standard for society. Though he criticized Catholic natural law for its too rigid notion of a fixed standard, Niebuhr nevertheless believed in "rational efforts to apply the moral obligation, implied in the love commandment, to the complexities of life and the fact of sin, that is to the situation created by the inclination of men to take advantage of each other."[3]

Similarly Ramsey, while he could not accept an autonomous natural law separate from Christian ethics, argued that the concept of love served as a principle that could be applied to social issues and could serve as a standard for all human beings. Thus in Ramsey's political ethic, "in-principled love" serves as a deontological principle to protect noncombatants in war from direct and indiscriminate killing.

Another example of a natural law position is evident in J. Philip Wogaman's thought.[4] In his book, *A Christian Method of Moral Judgment*, he describes the following set of general principles or presumptions: the goodness of created existence, the value of individual life, the unity of the human family in God and the equality of persons in God. Wogaman says these general presumptions flow from a Christian theological perspective, but once formulated as principles in this way, he uses them as universal standards to apply to social issues. Though these principles are not absolute, the burden of proof is on those who would violate them for the sake of some other more weighty ethical consideration. For example, although from a Christian point of view there is a general presumption against violence, this principle can be broken if a greater evil can be averted or a greater good come about through the use of violence. Again this principle is not justified on distinctive theological grounds, but on general rational grounds.

Democratic Liberalism

Since some forms of natural law ethics give support to democratic liberalism, we need to acknowledge that democratic liberalism is not completely separate from the previous paradigm. However, since it is a sufficiently powerful model in and of itself and in some sense is shared by all Western democracies, it must be described separately. Also narrative ethics is particularly critical of this type of ethic.

---

[3]Reinhold Niebuhr, *Faith and History* (New York, NY: Scribner's, 1951), 188-189.

[4]J. Philip Wogaman, *A Christian Method of Moral Judgment* (Philadelphia, PA: Westminster Press, 1976).

Two tenets characterize democratic liberalism. First the centrality of the individual. The autonomous person has certain rights that should not be violated and should be defended if threatened. Second, freedom is the primary value for the individual. This is the freedom to act as one chooses as long as that action does not violate the rights of others. These two modern doctrines have produced a society which is composed of persons who exercise their freedom as they choose, and who enter into contracts or agreements with each other. These contracts essentially provide for: minimal structures to preserve orderly interaction among people, primarily governed by the market place; a fair process to govern those interactions where individuals must pursue common projects, such as national defense and the general welfare; and a fair procedure that protects individual rights, such as speech, assembly and worship, and distributes fairly the goods and resources necessary in the pursuit of the common good.

The authors of *Habits of the Heart* describe this liberal view as a "thin consensus;" a view of justice where persons can agree about the procedures to follow in adjudicating disputes, but who do not share a substantive view of justice or a common vision for the institutional arrangement of society.[5] Hauerwas describes the position thus:

> A people do not need a shared history; all they need is a system of rules that will constitute procedures for resolving disputes as they pursue their various interests. Thus liberalism is a political philosophy committed to the proposition that a social order and corresponding mode of government can be formed on self-interest and consent.[6]

Within the United States both major political parties share the basic assumptions of this view, though there are some differences about the relative role of government in pursuing social goods and regulating individual freedom. The same can probably be said about most Western democracies except that

---

[5]Robert Bellah, et.al. *Habits of the Heart* (Berkeley, CA: University of California Press, 1985), 334.

[6]Stanley Hauerwas, *A Community of Character* (Notre Dame, IN: University of Notre Dame Press, 1981), 78.

the existence of stronger socialist political philosophies in some countries may make the differences in parties somewhat greater.

Narrative Ethics

Stanley Hauerwas' position is not easy to summarize. He is a very prolific writer and has not developed a full systematic statement of his position. One of his more recent works, however, *The Peaceable Kingdom*, does make some effort at being more methodical.

We can best describe Hauerwas' position by analyzing three concepts: narrative, community and character. According to Kenneth Carter "narrative is important to Hauerwas for three reasons: first, the narrative teaches us that we are creatures dependent upon God; second, the narrative forces us to admit our historicity; third, in the narrative we learn of God's self-revelation to us in Israel and in Jesus."[7] It is important to focus on the second understanding of narrative, the concept of historicity, before we elaborate Hauerwas' specific theological understanding.

Hauerwas argues that all ethics is necessarily narrative because every ethic is a qualified ethic shaped by our specific histories. In *The Peaceable Kingdom* he puts it this way:

> All ethical reflection occurs relative to a particular time and place. Not only do ethical problems change from one time to the next, but the very nature and structure of ethics is determined by the particularities of a community's history and convictions.[8]

Hauerwas argues, for example, that democratic liberalism can only be understood in terms of post-Enlightenment Western developments. He would say the same for any particular natural law ethic. Despite the claim of natural law ethics to universality, every ethic is qualified by the contingencies of time and place.

The Christian faith also can be apprehended only in the form of narrative or story, for the very way we come to know

---

[7]Kenneth Carter, "The Theological Ethics of Stanley Hauerwas: Christian Ethics and the Community of the Church," *Quarterly Review* (Winter, 1986): 65.

[8]Stanley Hauerwas, *The Peaceable Kingdom* (Notre Dame, IN: University of Notre Dame Press, 1983), 1.

God derives from how God has interacted with a people over time. We do not, therefore, come to understand the Christian faith through a set of principles or doctrines, nor by abstracting a meaning from the story which we put in non-narrative form. The story itself discloses to us who God is. Hauerwas says:

> The fact that we come to know God through the recounting of the story of Israel and the life of Jesus is decisive for our truthful understanding of the kind of God we worship as well as the world in which we exist. . . . Because the Christian story is an enacted story, liturgy is probably a much more important resource than are doctrines or creeds for helping us to hear, tell, and live the story of God.[9]

For Hauerwas, then, scripture is central to a Christian theological ethic. He says:

> The authority of scripture derives its intelligibility from the existence of a community that knows its life depends on faithful remembering of God's care of his creation through the calling of Israel and the life of Jesus.[10]

At this point it is crucial to note the importance of community in the appropriation and interpretation of scripture. Scripture does not present us with a *revealed morality* in the form of propositions or principles that can be abstracted from the total narrative framework, nor should scripture be translated into a universal ethic that makes sense to everyone. Scripture is to be interpreted by that community of persons which allows its life to be shaped by the story of God's interaction with God's people. Scripture does not contain some objective meaning inherent in the text, nor is the interpretation of scripture primarily a conceptual operation within the domain of the scholar. Hauerwas quotes John H. Yoder who argues that the Free Church view of scripture involves an ongoing conversational process in which, under the guidance of the spirit, people "gather around the Scripture in face of a given real moral challenge. Any description of the substance of ethical decision-making criteria is incomplete if this aspect of its communitarian and contemporary

---

[9]Ibid., 25-26.

[10]Hauerwas, *A Community of Character*, 53.

form is omitted."[11]

We see here the close interaction of narrative and community. Narrative teaches the community, the church, that its life is dependent upon God, that it is a community of grace, a gifted community. This empowers the community to live truthfully, to recognize sin and the need for repentance, as well as to live in faith and trust. Hauerwas believes that such a sense of dependency upon God is foundational to living peaceable lives. A gifted community is one which recognizes that it does not, nor should it try to, control the world. The belief that we are in charge of the world and that we are responsible for directing the course of world events is precisely the root of violence, says Hauerwas. Rather the church is called to live faithfully, in obedience to the character of God as revealed through the story of Israel and the life of Jesus. The church, therefore, exists as an alternative to the world, as a community where a different set of virtues shapes its character within the world. The first responsibility of the church, then, is not to change the world, but simply to be itself. By being itself, by living faithfully, the church fulfills its most important mission, that is, serving as a witness of the truth. In an article in *Christian Century* Hauerwas and William H. Willimon set out a series of brief statements in which they critique those approaches which seek to "translate Christian convictions into terms palatable to the world." They wish to "lay down a program, a vision, a paradigm for accommodating the world to the gospel."

> We confess that to us the church has an independent and intrinsic value in a way that we have not heard articulated by others. . . . We are not at all interested, as Richard John Neuhaus is, in contending that the church is a useful component in keeping constitutional democracy afloat. It may be, but that is neither the church's nor the Christian's first task. Our account of the church is (we admit) more imperialistic. Given our sanctificationist leanings, we believe that the sort of life required of Christians is too difficult and peculiar to survive without the church. This life challenges every other social order—including democracy. In this sense, we are more radical than either the liberal or the conservative camp.[12]

---

[11]John H. Yoder, as quoted by Hauerwas in *A Community of Character*, 54.

[12]Stanley Hauerwas and William H. Willimon, "Embarrassed by God's Pres-

Here emerges the connection to the third concept, character. The narrative, lived out by a community which takes that story as normative, gives shape to a certain kind of people. Thus Christian ethics is not first of all an ethic of rules that we seek to apply to the various quandaries we must face or the decisions we must make. Rather the Christian story socializes us into a set of virtues; it teaches us what it means to live well formed lives. We, therefore, do not *choose* an ethic, but we are *grasped* by a story which gives shape to our lives. Our freedom consists in the resources we are given to make the story our own. As Hauerwas puts it,

> we are beings who have the capacity to claim our lives by learning to grow in a truthful narrative. . . . Our character is a gift from others which we learn to claim as our own by recognizing it as a gift. . . . The Christian tradition holds us accountable, not to an abstract story, but to a body of people who have been formed by the life of Jesus. By learning to make his life our life we see we are free just to the extent that we learn to trust others and make ourselves available to be trusted by others. Such trust is possible because the story of his life, by the very way we learn it, requires that we recognize and accept the giftedness of our existence: I did not create myself but what I am has been made possible by others.[13]

Hauerwas' Critique of the Democratic Liberal and Natural Law Paradigms

For Hauerwas all ethics is necessarily historical, and hence qualified by contingencies of time and place. Both of the other paradigms assume that one can develop abstract universal principles that are not contingent. He believes that judgements cannot be justified apart from the agent who finds himself or herself in a particular historical and communal context. The natural law ethicist seeks to arrive at a decision by removing all contingent factors in order to develop a moral position that is impersonal, one which can be adopted by everyone. Hauerwas

---

ence," *Christian Century* 102 (30 January 1985): 98.

[13]Hauerwas, *The Peaceable Kingdom*, 43-46.

reasons that this is simply mistaken. He uses the example of abortion to show how factors of one's identity as a Christian believer and member of a faith community give shape to a very different description of the issue of abortion. In other words abortion is not a quandary which we settle by weighing the validity of abstract principles such as the sanctity of life of the fetus versus the rights of the mother, but our very description of the issue is shaped by our narrative and communal identity. What does this look like? First, a person belongs to a community which describes life as a gift of God. Second, members of that community can share and bear each other's burdens. Third, the church is a community that views children not as owned by an individual or couple but as a responsibility of the community. And fourth, the church is a community which learns how to suffer faithfully in the world, not primarily how to avoid suffering.

A Christian then should treat abortion not as an abstract discussion about the status of the fetus, or an abstract account of the clash of competing interests of fetus and mother, as is reflected in the societal debate about abortion. According to Hauerwas,

> Liberalism seeks a philosophical account of morality that can ground the rightness or wrongness of particular actions or behaviour in a "theory" divorced from any substantive commitments about what kind of people we are or should be—except perhaps to the extent that we should be rational or fair. . . . [Christians] failed to show . . . why abortion is an affront to our most basic convictions about what makes life meaningful and worthwhile. We tried to argue in terms of the "facts" or on the basis of "principles" and thus failed to make intelligible why such "facts" or "principles" were relevant in the first place. We have spent our time arguing abstractly about when human life does or does not begin. As a result, we have failed to challenge the basic presuppositions that force the debate to hinge on such abstraction. . . . If Christians are to make their moral and political convictions concerning abortion intelligible we must show how the meaning and prohibition of abortion is correlative to the stories of God and his people that form our basic convictions. We must indicate why it is that the Christian way of life forms people in a manner that makes abortion unthinkable. Ironically it is only when we have done this that we will have the basis for suggesting why the

fetus should be regarded as but another of God's children.[14]

Second, Hauerwas critiques both paradigms for making ethical quandaries the locus of ethics. He argues that the starting point of ethics should be the kind of people we are. Hence, the essence of Christian ethics entails a view of the virtues which is shaped by our narrative. Casuistry, from a Christian perspective, is not simply an individual struggling to determine the right action based on an abstract set of principles. It involves testing out how our basic commitments, which have made us into the kind of people we claim to be, should be carried out. That determination takes place in the context of communal discernment. The church not only is, but must be a community of moral discourse, that is, a community that sustains a rigorous analysis of the implications of its commitments across generations as it faces new challenges and situations.[15]

Third, Hauerwas criticizes both paradigms for reducing ethics to minimalist ethics. Both natural law ethics and democratic liberalism undermine any distinctively Christian ethic. Terms such as "the categorical imperative," the "ideal observer," "universalizability" or Rawls' "original position" all reflect an approach to ethics where we must learn to make ethical judgements from anyone's point of view. By such an abstract and formal account of ethics, the moral life is vacuous of significant substantive content, so that one can give an account of the moral life that is not subject to any community or tradition. In fact, a specifically Christian ethic is precisely what is to be avoided by such accounts of the moral enterprise.[16]

Fourth, the above criticisms are integrally connected to Hauerwas' challenge that the primary emphasis of Christian ethics should focus on being the church, not first of all on trying to change the world.

Fifth, Hauerwas argues that both liberalism and natural law theory lack a sufficiently social view of being human. This is

---

[14]Hauerwas, *A Community of Character*, 220-222.

[15]Hauerwas, *The Peaceable Kingdom*, 131.

[16]See Hauerwas, *Truthfulness and Tragedy* (Notre Dame, IN: University of Notre Dame Press, 1977), 16f.

certainly clear in the case of the democratic liberal paradigm which begins with the individual autonomous self. It is true that some natural law theories are based on a more social view of being human, a general theory of human rationality, for example, which bases the unity of all human beings on a common rationality. Hauerwas argues, however, that such a view abstracts us from our particular communal contexts, thus making proper ethical discernment impossible because it destroys those particular communities which give shape to our identity.

Critique of Narrative Ethics

As we said in the introduction, a number of problems have been raised about narrative ethics. I will address three issues in particular: the epistemological question, the charge of sectarianism and the connection of an ethic of virtue to action.

The Epistemological Issue

On what grounds does one determine whether an ethic is true or valid? If one appeals to the truth of the Christian narrative by saying that an ethic is valid if it is consistent with the story of how God has acted in history through Israel and the church, then one simply begs the question of truth. For on what grounds can one say that the Christian story is true? How is that story more true than another story? Does Hauerwas' position then lead to relativism? Does his ethic merely amount to the claim that our ethic is valid because it is grounded in a narrative *which we believe* to be true? Someone else can make a similar claim about his/her narrative. Is there any way to adjudicate between various stories? Is there any way to ask the question whether what two communities believe to be true is *really true*?

Hauerwas does not seem to have a way of solving this problem. He asserts that ethics always involves a "qualifier," that is, every ethic is shaped by a particular narrative context. That means there is no standpoint outside one's own narrative from which one could judge the truth of a narrative, for the narrative is itself the truth. Stated another way, the truth cannot be abstracted from the narrative to provide a standard outside the narrative from which to judge the truth. That there is a universal standard outside the narrative is the claim of a natural law paradigm. Though natural law ethicists admit that the determination of this universal standard is very difficult to arrive at, they claim that at least they have a method by which to explore the possibility of truth and counter the dangers of relativism.

We cannot adequately work through this difficulty in this short paper, but we can briefly sketch an approach to the problem by asking ourselves what it is about a narrative that leads us to adopt it as a true account of our lives.

Narrative is true if it does two things. First, it must empower us to make sense of our existence. We must ask whether it provides a framework of interpretation that can illuminate life, that can help us give an account of the nature of reality as we experience it. The difficulty with this criterion is that several alternative competing paradigms seem to be capable of powerfully illuminating human existence. We can, for example, think of the competing paradigms of the Hebraic prophetic view of life and a Greek tragic view of human existence. We can never solve the truth of a paradigm, but we can become aware of the alternatives and the crucial issues at stake as we choose to define our life in terms of one paradigm rather than another. It is true that in a very important sense, as Hauerwas says, we are chosen by a story that has become embodied within a community.

But the very existence of a pluralism of world views makes us aware of alternatives. In that context we must weigh the alternatives through the exercise of reason. The point is that the choice of a paradigm is not simply an arbitrary "leap of faith." The choice is made in the context of discerning what the crucial alternatives are, using reason to help determine why a particular paradigm more powerfully illuminates our life than another.

Secondly, a narrative can be said to be true only if it is fruitful, if it can empower us to live in the world in a creative and appropriate way. Does it help us sustain life and those crucial values which we consider central to human existence? Again we cannot get outside the circle, since the crucial values we deem important are given to us in our narrative. Nevertheless, as we said in elaborating the first point, we can come to know in a pluralistic world what the choices are. Reason must help us discern what the alternatives are and which of these most adequately meet the ethical test of being life sustaining.

But does this not violate Hauerwas' concept of narrative truth? Do we not in fact determine whether a narrative is true based on standards external to the narrative, that is, whether the narrative is functional in enabling us to interpret the world and live creatively in it? I think not. What we have here is a dialectic. We live by the truth of a particular narrative but a narrative whose truth we are constantly testing in dialogue with others who understand the world differently. I agree with Hauerwas that we cannot abstract ourselves from our narrative framework. We interpret the world from a particular standpoint. But we do that in conversation with other persons and communities who also are interpreting the world. In that sense we are constantly being forced to ask the question about what makes our narrative truthful and valid.

The natural law position is mistaken in believing that we can abstract ourselves from our particular narrative to arrive at some neutral or universal standpoint. However, the narrative ethic of Hauerwas also needs to recognize the insistence by a natural law ethic that we give an account of our ethic in the context of dialogue with truth-claims of others.

The Charge of Sectarianism

The issue of sectarianism is inseparably linked to the problem of determining the truth of a narrative. Hauerwas has rightly called on the church first of all to be the church, to live faithfully by the truth of its own story and not to water down its ethic by seeking to define itself in terms of what it has in common with all people. However, in being charged with a sectarian ethic of withdrawal from the world, he has been misunderstood. Hauerwas believes that the world must be understood in terms of the church, not the other way around. The world can be perceived properly only from the standpoint of the church's narrative and its grasp of the truth of the gospel. Having understood the world correctly the church can then be and act in the world in a way that is faithful to its own story. In other words, Hauerwas does not want the world to define the terms of the church's involvement in it. If that happens, then the church and its gospel simply become functional for other ends, such as preserving democracy and the values of Western civilization and preserving life in the face of the nuclear threat. Hauerwas is deeply concerned about nuclear war and a just society but not on the terms defined by the world.

It is crucial that the terms "church" and "world" be properly understood.[17] I find myself in agreement with Hauerwas when he refers to the church simultaneously on two levels. On one level he gives a normative definition. Church is those persons in a covenanted community whose intention it is to allow the Christian narrative to serve as the fundamental paradigm for their lives, a paradigm giving shape to their character. On the other level, church is appropriately given a variety of forms from the local congregation to larger denominational structures to ecumenical gatherings. In its social expression the story is enacted liturgically and lived out authentically in the church's program and members' ministry.

World can thus also be understood at these two levels. On the one hand it refers to persons whose fundamental paradigm is not the Christian story but some other story which gives meaning to their lives. World can also refer to institutional forms, such as families, colleges, the professions, political institutions, which are organized around other social purposes than those whose intention it is to liturgically enact or visibly express the Christian story. Such structures can be in essential harmony with, relatively neutral or indifferent to, in tension with or sometimes directly hostile to Christian intentionality. It is the task of the gathered community of Christians to discern where and how Christians can give most faithful expression to the Christian story within these structures, for example, as a father in a family, a teacher in a college or a representative to the city council. Hauerwas' point is that the church's primary agenda is "being" the church, that is, faithfully living out the Christian narrative. Its main purpose is not keeping democracy afloat,

---

[17]This paragraph was written after I read the two responses by John Friesen and Ted Grimsrud who appropriately raised questions about the confusion that can result from the terminology. I have chosen to stay with the terms, however, despite their "freight" because they are significant in the writings of Hauerwas, and because they point to something which must be said theologically.

raising and nurturing children or enhancing the profession of college teaching, even though all of those arenas may be appropriate loci and vehicles for expressing Christian intentionality. His view of church-world should not be confused with some traditional Mennonite ethnic distinctions which called for the separation of one group of people from another who were not members of the in-group. Nor should Hauerwas' understanding of church-world be confused with some interpretations of Anabaptism which identified certain areas of human culture such as the state or the arts as worldly because they are necessarily non-Christian or a threat to Christianity. For Hauerwas church (defined by one's intentionality) does not in advance exclude particular arenas of culture, but the church provides the framework for discerning how one lives and expresses oneself in the world.

However, by emphasizing so strongly that first of all the church must be the church, Hauerwas does not make it clear on what terms and how the church is to exercise its witness actively in the world. What does it in fact mean to "be" the church?

Presumably he is here referring to the way in which Christian people, both corporately and individually, act in the world—in their public vocations in the world of work, in their political responsibility as citizens or in their family life. Much work still needs to be done if the kind of ethic Hauerwas represents is going to avoid the charge of sectarianism. Hauerwas simply has not shown what it means concretely for the church to be the church as it lives *in the world*. The charge of sectarianism will only be counteracted when the church demonstrates how its involvement in the world can offer a creative and practical alternative to the typical approaches to war and peace, issues of social and racial justice, issues in medical ethics, problems of family life, environmental destruction and crime. It simply will not do to assert that the church must first be the church. Our being the church is given visible, concrete form in our daily living. That is how we "are" the church. Yet what this means explicitly in our family, worker and citizen relationships has yet to be determined.

We need imaginative proposals on how a distinctively Christian narrative framework can provide a perspective and course of action that is indeed an alternative to the typical proposals that come from either a liberal or conservative point of view. If Christians are not to be sectarian, they must enter the arena of rational discourse with persons of other viewpoints, employing the analysis of whatever academic or practical discipline is appropriate in speaking to issues confronted in the polis. In these arenas of public discourse we cannot simply repeat the Christian narrative and urge the practice of virtues that follow from the narrative. Christians must seek to demonstrate in what sense a Christian perspective can illuminate our public lives as citizens and offer creative alternatives to current approaches. I do not mean to say that our primary job is to be good citizens. Our task is to "be" the church, but that takes on flesh in how we exercise our citizenship. Hauerwas, in stressing the narrative framework of Christian ethics, has not shown us how to express that narrative vision in the arena of public life. Until he does that, he is subject to the charge of sectarianism, no matter how much he claims the contrary.

The Relationship of Character and Action

Hauerwas maintains that the first concern of ethics focuses on what kind of people we should be. Our decisions about what we should do, he argues, should be an outgrowth of our character. Our actions should be consistent with what it means to be Christian people whose identity is defined by the church. He is critical of the stress in contemporary ethics on ethical quandaries and case studies abstracted from their theological/ethical framework. He argues that most contemporary scholars approach ethics as if it involved a number of isolated problems: business ethics, social ethics, medical ethics, political ethics. Hence ethical reflection has no coherence, for we approach ethical issues without a normative vision of life, as if our ethical life involves isolated fragments, each demanding a separate analysis of what we should do in each case.

Hauerwas has rightly pointed out that we cannot abstract cases from their narrative framework, for the very way we describe or analyze an ethical issue is itself a function of the theological or philosophical framework we bring to the issue. In

my book, *Christian Peacemaking and International Conflict*,[18] I
point out that the very description of how the world works, with
its balance of power models versus transnational network models
and the relative weight given to the role of ordinary people
versus that of the elite in giving shape to international politics,
is integrally related to the theological paradigm we bring to
political ethics. We do not first have a neutral description of the
world, then bring to bear our theological/ethical framework. Our
theological orientation, our understanding of God, the way God
works in the world, the role of the church in the world—all are
ways of describing the world which have a profound effect on
our ethical analysis.

Despite the validity of much of what Hauerwas says about
the nature of ethics, his position needs modification to avoid
several problems. Critics argue that we must still make decisions
as Christians and Hauerwas has not shown us how we move
from an ethic of character to making actual decisions by weighing the rightness or wrongness of alternatives. Even though we
may have a clear sense of our narrative framework and know
what that means for the kind of people we are to be, that sense
of identity is not sufficient for determining what specific decisions we must make as Christian people seeking to be creative
witnesses in a world where we are confronted with hard choices
within political, social, economic or health institutions.

The fact is that the categories of narrative ethics do not
give very precise guidance for our decisions. The narrative
approach has been used by ethicists to argue for quite different
ethical outcomes on particular ethical questions. Hence, we still
need to develop an ethic of rules or principles that can guide us
in specific decisions. We cannot simply replace a theory of
obligation—a theory of what constitutes the rightness or wrongness of actions—with an ethic of virtue. What has happened, in
short, is that Hauerwas, in offering a corrective to the limitations
of quandary ethics, has himself developed a truncated ethic. An
ethic of character, as such, cannot adequately guide us in making
concrete ethical decisions.

---

[18]Duane K. Friesen, *Christian Peacemaking and International Conflict*
(Scottdale, PA: Herald Press, 1986).

This issue is connected with the problem of sectarianism. An ethic of virtue alone, therefore, cannot satisfactorily direct Christian people on how to act *in the world*. In order to act faithfully, we cannot avoid developing principles or rules that guide our actions. Although Hauerwas would deny it, one possible interpretation of his position is that he has developed an ethic of good intentions, one that calls for the practice of certain virtues, but he has failed to develop clarity about what acting on those virtues in the world might entail.

Again, I want to emphasize that we should not develop rules or principles abstracted from or independent of the Christian narrative. Rather, we should seek to describe those rules which give most authentic expression to Christian intentionality. The biblical literature is instructive here. It not only provides lists of virtues that are authentic expressions of Christian character—love, joy, peace, patience (Galatians 5:22)—but also gives numerous descriptions of what kinds of actions are appropriate. Paul's description of what it means "not to be conformed to this world" (Romans 12:2) includes exhortations to think soberly, use our gifts wisely, contribute to the needs of the saints, practice hospitality, bless those who persecute, repay no one evil for evil, feed our hungry enemies. A full account of Christian ethics, then, would not only describe the virtues but also give an account of those "rules" which can guide action. These should admittedly not be stated as eternal principles abstracted from the narrative, but should be continually revised descriptions by the discerning community of its basic rules of operation for that time and place.

Reflections on Anabaptist-Mennonite Ethics from the Narrative Paradigm

Several areas can be identified where fruitful dialogue can occur or linkage be made between Anabaptist-Mennonite ethics and the narrative approach.

Biblical Authority and the Truthfulness of Narrative

Anabaptist-Mennonite ethics has insisted on the authority

of the biblical story for ethics. Such a narrative framework for doing ethics has been integral to Mennonite ethics. What is needed, however, is more thorough analysis of what kind of authority this narrative has, and how that question of biblical authority is understood in relationship to epistemological issues raised above.[19]

We can think of the authority of a narrative in at least three different ways: as something we submit ourselves to simply because it has been given to us and we accept its truth apart from any rational assessment of it; as the framework for defining a community, the church, which we accept as a basis for our Christian identity; and as something we accept because it helps us "make sense" of our lives, as a framework for living that is also rationally intelligible. We need to work out how we understand this third sense of authority. It is this approach to narrative which can help sort out what we mean when we say a narrative is truthful and which will also help us deal more adequately with the epistemological problems raised about narrative ethics in general. I like the way H.R. Niebuhr puts the issue in his book, *The Meaning of Revelation*. He uses the phrase, "reasons of the heart," which refers to how the appropriation of revelation in our lives is not something contrary to reason, but is the way in which the story of God's action in history can make our lives intelligible.

> Revelation means for us that part of our inner history which illuminates the rest of it and which is itself intelligible. . . . The special occasion to which we appeal in the Christian church is called Jesus Christ, in whom we see the righteousness of God, his power and wisdom. But from that special occasion we also derive the concepts which make possible the elucidation of all the events in our history. Revelation means this intelligible event which makes all other events intelligible. Such a revelation, rather than being contrary to reason in our life, is the discovery of rational pattern in it. Revelation means the point at which we can begin to think and act as members of an intelligible and intelligent world of persons.[20]

---

[19]See also my lecture, "Biblical Authority: The Contemporary Theological Debate," given as part of the annual Bible Lectures at Bethel College, February 26-28, 1989, and published in *Mennonite Life* 26 (September 1989): 26-31.

[20]H. Richard Niebuhr, *The Meaning of Revelation* (New York, NY: The MacMillan Company, 1941), 68-69.

The important point is that the Christian narrative takes on authority insofar as the biblical view of life can help us make sense of our lives. Some appeals to the truth of a narrative appear to be arbitrary: that is the story I have been given and I believe it to be true regardless of what it says. The authority of a narrative and the exercise of reason are not opposites but they complement each other. In such a view our lives are involved in a constant dialectic of living in the memory of the story that has been handed down to us and in testing that story against our knowledge and experience of the world in which we live. In this sense the church and a community of reason are not opposites. The meaning of a community of reason is that we give consent to the truth, not because of the coercive power of authority but because the truth itself is compelling. But that is also the meaning of the church. We have responded to a God who has not compelled us out of fear but has called us through grace and love to respond freely.

Of course, we can not rationally demonstrate a narrative to be true beyond doubt. As mentioned earlier, quite compelling reasons can be given for alternative narrative interpretations of the world. We cannot avoid commitment, a certain leap that goes beyond reason. However, even though a narrative in its most fundamental sense carries us beyond reason, that does not make the narrative contrary to reason. "Faith seeking understanding" is a central, ongoing task of theology.

A narrative theology also does not imply a relativist position, in which one narrative may be as true as another, and that therefore we cannot presume to claim the Christian narrative as true and commend it to others. To claim the Christian story as one's own is to affirm the God who is God of all people, whose disclosure is manifested supremely in Jesus Christ. That story can be confessed and commended to others as "true" by stating the story as intelligently as possible. This confession must, however, be made in humility and in full awareness that our own commitments go beyond reason. We must therefore make our own confession in a context of readiness to *listen* to others who may give witness to another narrative interpretation of the world.

A genuinely relativist position would not really be committed to the dialogical process, for in advance one would hold truth to be relative to each person's standpoint. Paradoxically, genuine engagement can come if, in the context of respectful speaking and listening, one shares one's own narrative as true and recognizes that the other's narrative entails similar claims.

Church-World and Narrative Ethics[21]

For Hauerwas the world is to be described and understood from the standpoint of the church's narrative, not the other way around. His approach to the relationship between church and world can also speak to a long-standing debate centred on the nature of the Anabaptist-Mennonite church-world dualism.

One approach to this dualism, seen for example in Guy Hershberger and revived in contemporary Mennonite ethics by Ted Koontz,[22] has been to develop a two-level ethic. The norms of Christian discipleship apply to Christians, and another standard is applicable to the world, particularly in relationship to political institutions. In such a dualism Mennonite ethics is vulnerable to the charge of sectarianism since one ethic, which the church cannot practice, applies to the world, another ethic applies to the church which inevitably must "withdraw" from those institutions where a worldly ethic is practised.

For Hauerwas there is only one norm for truth, only one standard of ethics. That is the truth revealed through the narrative of God's action in Israel and Jesus Christ. There is not one level of worldly ethics or natural law that can be applied to the state or other institutions alongside the narrative ethic for Christians. There are not two gods, one who works through the persuasive love of Christ and another who uses coercion to keep order in the world. Yet Hauerwas does not dissolve this dualism. The church which lives by the narrative revealed through the story of Jesus is in tension with a world which lives by a different standard. But that different worldly standard can never be

---

[21]Note the clarification of the terminology of church-world, supra., 237.

[22]See especially Guy F. Hershberger, *War, Peace, and Nonresistance* (Scottdale, PA: Herald Press, 1953) and Ted Koontz, "Mennonites and the State: Preliminary Reflections," in *Essays on Peace Theology and Witness*, ed. Willard M. Swartley (Elkhart, IN: Institute of Mennonite Studies, 1988).

legitimated on its own terms, but must always be understood and critiqued from the standpoint of the one truth revealed in Jesus Christ.

Thus in his book, *Against the Nations*,[23] Hauerwas challenges the whole notion of war as a legitimate institution serving God's purposes before the full manifestation of the Kingdom of God. From the standpoint of the God who has been revealed in Jesus Christ, war as an institution has been delegitimized. Thus a Christian ethic that seeks to give testimony in the world from the standpoint of its own narrative does not adjust its ethic to the realities of war in a sinful world. That is precisely what the just war position has always done. Rather Christians witness in the world by exercising their imaginations to contribute to thinking about alternative ways of dealing with human conflict without resorting to war. In this way we move beyond sectarianism, testifying in the world out of the framework of our own narrative, defining the world in terms of the church rather than the church in terms of the world.

My own book, *Christian Peacemaking and International Conflict*, is an effort to work out of a narrative framework that describes the problem of international politics in terms of that narrative framework. I describe and interpret international politics in terms of Christian revelation rather than from the accepted standpoint of the world of secular political science. However, doing so involved a dialectic where I considered various secular understandings of politics and tested these interpretations in light of a Christian paradigm. I read as heavily in the social sciences and in political science as I did in Christian theology and ethics, and then attempted to state in the language of public discourse how a Christian perspective might interpret international politics and act out of that interpretation *in the world* of international politics. That effort involved a discerning dialogical process in which my understanding of politics was in part given shape by empirical and critical reflection from a Christian narrative point of view. In the process I assessed those aspects of political world views which reflected underlying

---

[23]Stanley Hauerwas, *Against the Nations: War and Survival in a Liberal Society* (Minneapolis, MN: Winston Press, 1985).

philosophical assumptions about the human or normative views of how political life must or should be organized to discern what is in harmony with, relatively neutral, in tension with or hostile to a Christian interpretation of the world. The goal of such analysis is not to find ways for Christians to run the world more successfully than others, but how Christians can live faithfully in the context of citizenship.

One can see how closely the church-world issue is tied to the epistemological issue. We cannot simply work deductively, taking our own narrative as true "come hell or high water;" then apply that ethic to the world. Rather we must enter into dialogue with other descriptions of the world in order to discern how the narrative can be applied in such a way as to intelligibly interpret the world. Only then is it possible to be a witness in the world, offering models and creative alternatives to the ruts in which the world is stuck. Most Christians are quite unsuccessful in this enterprise because they have allowed the world to define reality for the church. Many Christians who stress the priority of the church, however, have not done the hard job of imagining, describing and then acting out alternative models that could become attractive to the world. This imagining and acting out creative alternatives is precisely what the gospel is about. But it will only be seen as good news pointing to a way out of the ruts in which the world is stuck if that narrative can be made intelligible to others. We must work out descriptions of the world that are attractive and can evoke consent. The God we have come to know in Jesus Christ works in the world in that way. Such an approach does not guarantee success but it is the only approach consistent with the truth as we have come to know it.

Harry Huebner*

CHRISTIAN PACIFISM AND THE CHARACTER OF GOD**

Several years ago when I lived and worked in Jerusalem, and was trying to think theologically in the midst of a raging conflict, I was frequently reminded of the close connection between theology and ethics. Two experiences stand out. First, in the spring of 1983 I attended the Tantur Lectures on "The Possession and Use of Nuclear Weapons in Light of Torah, Gospel and Shari'a." They were delivered by leaders from each of the three religions, Islam, Judaism and Christianity. Their arguments were virtually identical. Each managed somehow to give his religious group special status before God and the world, and each invoked God to justify his position. For example, the Jewish rabbi concluded, "If anyone has a right to possess nuclear weapons, to be prepared to deter murderous aggression, Israel is the country that irrefutably should have such a right."[1] It was as though each leader was saying, "God and the world could not possibly exist without us. God's choosing us has legitimated our struggle for survival if but for the defence of God. Hence there is no morality in relation to which our own survival can be risked."

The most amazing thing with this way of thinking about God and ethics is not self-interest in the survival of a people— that is understandable. But this "tribal-God logic" distorts what is supposed to be the very core of monotheism: that God gives *us* life, meaning and protection. We do not save God; God saves

---

*Harry Huebner is Associate Professor of Philosophy and Theology at Canadian Mennonite Bible College, Winnipeg, Manitoba.

**The author would like to thank Marlin Miller, President of Goshen Biblical Seminary, Elkhart, Indiana, and Ray Gingerich, Professor of Church Studies, Eastern Mennonite College, Harrisonburg, Virginia, for their critical responses to this essay at the Symposium.

[1]Donald Nicholl, ed. *Tantur Lectures 1983* (Jerusalem: Ecumenical Institute for Theological Research, 1983), 18.

us. God is the ontological and moral ground of all life, not just ours *contra* others. A fundamental reversal of ontological dependence has taken place. By suggesting that we are indispensable to God, we are implying that God's being and "success" somehow depend on us and our efforts, and that our life is inherently more valuable than the life of those we call God's (and our) enemies.

The second experience relates to the other side of the same logical shekel. While in dialogue with persons of other faiths, I discovered that often my own religious and intellectual commonality lay less with my Christian kinsfolk than with fellow pacifists, whether Muslims, Jews or Christians. At first this felt like I was betraying my strong ecclesiological convictions, but on reflection I began to see why this was the case. The common vision among us pacifists had its source in a similar understanding of God as one who is universal and hence does not need one people's defence against another. Hence, we managed to transcend many of our religious differences. For me this was a remarkable discovery.

I share these experiences here not because I want to talk about Christian ethics in relation to other religions, nor because I want to talk about God from the general monotheistic perspective, nor even because I want to assert a necessary connection between religion and ethics, but because these experiences highlighted for me a very important and often ignored emphasis on the relationship between theology and ethics. Ever since Immanuel Kant's *Religion Within the Limits of Pure Reason*, it has been fashionable to think that the way ethics and theology relate is to fit one's view of God into whatever view of ethics one has. As one who is interested in taking theology seriously, this has always struck me as peculiar. Surely our view of ethics must flow from our clearest understanding of who God is.

The major impetus for writing this essay, therefore, goes beyond my personal experience with conflict. At the systematic level it is a response to two common criticisms of Christian pacifism which I hold to be misguided. First is the criticism by Christian non-pacifists who argue that pacifism only makes sense from the standpoint of a sectarian ecclesiology which freely admits the irrelevance of its ethic for society at large.[2] If the moral ground of pacifism is in fact rooted in the being of God this "sectarian criticism" is undercut. A second position is put forward by some pacifists who want it both ways. They argue that, although pacifism is derived from Christian discipleship, disciples nevertheless can and should advise non-church structures, like governments, on ethical matters. When they do, however, they must be careful not to be too pacifist since this may in fact lead to increased violence. They argue that when speaking to governments one cannot rely on the ethic of the church. For a church community the pacifist option may well be the best, but in a world of power-brokerage and compromise, it cannot be applied.[3] Such an argument assumes that there is a dual moral source from which pacifism is but one strand. This view is antagonistic to the thesis of this paper.

Permit me one final comment to locate our subject. The argument is often made that narrative ethics[4] implies an inherent relativism because it cannot escape the diversity of narratives which forms its base. My claim is that to deal successfully with this charge the narrative approach must focus more attention than it has on the discussion of the main character in its narrative.[5] Unless our view of God morally undergirds our pacifist claim, this particular approach to ethics loses its moral claim. And if our argument succeeds, the charge of relativism against narrative ethics cannot be sustained.

In this paper I will therefore engage the question, "Which God ought we to obey and why?"[6] I want to show that how

---

[2]For a helpful example of the current form of this debate see especially the "Introduction" in *Christian Existence Today: Essays on Church, World and Living in Between* by Stanley Hauerwas (Durham, NC: The Labyrinth Press, 1988).

[3]See for example, Ted Koontz, "Mennonites and the State: Preliminary Reflections," in *Essays on Peace Theology and Witness*, ed. Willard Swartley (Elkhart, IN: Institute of Mennonite Studies, 1988).

[4]By "narrative ethics" I mean that approach to the discipline made popular by such scholars as Hans Frei, Alasdair MacIntyre, John H. Yoder, Stanley Hauerwas, James McClendon, *inter alia*.

[5]See my article "An Ethic of Character: The Normative Form of the Christian Life According to Stanley Hauerwas" and Hauerwas' response "On God: Ethics and the Power to Act in History," both in *Essays in Peace Theology and Witness*, ed. Willard Swartley, 179-203, 204-209.

[6]For a helpful study of this question, see Alasdair MacIntyre's article by this

theology and ethics are related influences the way we think of the moral enterprise, especially pacifism. This will lead to a discussion of how the content of Christian ethics gets shaped when we take the Christian character of God seriously.

Theology and Ethics: Two Dominant Models

Gordon Kaufman, an American Mennonite theologian, wrote an article in 1972 entitled, "Two Models of Transcendence" in which he identified the two dominant models of theology as "teleological transcendence" and "interpersonal transcendence."[7] The teleological model has its roots in the Greek philosophy of being and is made popular by Roman Catholicism. It is also the dominant approach of some Protestant theologians like Paul Tillich, although usually Protestants have rejected this approach. In this view finite reality is seen as being grounded in ultimate reality. God becomes best understood through an analysis of the structures of being. God's being makes God's activities intelligible.

On this model, nature is the dominant category. The argument is that God has created an ordered world to which even God is wilfully bound. All that exists is governed by the "form" which shapes "matter" towards its real *telos* (end). We therefore see the will of God not so much in the free agency of God's actions but in the very structure of being itself, in God's being as well as in the created order. This does not mean that God cannot act, but that the activity of God is best seen through the structure of being.

On the interpersonal model, God is seen "as an autonomous

---

title in *Faith and Philosophy* 3 (October 1986): 359-371.

[7]In Gordon Kaufman, *God the Problem* (Cambridge, MA.: Harvard University Press, 1972), 72-81. A comparable and more recent statement of this polarity is found in George Lindbeck, *The Nature of Doctrine: Religion and Theology in a Postliberal Age* (Philadelphia, PA: Westminster Press, 1984). Lindbeck calls the two types of theology "cognitive-propositional" and "experiential-expressive." Although there are distinct differences between Lindbeck and Kaufman, both are attempting to identify the thought structures that lie behind what is commonly called the theology of nature and the theology of history. Lindbeck is especially interested in developing the "cultural-linguistic model" which is to bring the two into logical coherence.

agent capable of genuinely free acts."[8] Karl Barth has no doubt been the leading Protestant proponent of this view. The success of this model was due in part to its easy integration with modern biblical theology. G. Ernest Wright's "God who acts" and Barth's "wholly other God" are conceived in very similar ways. On this model God becomes known to us by observing how God has acted in the past and is acting in the present. God's actions reveal God's being. Here history and action rather than nature and being are the dominant categories.[9] While the two approaches could be discussed on the merits of their theological adequacy, we are here interested in their impact on ethics. And the impact is significant.

On the theology of nature model, the way things really are becomes the standard for how they ought to be. That is, being determines action. As St. Thomas Aquinas via Aristotle might state it, once we have come to know what the natural *telos* of being human is, then all we need to do is act in keeping with it. Or once we have come to know what the *telos* of marriage, or teaching, or business is, then we can know how to engage in each morally. This "coming to know" is itself a natural process; it happens via reason and critical reflection.

On this model we are called to fit into what God has ordered as good. Goodness is given through the structure of being itself and is not created by us; nor is it shown to us by way of God's special acts in history. On this view God's freedom and creativity are seen in God's detachedness from the physical order, since goodness has its source in the non-physical. Our freedom and creativity are seen as secondary categories to discipline and training. We are called to act not on the basis of our own ingenuity, but in keeping with what we have come to see as real. Our task is directed at getting ourselves to understand being and then "ordering" our actions and character into this understanding.

On the theology of history model, the task of ethical

---

[8]Ibid., 78.

[9]James Gustafson, an American ethicist, recently gave the Hanley Memorial Lectures at the University of Manitoba, Winnipeg, Manitoba in which he spoke of the implications of these two models for Christian ethics. I am indebted to his lecture entitled, "Ideas of God and Ethics," delivered October 26, 1988, for some of the ideas in this section.

construction is quite different. Here action determines being. God is what God does, and we are what we do. Since God is seen primarily as one who acts in history, we as moral beings must somehow relate ourselves to these acts. What God does and has done becomes normative for our actions. As God is free, so we are free. As God is moving history to its completion in time, so we are called to participate in this process which may be understood as liberation, humanization, democratization or obedience. Our ethical self-understanding is grounded on the *Imago Dei* and demands that we collaborate in the process of moving history towards the goal as we come to see it. In doing this we see ourselves as participating in God's history.

When we examine the workings of the historical model in greater detail, we notice some important refinements. Most Christian ethicists want to put limits on our imitation of God's acts. We are all too conscious of "The Fall" which entails a false imitation of God. There are some things which God does which we should not do. But we are not agreed on which actions of God we may imitate. For example, in the area of medical ethics, there are those who say that at life's limits, at birth and at death, God alone has jurisdiction. Others say that, since we already find ourselves working with God anyway, even here we ought to emulate the way God acts in these matters. Or, in areas of political ethics, some say that we should fight wars in certain situations to bring about justice, because this is the way God does it. Our involvement in war is therefore but a participation in God's justice. On the other side of the argument are those who contend that, although God does fight wars, we may not.

Christian ethicists rarely operate exclusively in either the history or the nature camp. Yet most give primary allegiance, consciously or otherwise, to one or the other approach. What is most significant, however, is that the drive behind much of the current serious writing in both theological method and Christian ethics, like the work of Lindbeck and Hauerwas, is the attempt to bring these two models into some kind of critical coherence. Because we have felt it necessary to choose between these two approaches, viable ways of speaking about the relationship of God's moral being and ours have eluded our grasp.

Each approach, when seen over against the other, has major

deficiencies. On the one hand, since history is the realm of freedom and contingency, and since from this perspective God is seen as autonomous free agent, this approach cannot be of much help in answering the question of God's moral character. If God is free in the sense implied, then God may choose to act in the future in a manner quite different from the past. After all, "character determination" requires rational construction on the part of the reader of the story. History alone cannot produce character. Yet, positively, if we did not learn the content of God's character via the Christ event—an act of history—the Christian faith would lose moral power over its disciples.

On the other hand, since the theology of nature demands a metaphysical dualism of the natural and the supernatural, moral continuity is rendered difficult from the start. Moreover, since normativity is granted to nature, the historical Christ event becomes all but irrelevant. Yet, positively, the language of God's steadfast character—the language of being—is absolutely essential in order for us to have faith and hope.

The narrative approach to ethics provides us with a context for speaking meaningfully about the character of God. God is the main character in the Christian narrative. The special moral term "character" is a concept which enables us to understand actions as belonging to an agent. Character is the "qualification of our self agency."[10] When ascribed to God, it enables us to understand God's being in relation to ours. Pure history only tells us what God does, while pure nature at most discloses God's abstract existence. Narrative ethics provides the framework for understanding God via a process of coming to see certain acts as uniquely God's. In this way our story can become essentially linked to God's story.

God and Pacifism in Anabaptist Thought

In an attempt to evaluate Christian pacifism in light of the above discussion of ethics, it is instructive to note how the

---

[10]Stanley Hauerwas, *Vision and Virtue: Essays in Critical Ethical Reflection* (Notre Dame, IN: University of Notre Dame Press, 1974), 55.

nature-history dynamic gets expressed in sixteenth-century Anabaptist theology. At the outset we must bear in mind that on the one hand they, along with the mainline reformers, rejected the Catholic tradition and the natural theology which was part of it; on the other hand they found themselves critical of the mainline radical historicization of the incarnation which lacked the basis for affirming the timeless and full normativity of Jesus as the way of all disciples. This double critique left them with few resources for shaping their theology.

The Anabaptists did not speak much about God, certainly not in abstract philosophical language. The argument has been made that they simply accepted the standard view of God and hence did not need to address the matter. Although this interpretation is really quite doubtful, we do find a significant diversity of views on how God's character and ours relate. It may well be argued that, even though the Anabaptists were not agreed on a precise alternative formulation, they clearly had considerable discomfort with the traditional way of stating this relationship. Moreover, how the nature of pacifism gets formulated hinges on this issue.

Let us examine a few of their arguments.

> The sword is an ordering of God outside the perfection of Christ. It punishes and kills the wicked and rewards and protects the good. In the law the sword is established over the wicked for punishment and for death, and the secular rulers are established to wield the same. But within the perfection of Christ only the ban is used for the admonition and exclusion of the one who has sinned, without the death of the flesh, simply the warning and the command to sin no more.[11]

> [The government] is a servant of God, the protector of the innocent and the righteous, an avenger of evil, having received power from God on earth to use it accordingly. This is the true Christian government.[12]

---

[11]"The Schleitheim Brotherly Union," trans. John H. Yoder, in *The Legacy of Michael Sattler* (Scottdale, PA: Herald Press, 1973), 39.

[12]Bernard Rothmann, in *Anabaptism in Outline*, ed. Walter Klaassen (Scottdale, PA: Herald Press, 1981), 253 (hereafter cited as Klaassen). One could add other voices which express a similar theology, for example, Pilgram Marpeck. "I admit worldly, carnal, and earthly rulers as servants of God in earthly matters, but not in the kingdom of Christ. According to the words of Paul, to them rightfully belongs all carnal honour, fear, obedience, tax, toll, and tribute. However

The strong biblicism of these writers seems to have bound some Anabaptists to a canonical syncretism which required them to speak of God in terms of the aggregate of all past divine acts. In other words, here they simply accepted the mainline reformers' wholesale rejection of natural theology in favour of a historical-revelational approach. God is what God does. Hence God is seen as morally dualistic. That is, God uses both the sword and the love of Christ to deal with sin, because this is the way the Bible tells the story.

In this way of thinking about God, the Anabaptists were virtually indistinguishable from Martin Luther. Luther also held that God could use either violence or forgiveness as a way of dealing with sin. In the church God's agency finds expression through love and forgiveness, while in the state it is expressed through the sword and violence.

Although these Anabaptists agreed with Luther on divine moral dualism, they nevertheless vigorously disagreed with his moral dualism for Christians. For Luther, what is right for us is rooted in the divine. He believed in divine-human-moral-continuity. Hence, just as God could deal with sin in two ways, so could Christians. On his model, as long as we are clear whether we are in the arena of the church or of the state, we will also be clear on how to act.

With this conclusion the Anabaptists disagreed. They believed that we are called to live only one way, in accordance with the way of Jesus. We are to deal with sin only through forgiveness and the ban. After all, Christians are to be the body of Christ. While God has the prerogative of dealing with sin in whatever way God wishes—God is autonomous free agent—Christians are called to deal with sin only by way of the cross of Jesus Christ.

When we examine the inherent logic of this debate, it should surprise us to see discipleship Christians espouse this kind of discontinuity between who God is and what we ought to do. After all, to suggest that Jesus is normative for us while not

---

when such persons who hold authority become Christian (which I heartily wish and pray for) they may not use the aforementioned carnal force, sovereignty or ruling in the kingdom of Christ. It cannot be upheld by any scripture." Klaassen, 251.

fully revelatory of God, results in enormous trinitarian and christological problems.[13] From the standpoint of simple consistency,
therefore, Luther makes much more sense. His ethic is at least
morally grounded in God, however inadequate his conception of
God might be. The Anabaptists in question, on the other hand,
based their ethic on obedience to Jesus Christ alone.

It should therefore not surprise us to discover a lack of
unanimity among the Anabaptists on this way of stating the
relationship between God's character and ours. A quick reading
of the literature suggests at least three different views.[14]

The first we might call "divine-human-moral-discontinuity-
pacifism." This is the view represented by the above statements
suggesting that, although God is morally dualistic, Christians
should be disciples of Christ and adherents only to the way of
Jesus. This may well be the most prevalent view among the
Anabaptists. It is certainly the one most commonly accepted as
representing their thought.

The second view may be called "divine-human-moral-
continuity-non-pacifism." This is the view represented by writers
like Balthasar Hubmaier who argue, along with Luther, that
since God uses the sword, so may we. Hubmaier says, for
example:

> The judge too may and ought to be a Christian even though
> the contentious parties sin and are not prepared to be
> wronged. Thus also a Christian may—according to the order
> of God—bear the sword in God's stead against the evildoer

---

[13]With the denial of the full revelation of God in Christ comes the collapse
of the doctrine of the incarnation. Unless the trinitarian controversy is seen in
purely metaphysical terms, which I cannot imagine many Anabaptists accepting,
the affirmation of the sameness of the Son and the Father entailed the claim of
the revelation of God's moral character in Christ. The designation of the ebionic
and docetic views of Jesus as heretical reenforces the necessity of a proper
christology implying that Jesus is "fully God and fully man." Such continuity of
Father and Son is also found, not surprisingly, in Anabaptist writings, to wit.,
Pilgrim Marpeck, ". . . the Son makes the Father known, and the Father makes
known and reveals the Son. The elect are glorified in them, just as the Father and
Son are glorified in themselves." *The Writings of Pilgrim Marpeck*, ed. William
Klassen and Walter Klaassen (Scottdale, PA: Herald Press, 1978), 435.

[14]Ray Gingerich, in his response to this essay at the Symposium suggests a
fourth possible view which he calls "*now* moral-discontinuity-pacifism but *then*
moral-continuity-non-pacifism." He suggests that this characterizes "the chiliasts
such as Hans Hut who taught a 'sheathed sword' until the Final Day at which
time Christ's followers will participate in the bloody over-throw of the evil rulers,
thus preparing the scene for Christ's reign."

and punish him. For it has been so ordered by God because of wickedness for the protection of the pious (Romans 13).[15]

The third approach, which may be called, "divine-human-moral-continuity-pacifism," is the least well-known and, from the standpoint of our thesis, the most interesting. Although this view is not well developed and not even always clearly presented, its seeds and its rudimentary structure are discernible. In this argument the way of Jesus is the way of God; therefore discipleship of Jesus is discipleship of God. Hans Denck is one of its representatives.

> For man imitates God, takes on the traits of the divine generation, as one who is the son of God and coheir with Christ. . . . All Christians . . . are in God, like unto Christ and equal to him, in such a way that what refers to one also refers to the other. As Christ does, so do they also. And thus they have Christ as Lord and Master, for the reason that he is the most perfect mirror of his Father. . . .[16]

It is significant to note that this way of speaking about God and ethics led Denck to speak about power and government differently from the other Anabaptists. Power is not evil because it is rooted in the goodness of God, and rulers do the will of God when they act in keeping with the character of God as revealed in Christ. For example he says:

> It is not that power in itself is wrong seen from the perspective of the evil world, for (the government) serves God in his wrath, but rather that love teaches her children a better way, namely to serve the graciousness of God. . . . And in so far as it were possible for a government to act in (love) it could well be Christian in its office. Since however the world will not tolerate it, a friend of God should not be in government but out of it, that is if he desires to keep Christ as a lord and master.[17]

---

[15]Klaassen, 246

[16]"Whether God is the Cause of Evil," in *Spiritual and Anabaptist Writers*, ed. George Williams (Philadelphia, PA: Westminster Press, 1957), 99-100. One finds similar logic in other Anabaptist writings, for example, Peter Rideman, who says, ". . . the twigs are of the same character as the root, and bear corresponding fruit. . . . Thus doth man become one with God and God with him, even as the father with his son. . . ." *Account of our Religion, Doctrine and Faith* (New York, NY: Plough Publishing House, 1970), 62. Or again, "For if a man is to be renewed again into the likeness of God, he must put off all that leads him from him . . . for he cannot otherwise attain God's likeness." Ibid., 89.

[17]Klaassen, 249. The reference to the government serving "God in his wrath"

Denck here speaks of ethics from the point of view of a single moral source: namely the character of God. It is now no longer permissible to say that the church is called to live by the rule of Christ whereas God provides another norm for the rulers of the nation. There is but one moral source and that is the love of God as revealed in Jesus the Christ.

Menno Simons' pacifism presupposes a similar kind of divine-human-moral-continuity. He puts it thus:

> How could the true brethren and sisters of Jesus Christ, the well-disposed children of God, who with Christ Jesus are born of God the Father and the powerful seed of his divine Word in Jesus Christ, who are regenerated by Christ, partake of his Spirit and nature, who have been made like unto Him, are Christians and heavenly minded—how can such people teach or stage turmoil of any kind. . . . Again, in peace we are called of God.[18]

As with Denck, moral continuity logic pushes Menno to challenge government leaders to act according to the rule of Christ. He explicitly affirms the unity of the moral source by arguing that it is nonsense to assert Christ as king over the church but not the world.[19] This enables him to address the leaders boldly.

> O highly renowned, noble lords, believe Christ's Word, fear God's wrath, love righteousness, do justice to widows and orphans, judge rightly between a man and his neighbor, fear no man's highness, despise no man's littleness, hate all avarice, punish with reason, allow the Word of God to be taught freely, hinder no one from walking in the truth, bow to the scepter of him who called you to this high service. Then shall

---

does not seem to imply a dualistic divine character for Denck. His suggestion appears to be that the evil power of the government is not ultimate, and hence must eventually self-destruct, whereas the power of love is ultimate and therefore will eventually be victorious. That Christians cannot serve in government is therefore not a matter of structural necessity, but is determined by what an evil world will or will not tolerate. The world, which empirically does not believe that the love of God is the superior power, will not easily risk the penultimate negative consequences of the life of discipleship.

[18]*The Complete Writings of Menno Simons*, ed. and trans. J. C. Wenger (Scottdale, PA: Herald Press, 1956), 423.

[19]He says ". . . it is clear that Almighty God has made His Son Christ Jesus our Lord King both of the earth and of his faithful church. That Christ is the King of all the earth is abundantly testified to by the Scriptures. . . . As certainly as Christ is God, so certainly is He King of all the earth." *Complete Writings*, 34f.

your throne stand firm forever.[20]

Denck, Menno and others like Rideman, speak a language of pacifism grounded in the unity of God as revealed in the Christ event.[21] In order to overcome the divine moral dualism of much of the then current theology, they had to transcend the historicism of the mainline reformers. They did this by a simple, perhaps even unconscious, assumption that in Christ Jesus we come to know not merely another side of God, but we come to know the very character of God. So, for Christians, divine epistemology cannot be represented by the phrase "God is what God does." Instead, after the Christ event, God's actions must be seen as emanating from God's being as disclosed in Jesus, the Christ.

Yet clearly the Anabaptist pacifists were not united in arguing that their pacifism was grounded in divine-human-moral-continuity. Most represent a pacifism based on moral discontinuity. But this may be due to an unintended deficiency rather than a careful working out of a position. The failure to develop one's theology fully is not necessarily an indictment of a persecuted people who are forced to write their theology on the run. Moreover, the Anabaptists had legitimately grown suspicious of first trying to get their theology straight before being able to live the ethic of Jesus. They were right in declaring that the time for right living had come even though not all the theological niceties were in place.

In any event, consistency of theology and ethics and clarity of appropriate divine metaphors are of great significance for us in the current debate on Christian ethics. Hence, the task of further clarifying the theological basis for pacifism is left to us. Curiously, the rationale undergirding this quest today is identical to that of the reformation in that the meaning and integrity of the church are once more at stake.[22] It is not difficult for the

---

[20]Menno Simons, *Complete Writings*, 193.

[21]Our thesis here is not that the moral continuity view of pacifism is represented only by these writers and not by others, nor that these writers represent this view consistently throughout their works; rather that there is ample evidence of this view of pacifism to be found throughout Anabaptist thought, although it is not systematically developed.

[22]Yoder says of the church of the reformation that "The fallenness by virtue

modern imagination to concoct interpretations of being Christian which are virtually vacuous of theological content. We need to engage in a comprehensive process of constructing a theological ethic for the church appropriate to the story of Jesus, the Christ. And if such an ethic is not rooted in the character of God, then it lacks the power and rationale which can make it believable; even more important, then it lacks the ontological ground which makes it true.

The agenda of modern Christian ethics requires that the divine-human-moral-continuity model be made intelligible. In doing this we will need to find ways of speaking about God acting in history from an intentionally moral base. The first step towards this is to examine whether the current way of speaking about God in modern theology helps us in this regard.

The Character of God

Perhaps Schubert Ogden was right when he said some twenty-five years ago that "the reality of God has now become the central theological problem."[23] Certainly the past two decades of theological writing have seen a remarkable surge of interest in rethinking God-language.[24] Moreover, the direction in which

---

of which it is held that the church is in need of radical reformation is not merely an accumulation of a series of unrelated mistakes but a fundamental flaw of structure and strategy. The church of the Middle Ages had come to be marked by the alliance of the clergy with the sword, with wealth, and with hierarchy." *The Priestly Kingdom: Social Ethics as Gospel* (Notre Dame, IN: University of Notre Dame Press, 1984), 107. We note that this is not an altogether inaccurate account of the modern church.

[23]Schubert Ogden, *The Reality of God and Other Essays* (New York, NY: Harper and Row, 1963), 1.

[24]A few of the important books on this topic are: Jürgen Moltmann, *The Crucified God* (London: SCM Press, 1974); James H. Cone, *The God of the Oppressed* (New York, NY: Seabury Press, 1975); Jung Young Lee, *God Suffers for Us* (The Hague: Martinus Nijhoff, 1974); C. S. Song, *The Compassionate God* (Maryknoll, NY: Orbis Books, 1982); Axel D. Steuer & James Wm. McClendon, eds. *Is God GOD?* (Nashville, TN: Abingdon Press, 1981); Rosemary Radford Ruether, *Sexism and God-Talk: Toward a Feminist Theology* (Boston, MA: Beacon Press, 1983); Terence E. Fretheim, *The Suffering of God: An Old Testament Perspective* (Philadelphia, PA: Fortress Press, 1984); Warren MacWilliams, *The Passion of God: Divine Suffering in Contemporary Protestant Theology* (Macon, GA.: Mercer University Press, 1985); Douglas Hall, *Imaging God: Dominion as Stewardship* (Grand Rapids, MI: Eerdmans Publishing Company, 1986); Monika

much of this effort has gone is precisely to address the kind of ambiguity we find within Anabaptist theology. Is the God of Jesus Christ best understood as one who rules from two moral platforms, or does *theologia crucis* (theology of the cross) show us another way? The move by many contemporary theologians has been away from a God of dominance and independence to a God of compassion and suffering.

Already forty-five years ago, Dietrich Bonhoeffer, then in prison for his political peace activities, argued that discipleship Christianity must rethink the traditional characterization of God. He believed that the usual attributes of God spoken about in systematic theology textbooks were inadequate. He argued that since God is decisively revealed in Jesus Christ, we cannot talk of God as one who saves us from a distance, without "getting involved." Salvation made concrete in the life and death of Christ has nothing to do with dominance and control over us. The cross of Christ saves us in that God becomes present to us in compassion and hope. The story of the cross is the story of the ultimate extent of God's presence with human misery and sin.[25] Hence "weakness of God" and "suffering of God" are more appropriate God-metaphors than are the traditional power images. For Bonhoeffer there is no appropriate language of God which does not have its roots in the character of Jesus Christ.

Recently theologians have attempted to unravel the implications of this kind of God-talk which turns much of traditional theology on its head. Greek dualism and medieval theology have taught us that God *qua* God is incapable of suffering, and that weakness and passion are evil. But if this is so, how can Jesus tell us anything at all about who God is? Jesus is at the very core the one who suffers for others.[26] The themes of suffering,

---

K. Hellwig, *Jesus: The Compassion of God* (Wilmington, DE.: Michael Glazier, Inc., 1986); Sallie McFague, *Models of God: Theology for an Ecological Nuclear Age* (Philadelphia, PA: Fortress Press, 1987).

[25]See especially his *Letters and Papers From Prison*, New Greatly Enlarged Edition, ed. E. Bethge (New York, NY: MacMillan and Company, 1972), 361ff.

[26]The way this tension between Jesus' suffering and God's passivity has been handled in traditional theology is by arguing that Jesus as man suffers, but Jesus as God cannot. ". . . Suffering, indeed overflowing suffering in Christ, but as man, not as God." Baron Friedrich von Hügel, *Essays and Addresses on the Philosophy of Religion* (London: J.M. Dent & Sons, 1929), 199. The problem with this kind

servanthood and defencelessness abound in the gospels.

Jürgen Moltmann was one of the first mainline Western theologians to take these comments seriously. He does so by distinguishing between *apathetic theology* and *pathetic theology.* The former has its roots in the Greek philosophy of being, the latter in the Jewish philosophy of history. He distinguishes these two theologies as follows:

> In the physical sense *apatheia* means unchangeableness; in the psychological sense, insensitivity; and in the ethical sense, freedom. In contrast to this, *pathos* denotes need, compulsion, drives, dependence, lower passions and unwilled suffering. . . . The apathic God could therefore be understood as the free God who freed others for himself.[27]

Moltmann then rejects apathetic theology and embraces Abraham Heschel's notion of the "pathos of God." He argues that on this basis it is possible to "not think of God in his absoluteness and freedom,"[28] but rather in his concrete suffering presence among us. This is what makes possible the *theologia crucis* in which there is a direct correspondence between the pathos of God and the *sympatheia* of the people. The cross becomes the symbol which binds the people into a covenant relationship with each other and collectively to the God who is willing to suffer humiliation in being among the people.

But this is only the beginning of the contemporary discussion. Much more is to come. One can readily identify at least six areas of theology where God-talk literature has mushroomed in the past two decades.[29] First, in contemporary process theology with mentors like Charles Hartshorne. He criticizes traditional abstract concepts like omnipotence, omniscience and immutability and emphasizes God's presence in human history.[30]

---

of solution, however, is that then the core of the Gospel, the cross, loses its revelatory significance.

[27]Moltmann, *The Crucified God*, 267-9.

[28]Ibid., 271.

[29]Two helpful resources here are Daniel Day Williams, *What Present Day Theologians Are Thinking*, 3rd ed. (New York, NY: Harper and Row, 1967), 172; and Warren McWilliams, *The Passion of God: Divine Suffering in Contemporary Protestant Theology* (Macon, GA.: Mercer University Press, 1985), 15f.

[30]See especially Charles Hartshorne, *Omnipotence and Other Theological*

Second, in contemporary biblical theology, where both Old Testament and New Testament theologians have emphasized the de-Hellenization of God-talk.[31] Third, in Latin American liberation theology where theologians find it necessary to critique classical Roman Catholicism's view of natural theology and God-talk, in favour of liberation language much more closely related to Bonhoeffer's God of weakness.[32] Fourth, in Asian liberation theologies. Kazoh Kitamori, for example, offers a corrective to the Western liberal view of the love of God by expounding on the significance of the "pain of God."[33] Fifth, in feminist theology where divine power paradigms and salvation theories have undergone a radical reworking.[34] Sixth, in a new atonement theology in which God's salvific act via the cross is spoken about in ways quite different from orthodox theological salvation theories.[35]

There is much that is exciting and right about these new ways of understanding God. They offer a helpful corrective to some of the traditional metaphors. But it is significant to note that this transformation of theological language is brought about, as Moltmann clearly noted, by a profound rejection of "being theology." Almost every theologian following the Moltmann tradition begins the task of theological reconstruction with a repudiation of natural theology in favour of the historical approach. This gives cause for reflection.

Mistakes (Albany, NY: State University of New York Press, 1984).

[31]See for example, Brevard S. Childs, *Biblical Theology in Crisis* (Philadelphia, PA: Westminster Press, 1970), 44ff. See also Terence E. Fretheim, *The Suffering of God: An Old Testament Perspective* (Philadelphia, PA: Fortress Press, 1984), and Kenneth Bailey, *God Is . . .* (Monroeville, PA.: Youth Club Program Inc., 1976).

[32]See especially Gustavo Gutierrez, *The Power of the Poor in History* (Maryknoll, NY: Orbis Books, 1983), 222-233.

[33]See Kazoh Kitamori, *Theology of the Pain of God*, trans. M.E. Bratcher (Richmond, VA: John Knox Press, 1965).

[34]See especially Sheila G. Davaney, *Divine Power: A Study of Karl Barth and Charles Hartshorne* (Philadelphia, PA: Fortress Press, 1986); Rosemary Radford Ruether, *Sexism and God-Talk: Toward a Feminist Theology* (Boston, MA: Beacon Press, 1983); and Pam McAllister, ed. *Reweaving the Web of Life: Feminism and Non-Violence* (Philadelphia, PA: New Society Publishers, 1982).

[35]See John Driver, *Understanding the Atonement for the Mission of the Church* (Scottdale, PA: Herald Press, 1986) and C. Norman Kraus, *Jesus Christ Our Lord: Christology from a Disciple's Perspective* (Scottdale, PA: Herald Press, 1987).

One should at least ask whether these theologians are not walking a razor's edge between being prophetic and merely being smitten by the spirit of modernity. I suggest that there is cause to be far more critical in sorting out some of the underlying implications of this shift from nature to history. One cannot help but wonder whether they may not have rejected too much. After all, there were some things which the Greeks had right.

One of these, I contend, is the structure of ethical language. They talked about ethics in terms of character and virtues. Theologies rooted in history have not been successful in providing a legitimate basis for ethics, and consequently are unable to propose a meaningful ethical language. The wholesale rejection of "being theology" has had the impact of relegating ethical discussion to relational ethics and values language, which cannot be the basis for Christian ethics. If we are unable to find a way of talking about who we are and what obligations are derived from our being Christian people, and if we are only able to speak about where we want to go on the basis of where we have come from, or even on the basis of what God is doing, Christian ethics remains hopeless. It may well have been quite legitimate to reject some of the traditional divine metaphors of independence and dominance, but if compassion, suffering and pathos are not grounded in the reality of being—God's and ours—then it turns out to be merely another way of telling the story. It should therefore not be surprising to us that this significant convergence of God-metaphors has met with uncharacteristic resolve to avoid explicit talk about ethics altogether.

To identify the route through this problem, two important concepts are in need of discussion: freedom and power. Both are basic to the discussion of ethics and theology. Both are especially important for our discussion of Christian pacifism. These are not the only notions in need of further clarification but they are two important ones around which much of the confusion revolves.

There are two reasons why we might begin here. First, whenever these two concepts are uncritically viewed from either the perspective of history or of nature, it becomes impossible to understand the biblical God and the Christian life properly. God's freedom and ours become meaningless if we see freedom simply as the unimpeded ability to act. Terence Fretheim, an Old

Testament scholar, puts it this way: "As in any relationship of integrity, God will have to give up some things for the sake of the relationship. Thus, God will have to give up some freedom. Any commitment or promise within a relationship entails a limitation of freedom."[36] Further, in dialogue with Walter Brueggemann's contention that the power of God is not "contained in the best assessment of worldly possibility," Fretheim contends that "God cannot use power in such a way as to violate a promise God has made; that would mean unfaithfulness."[37]

Second, this reinterpretation of God-talk sometimes sounds like God is being made subject to our limited understanding. To suggest that God can no longer be seen as free or that it is false to see God as omnipotent raises the question of whether this whole effort is not mere hubris from the start. It becomes very important that we clarify in what sense it is meaningful to speak about power and freedom regarding both God and human beings. After all, if the primordiality of God as the source and ground of all life and meaning is not fundamentally guaranteed, then the whole discussion of the relationship between theology and Christian ethics becomes misguided and superfluous.

Freedom and Power

Succinctly stated, the problem of freedom is this: On the one hand, freedom on the historical model is understood almost entirely as freedom to choose how to act. On this view, we think of freedom as the unrestricted ability to decide. We are seen as unfree insofar as we are under the "power" of others or even of our own history. On the other hand, freedom on the nature model implies divine unrelatedness to this world. Both views are fundamentally problematic for God and Christian ethics. The above contemporary theologians are quite right in rejecting the latter, but they are wrong in their uncritical embrace of the former.

---

[36]Terence Fretheim, *The Suffering of God*, 36.
[37]Ibid., 72.

Similar comments can be made about power. Power is today understood primarily on the historical model. It is interesting that Plato's definition of power as being[38] is hardly even intelligible to the modern mind. We like to think that the ones who can control history are the powerful ones. Those who cannot, lack power. When we act and bring something about, we have power. Power is dominance and control. Power is effectiveness. Given the obvious problems this view of power poses for Christian ethics, some think it necessary to talk about Christian faithfulness in the language of powerlessness.[39] But this brings with it its own set of problems. True powerlessness is death.

Both freedom and power must be reconceived from the standpoint of proper Christian theology. Character language, qualifying both God and us, is helpful at this point.

We need to distinguish between two ways of talking about freedom: linear freedom and character freedom. To talk of freedom only in the context of acts and decisions means that we understand ourselves (and God) as free to the extent that nothing inhibits us (and God) from doing what we want to do. But to state it this way is to think of freedom as a linear connection of events which are freely ours (or God's) only in the sense that they emanate from our (or God's) will. On this view, our actions determine our being and nothing but the desire of the self determines our actions. This view enslaves us to the "passions of the flesh." This is the very opposite of the way the writer to Galatians, for example, conceives of freedom.

Character freedom speaks about freedom quite differently. Its context is that of being a self, or having a character. It prescribes a boundary to freedom, namely character.[40] Hence, if one is an honest person, one is no longer free to lie. If one is a

---

[38]See Plato, "Sophist," in *The Dialogues of Plato*, vol II, trans. B. Jowett (New York, NY: Random House, 1937), where he says "I hold that the definition of being is simply power," 255.

[39]See for example, John Howard Yoder's *The Politics of Jesus* (Grand Rapids, MI: Eerdmans Publishing Company, 1972), 244 *et passim*. It should be said in fairness to Yoder that his later writings, for example, *The Priestly Kingdom* address the issue of power quite differently.

[40]For a helpful study of the relationship of freedom and character see Stanley Hauerwas, *The Peaceable Kingdom: A Primer in Christian Ethics* (Notre Dame, IN: University of Notre Dame Press, 1983), 35-49.

pacifist, one is not free to go to war. One has, in effect, surrendered one's (linear) freedom to tell lies and go to war. But the reason we are willing to make such sacrifices is because we have faith that in doing so we will gain and maintain (character) freedom. One believes in the goodness of certain virtues. Of course, if one had no such faith, one would see freedom only in the linear sense. This approach assumes that one's being determines one's actions and that one's being is shaped by one's moral/religious commitment and training.

To think of God as a free moral agent in the linear freedom sense is problematic. It means that very little can be said about the content of God's acts, other than that God has acted in the past and that God continues to act. There is nothing which guarantees that God might not choose to act differently the next time around. To speak of God as acting freely in the character sense is quite different. Now God is self-bound to God's character. To understand God as free in this sense means that we look for patterns of consistency in God's actions. We try to understand God precisely by what God is bound to: God's faithfulness, steadfastness and predictability and these qualities are all in tension with linear freedom. It means further that now we must sort out what acts fall outside the parameters of core divine virtues; that is, which acts commonly ascribed to God are "out of character" or not really God's acts.

For ethics to be Christian, Jesus must be seen as the central figure in shaping our understanding of the character of God. Since Jesus shows us the moral character of God, we must reconstruct our understanding of the story of God's acts from the standpoint of the character of Jesus.

This is not to suggest that we begin this process from scratch, ignoring the story of God's acts prior to Jesus. The story of Jesus told in this way makes no sense. The story of Jesus has meaning only within the story of the children of Israel. But that does mean that, since we confess Jesus as the Christ, the way Jesus portrays life and its failings—how Jesus deals with human sin—is God's way of doing so. On this basis divine-human-moral-discontinuity-pacifism is no longer tenable. Now the rationale for our pacifism is rooted in the very character of God.

We need to be careful to interpret this properly. The

temptation is to understand moral continuity on the historical model which would suggest that we should simply imitate the acts of God. But this is the very sin of the Fall in Genesis. The narrative-character approach sees it quite differently. Here the continuity is not act-continuity but character-continuity. This way of putting it is consistent with the multiple biblical imagery: "put on the whole armour of God" (Ephesians 6:11), "be ye perfect as your heavenly Father is perfect" (Matthew 5:48), "you shall be holy, for I am holy" (1 Peter 1:16; Leviticus 19:2).[41] It is not necessarily Christian to do what God does. The very content of our actions is to emanate from the virtues of God which we are called to make our own.

Similarly, we need to distinguish between two kinds of power: linear power and character power. Power is normally seen as the capacity to bring about change. But how change is brought about defines the nature of the power used. The character of the biblical God seems more concerned about *how* change occurs than *that* it occurs. False power can bring death, while true power can bring life.

Linear power is the capacity to bring about change through creating an influence, exerting a force, through manipulation and dominance. Bernard Loomer says of this form of power that it is "thoroughly masculine in character."[42] On this model, being influenced by someone or something outside oneself is seen as weakness. Dependency is seen as a threat to one's personal being and integrity. Hence relationships where dominance is always the core objective inevitably lead to conflict. When control is good and dependence is weakness, then estrangement and conflict are inevitable.

Character power is the capacity to bring about change by representing moral truth in one's being. The preoccupation with

---

[41]Many additional biblical references to "imitating" the character, or virtues, of God can be found. *Inter alia*, ". . . forgiving one another as God in Christ forgave you" (Ephesians 4:32); "Be merciful, even as your Father is merciful" (Luke 6:36); ". . . should not you have had mercy on your fellow servant, as I had mercy on you?" (Matthew 19:32); "Beloved, if God so loved us, we also ought to love one another" (1 John 4:11). For a helpful discussion of this theme see Yoder, *The Politics of Jesus*, 116-120.

[42]Bernard Loomer, "Two Conceptions of Power," *Process Studies* 6 (Spring 1976): 9.

direct agency gives way to a concern for the proper embodiment of truth. It does not follow from this that one does not want change to occur, but rather that one believes that unless power is based on truth, the change it brings about is not redemptive. On this model, we can simultaneously sacrifice consequences and be assured of moral outcome.[43]

Character power sees the individual as a communal self, created in the context of interaction with other selves. It is at once an openness to others and a capacity to sustain close relationships with others. It is the power of being present to one another. It is based on the belief that only truth will triumph and that its embodiment in moral character is its power.

The modern autonomous God of history and the traditional omnipotent God of being, are both not large enough to merit our faith and devotion. The suffering servant God of Jesus Christ—the one who comes to us in forgiveness and compassion; the one who is willing to accept defeat at the cross instead of loss of character; the one who defencelessly embodies agape in a sinful and hostile world; the one who gives life freely; the one who exercises power for others redemptively—this one is the God who has power to save us from death.[44] By embracing the openness to have our being shaped by this character, we risk the encounter of real power and freedom.

Herein also lies the clue for our understanding of Christian pacifism. We are pacifists not merely because we are told to be so by one whom we claim as Lord, but because our Lord shows us the being of God—one who wills to rule the world via the cross. The cross is not an accident of history. It is the expected

---

[43]Loomer identifies the second form of power as "relational power." Much of what he says here is convincing, but I do not believe, given his heavy reliance upon process thought, that he is successful in giving Christian content to the concept of power. He fails to take Jesus seriously precisely at this point. His source is "relational" instead of christological. Because of this, "relational power" is that power which allows us to bring about all those things which we want without the employ of linear power. Character power is not like that. It is willing to sacrifice those things which cannot be brought about without violation of character.

[44]A helpful discussion of God in similar language can be found in Hendrikus Berkhof, *Christian Faith: An Introduction to the Study of the Faith* (Grand Rapids, MI: Eerdmans Publishing Company, 1979). See especially his section under "God" entitled "The Defenceless Superior Power," 133-140.

consequent of the defenceless and agape God meeting human selfishness and *Angst*. But this embodiment of the source of life itself cannot be destroyed. It arises again and again in new life forms to be ever present to sin and hostility, until all evil is overcome.

Conclusion

I want to be totally clear on what my argument has been and what it implies concretely for the theological community called church. I have argued that Christian pacifism is untenable when based on a theology of history or a theology of nature. Both drive a wedge between the way of Jesus and the way of God; the former by misinterpreting freedom, God's and ours, and the latter by presupposing a false metaphysical dualism. In response, I have tried to show that the defenceless, suffering Christ of the gospels is the embodiment of the character of God. To establish this claim is to undercut the most basic of all theological arguments against Christian pacifism, namely, that the way of Jesus is but one way of God, among others. To accept the moral continuity of God and Christ is to accept the truth of the singularity of the nonviolent way of God revealed through Jesus Christ. Hence, pacifism can be believed, it works and is life sustaining, because it is rooted in the ontological source of life itself.

The biblical story tells us that God wills to rule the world through the servant community. We, along with our Anabaptist forebears, still find it tempting to empower God to rule the Christian community in love and the world by an "out of character" dominant power, because we find it so hard to believe that the defencelessness of Jesus shows us the character of God. To accept servanthood as a real power, or better, as ultimate power, is very difficult. This way of understanding God and pacifism has some concrete implications for how we conceive of the church. First, it permits us to understand the church as the body incarnate whose primary task is to be what it professes to be. Hence, our task is not first of all to accomplish some goal; our task is rather to keep our identity from being eroded into something other than our true identity as the body of Christ. We are called to embody the truth of God's character in a sinful and hostile world. This is our power. In the words of Stanley Hauerwas, the "task of the church is to be the church."[45] We are challenged to be peacemakers as God is peacemaker by taking up the defenceless posture of representing the character of love and compassion to those around us. Since the power of God's being is ultimate power, the quest towards its embodiment is the ultimate honour and task of the church.

Second, it points us in the direction which helps us remain faithful in our call. Our primary resource is the text, and our commitment is our attachment to the text. Our modern imagination tempts us into thinking that being the church means being true to our own selves. This is a profound mistake. For the church to be the church, we must bind ourselves to the story which gives meaning to "following after Jesus." Lindbeck is right in suggesting that "intratextuality" is the post-modern answer to the problematic autonomy of modern liberalism.[46] To come to know the true character of God, we must read and re-read the story in which God is the central character.

But intratextuality is not only the epistemological answer, it is also the ethical answer. Learning to know the God of the biblical text is ultimately a matter of acquiring both the linguistic and the moral skills appropriate to the life ruled by God. This is not easy. It requires commitment and persistent learning. It requires the discipline of character training according to the Christian virtues. It requires nothing less than the faithfulness of the community called church which alone can muster the theological-moral acumen of avoiding canonical syncretism on the one hand, which, at best, allows for a comprehensive telling of the story, and using selective eisegesis on the other hand, which can build whatever case it wishes on the basis of particular interests brought to the text.[47]

---

[45]Stanley Hauerwas, *The Peaceable Kingdom*, 99.

[46]George Lindbeck, *The Nature of Theology*, 113ff.

[47]The limits of this paper prohibit me from addressing this matter of the relationship of biblical text to faithful community, but a few words must be said. I both agree and disagree with the "canonical critics" like Brevard Childs and James A. Sanders on the matter of biblical interpretation. (See also Waldemar Janzen's article "A Canonical Rethinking of the Anabaptist-Mennonite New Testament Orientation," supra 90). I agree with Janzen's concern for finding

Some may still wonder how such an apparently sectarian view of the church can provide a serious answer to the social ills of the world. The charge of sectarianism is still all too prevalent, yet it is made from a highly selective viewpoint. I have tried to show that Christian pacifism is not merely good for those who accept the full teachings of the man from Galilee, but it is good for all, because the man from Galilee has shown us what is good according to God's definition of goodness. The God of Jesus Christ is the God of all peoples. It is therefore the mainline ethicists' position, not ours, which is truly sectarian, since the former argues that the ethic of the man from Galilee only sometimes applies as a criterion of human conduct. An ethic rooted in God cannot be sectarian.

Compassion and peace are no less apropos to conflicts of the Middle East and the inner city than to disciples in the congregation. The disciple's task is to work at giving true expression to the grace which culminated in the cross. If there is any truth in the efforts of the disciples who bind themselves to the text and to one another in worship and training, praise be to God. Then we may pray in word and life:

Thy Kingdom come
Thy will be done
On earth as it is in heaven.

---

models that help us understand continuity between the two testaments of the canon. Nevertheless, I find his recourse to "canonical criticism" in establishing this claim unconvincing. An approach characterized by "interfacing and dialogue between texts" (supra 112) and as one in which we "should consider all themes within the boundaries of the whole canon and discern with respect to each theme where the most important biblical treatments affecting it can be found" (supra 107) is problematic unless the church, which must remain the interpreting community, is permitted to violate this very principle. The Bible cannot read itself, and it is not canon until it is read by a faithful community. Hence how it is read must at least to some degree be determined by that community. When the text is left to interpret itself, or when its checks are merely other parts of the same text, then we are in danger of "democratizing" its truth at the expense of depreciating its power in forming a community capable of being the church. "Canonical criticism" is therefore in danger of becoming "canonical syncretism," where every story or part of a text is read with equal normativity. If the story of Jesus cannot function as "an internal norm having priority" (supra 108), as Janzen says no text can, then it is difficult to see how even the Old Testament can have normativity for Christians. We need to remind ourselves that Jesus read the scriptures through normative-critical eyes. This is what gave him the basis for a critique of tradition.

VI. Practical Theology

Peter C. Erb[*]

TRADITIONAL SPIRITUALITY AND MENNONITE LIFE[**]

Within the last fifteen years spirituality has become a popular concern for Mennonites. It was little known in our circles before the mid-1970s, but by the early 1980s there were few Mennonite church colleges or seminaries in North America which were not developing programs in spiritual formation, wooing some ever-in-demand lecturer on breathing exercises or packing off a recalcitrant faculty member to a weekend Jesuit retreat. Nor has interest in the topic been limited to academic settings. Among conference and local church leaders and within Mennonite congregations the last decade has witnessed a steady growth in the formation of groups and structures devoted to the nurturing of prayer life and other aspects of spirituality. Also, more and more individuals have taken up the topic for personal study and meditation.

However one chooses to characterize this interest among Mennonites (and Mennonites are not atypical in this respect), two initial problems must be treated. The first concerns the definition of the term, spirituality; the second, has to do with implications for Mennonite polity and theology which result from the introduction of traditional spiritual concerns into the Mennonite community. Unless some clarity is reached on these two issues, the contemporary interest in spirituality will per-petuate confusions, already threatening to destroy the ends which those interested in reaffirming the spiritual life among Men-nonites are seeking. This essay endeavours to clarify the nature of this seeming threat to our polity and theology and, by

[*]Peter C. Erb is Professor of Religion and Culture at Wilfrid Laurier University in Waterloo, Ontario.

[**]The author would like to thank Sig Polle, Assistant Professor of Practical Theology, Canadian Mennonite Bible College, Winnipeg, Manitoba, and Peter Pauls, Professor of English, University of Winnipeg, Winnipeg, Manitoba, for their critical responses to this essay at the Symposium.

reflecting on the definition of the term "spirituality" suggests some directions for overcoming this threat while strengthening the central elements of the Mennonite faith itself.[1]

Dangers in Recovering the Spiritual Tradition

It may be useful to begin our discussion, in the fashion of the legendary Oxford philosopher, with an imaginary concrete example. An MDiv (Master of Divinity graduate) arrives fresh from northern Indiana as pastor to the Inkermann Mennonite church. He ranked first in the "Celebrating Spiritual Disciplines" seminar. On his arrival in the new congregation he forms a spirituality group and encourages individuals to meditate daily. Within months some members of the group are relaxing the tumult of their lives at will, praying at regular intervals, meditating on the scriptures, attending retreats and reading a plethora of texts from Loyola's *Spiritual Exercises* and anything by Thomas Merton to made-for-the-trade Jungian self-help guides and rabid Matthew Fox ramblings.

Our hypothetical MDiv has also graduated at the head of his Clinical Pastoral Training class and is able to meet the needs of group members suffering from serious psychological and social difficulties. Further, the Inkermann group is composed of mature individuals who are genuinely seeking a deeper spiritual life and are filled with a healthy humility and sensitivity towards their co-believers who remain outside of their small group. But within a week of the establishment of the group, perceptions in the congregation have changed. One does not need to be a specialist in the sociology of knowledge to recognize that to define one group or even one person within a larger body as having special interest in spirituality, implicitly defines those who remain outside that group (in spite of the best intentions of those within

---

[1]For the purposes of this essay, I set aside the extensive difficulties in defining "Mennonite" and treat only three Mennonite themes: baptism, the active expression of love for others in the name of Christ and the peace concern which includes this expression. Underlying the central thesis is a radically enlarged theology of the Lord's Supper, the nature of the Church and her tradition which requires further expansion.

it) as, at the least, less interested in spiritual life, and, at the worst, spiritually dead. To a large degree our Inkermann group repeats the Pietist problem in which the reborn reduced the definition of piety to active membership in conventicles and implicitly forced a distinction between true over-against hypocritical Christians.[2]

But the dualistic result is only part of the problem. The Inkermann spirituality group works essentially outside of the Mennonite tradition. Its resource books are written by non-Christians or by Christians whose primary intent in writing is to compile psychological or self-help guides. As such much of the literature is directed first to the individual and only thereafter to the community. The essence of spirituality in this sense is found in the mystical path of "the alone to the Alone" and communal prayer comes to be understood as the sum of the individuals involved in it rather than as a whole in which the individuals are subsumed. Moreover, when explicitly traditional Christian books are used, they are taken from varying traditions and the theological implications are seldom considered. The result is a highly diverse theological syncretism whose well-polished surface reflects only the hoped-for coherence and unity in the faces of all who look admiringly upon it. Almost inevitably our Inkermann group falls into a simplistic ecumenism, according to which it groups all spiritual texts together as one and posits a true, spiritual Christianity as reflected in groups like itself throughout all ages and denominations.[3] And inevitably the group reshapes traditional Mennonite concerns according to its new models.

The Inkermann group is nevertheless Mennonite. Its members have a strong sense of their Mennonite identity and history. They do not wish to lose the great wealth which their tradition has bequeathed to them and other Christians through them. As typical Mennonites they seek, then, to "return" to their past, searching for a lost resource in '60s concerns, '50s visions,

---

[2]For details and bibliography on this common Pietist pattern see the introduction to my *Pietists* (New York, NY: Paulist Press, 1983).

[3]The Pietist, Gottfried Arnold, in particular, developed this type of ecumenism to the fullest. See my *Pietists, Protestants, and Mysticism: The Use of Late Medieval Texts in the Work of Gottfried Arnold* (Metuchen, NJ: Scarecrow Press, 1989) for details.

eighteenth-century pietism, and, above all, the certain truth of original sixteenth-century Anabaptist spirituality (which must, of course, first be rediscovered). And when all this fails, there is yet another hope, still based on the return model—a return to the traditional spirituality of the Catholic Middle Ages.

The Problem of Return

For Mennonites, the "return" model is a common one. We supposedly returned to the New Testament church in the sixteenth century, and to the true pattern of sixteenth-century Anabaptist communities in the twentieth. But such returns, although profiting us much in some cases, can also limit our religious life in others. We cannot now expect that a sudden concern to recover a lost spiritual tradition will improve the situation. Such a concern will simply place a group of specialists in medieval, baroque Catholic or Pietist spirituality beside the specialists in biblical and archaic Anabaptist texts which we have produced with our other model, and perpetuate another form of scholastic authoritarianism within our hoped-for egalitarian community. By doing this we will simply continue the practice of making our historians our theologians. To replace bishops with antiquarians is as dangerous an action as to replace pastors with therapists; it is in effect to remove comely theology from the chatter of the marketplace and force her to market her adorned beauty in popular kingly courts.

And there is yet a greater problem. All "return" talk is caught up in the supposition that human life has been essentially permanent throughout history, and that all first- or sixteenth-century texts can be applied simply to twentieth-century situations with only a minimum of interpretation. Pietism, for example, was fitted for a household economy before the industrial and post-industrial revolutions. Its approaches can no more be rejected over against Anabaptism (existing in yet another type of socioeconomic structure) as Friedmann attempted,[4] nor accepted as in some form consistent with it. And

---

[4]See Robert Friedmann, *Mennonite Piety through the Centuries* (Goshen, IN:

the readers of T.S. Eliot's *Four Quartets*, revelling in the rhythms of:

> Sin is behovely but
> All shall be well, and
> All manner of thing shall be well[5]

do not return to Julian of Norwich and 1393. To thrill to her language in the late twentieth century is not to dwell with her as a fourteenth-century anchoress, enclosed in a cell on a church wall and communicating only through an iron grid.[6]

"Return" is an historical term, often bound together with recovery language. We return to a previous place or we attempt to recover something of a lost past, too often ignoring the full dimensions of the spiritual state of both the recoverer and the thing to be recovered. The daily prayer patterns established in pre-capitalist medieval or pre-industrialist Pietist spirituality are often initially attractive, but they were shaped by and served to support a socioeconomic reality much different from our own. If imported unreflectively such patterns will buttress sociopolitical, theological and spiritual worldviews at variance with those which we as importers might think we are supporting. A spiritual action may be fitting in one instance and totally out of place in another, in which case, if thoughtlessly introduced, it can destroy with viral intensity the system intended for renewal. For Mennonites the individualistic directions of some aspects of medieval and pietist material, broken away from the highly communal structures in which they are developed and practised, can be particularly problematic.

There is a final problem with the "return" model: such language supposes that there is a singular object to which a return can be made. In the case of spirituality, as the term is popularly used, nothing could be further from the truth. The use of the term in the singular inevitably leads to confusion. We

---

Mennonite Historical Society, 1949).

[5]T.S. Eliot, "Little Gidding," in *Four Quartets* (London: Faber and Faber, 1963), 166-168.

[6]See Julian of Norwich, *Showings*, trans. Edmund Colledge and James Walsh (New York, NY: Paulist Press, 1978).

must learn to speak of spiritualities, rather than spirituality. Even with a limiting adjective, medieval spirituality, for example, it exists only as a generic term. As such it binds together so many disparate figures that to speak of a return to medieval spirituality is to return to at least a dozen distinctive groups, characterized by such peculiar figures as the libidinous Peter Abelard, the erratic Joachim of Flora, the dumb-ox Thomas Aquinas and the near-heretical Margery Kempe. Even a term like Rhenish mysticism does great disservice to the philosophic complexities of an Eckhart, the moral intensity of a Tauler and the courtly sensitivity of a Seuse.

Re-forming our Definitions

Problems inherent in return language are not only those of our Mennonite tradition. They have been with Christianity from the earliest centuries. But along with return language Christianity has also developed a language of reform.[7] Return focuses on the past as origin; reform on the past as development. Return theologies must thus trust the truth of the origin—in Christianity's case, of the New Testament church, of the verbal accuracy of the New Testament documents or of the findings of New Testament scholars. To reform is to shape the present in light of the past. With the attention thus off the past as point of origin, reform theologies must trust tradition. Return presupposes the possibility of a renewal; reform attends not to the recovery of an earlier element into the present but to the practical restructuring of the present *in line with* the direction of

---

[7]On the use of "reform" and "return" in early Christianity, see especially the classic work by Gerhart B. Ladner, *The Idea of Reform* (New York, NY: Harper and Row, 1967). The meanings given to the terms in the discussion which follows owe much to Tübingen theology as developed in the early nineteenth century by Johann Adam Möhler and Johannes Kuhn. Cf. Walter Kasper, "Vertsändnis der Theologie damals und heute," in *Glaube im Wandel der Geschichte* (Mainz: Matthias Gruenewald, 1973), 9-38, and John Henry Newman, *An Essay on the Development of Christian Doctrine: The Edition of 1845*, ed. J.M. Cameron (Harmondsworth: Penguin, 1974). It is in this context that my comments on memory and tradition in "A Patristic and Medieval Perspective on the Nurturing of Faith," in *Perspectives in the Nurturing of the Faith*, ed. Leland Harder (Elkhart, IN: Institute of Mennonite Studies, 1983), 91-127 are to be interpreted.

the tradition, but not *the same as* one part of that tradition. An individual can return to a specific point; it takes two individuals, a community, to reform. Return must posit a single past and perfect Archimedean point; for return the present is always wrong. Reform, on the other hand, while acknowledging its sinful present, cannot accept as realistic that there was ever a pure point in human history, untouched by the original fall. With gnostic certainty, return can thus exist by teaching the salvific truth of a completed story of past events, whereas reform must remain satisfied by passing on in faith a yet uncompleted tradition.

Reform rejects nothing but works out of its present. It therefore requires a practical understanding of its present and a detailed knowledge of the whole of its past. It lives with probabilities, not necessities, since the past, according to which it makes its judgements, is so large that it cannot ever hope to portray it precisely and act with according precision. It does not believe that one can ever know how something actually happened (in this sense it is ahistorical, upholding tradition over history), trusting itself to be continuous with the tradition. Reform then allows the possibility of accepting all parts of the tradition, even those which are discontinuous, and of asking and receiving communal forgiveness for them.

For Mennonites such a view of reform means that we can look at a past greater than the Anabaptist, not leaving that past and at the same time not running away from the present into a rural or medieval Shangrala. To reform is to enlarge perspectives, to accept a real development of doctrine. To treat "Traditional Spirituality and Mennonite Life" then is to treat the reform of spirituality within, not aside from, a Mennonite context. But the question remains, "Where to begin?" and the most useful beginning appears to be a definition of spirituality.

Defining Spirituality

Over the past two decades the use of the term spirituality has grown ever more opaque. It is now used in such a broad sense that it refers to some unknowable, unquantifiable quality, inspiring or directing any individual or group, or characterizing that group's or individual's identity. And when the term is limited to a religious and, more particularly, Christian setting, it is usually understood within one of two frameworks. In the first, it refers almost exclusively to religious experience, descriptions of such experience and prescriptions for its achievement. In a second, closely-related sense, it refers to aspects of what has traditionally been called spiritual formation. In this case it is generally understood in some way or other within a psychological context and, thus, as a mode of Christian psychotherapy.

An initial foray into the literature on spirituality suggests that the definitional problem can be easily solved. The most recent attempt at a full history of spirituality, for example, opens as follows:

> Christian spirituality (or any other spirituality) is distinguished from dogma by the fact that, instead of studying or describing the objects of belief as if it were in the abstract, it studies the reactions which these objects arouse in the religious consciousness. . . . We still need to indicate the place of spiritual theology in relation to moral theology. . . . It is not by its concern with perfection that spirituality is to be distinguished from morality. But while the latter examines all human actions in relation to their ultimate end, whether this reference be explicit or not, spirituality concentrates on those in which the reference to God is not only explicit but immediate. It concentrates, that is, above all, on prayer and on everything connected with prayer in the ascetical and mystical life—in other words, on religious exercises as well as on religious experience.[8]

This definition follows in large part that of earlier ones[9] and is often repeated.[10]

But even this definition proves inadequate since the word "prayer" is often unduly limited in modern usage to petitionary

---

[8]Louis Bouyer, *The Spirituality of the New Testament and the Early Fathers*, trans. Mary P. Ryan (New York, NY: Desclee Press, 1963), vi-ix.

[9]P. Pourrat, *Christian Spirituality*, trans. W.H. Mitchell and S.P. Jacques (London: Burns, Oates and Washbourne, 1922), I, v.

[10]See Louis Bouyer, *Introduction to Spirituality*, trans. Mary P. Ryan (New York, NY: Desclee Press, 1961).

or other statements directed immediately to the Divine and to the ritual settings or practices of such statements rather than to the central motivating source of the prayer life proper. For spirituality finally does not define the many surface forms: routine daily prayer, liturgical acts, meditational practice or fasting. Indeed, even the much discussed interior journey and the quest for mystical union—the pattern which tends to be understood as primary in contemporary spiritual texts—is also only a form. The underlying structure and motivating force of the spiritual life lies deeper. According to the Christian tradition spirituality arises out of the endeavour to fulfill the greatest of all the commandments, namely, "to love God with all one's heart and mind and strength and soul and one's neighbour as oneself." This commandment to love is the "one thing necessary," the *unum necessarium* for which Christ praised Mary in Luke 10:42. From the late patristic period until well into the twentieth century it was this text which provided the biblical basis for all discussions regarding what we today refer to as spirituality. It is thus to this text that we must now direct our attention.

Spirituality and the "One Thing Necessary"

Spirituality is the "one thing necessary," but how are we to understand this "one thing?" The practice of contemporary critics has been to treat separately Luke's great interpolation in chapter 10 which includes both the Good Samaritan and the Martha-Mary stories. There is, however, strong evidence in the manuscripts and in the structure of Luke's narrative that the two stories must be interpreted together with the lawyer's question which initiates the parable of the Good Samaritan.[11]

At the opening of the section, the lawyer asks: "What must I do to inherit eternal life?" The answer has two parts. What must be done to live (note the change of direction from the lawyer's "inherit eternal life") is, first, to love God with all heart,

---

[11]For a full discussion of the textual problem in Luke 10:42, see my "The Contemplative Life as *Unum Necessarium*: In Defense of a Traditional Reading of Luke 10:42," *Mystics Quarterly* 11 (1985), 161-164.

soul, mind and strength and second, to love neighbour as self. The lawyer has fully understood that to gain eternal life he must follow both commandments. Continuing his test of Jesus, he now asks for a definition of neighbour, avoiding the broader implications of the first commandment by focusing on the second. In answer Jesus tells the story of the Samaritan and presents the admonition, "Go and do likewise" (Luke 10:37). Immediately thereafter the group is "in the going" and the enactment of the message of the Good Samaritan is first carried out by Martha.

The Samaritan's and Martha's actions are directed toward the love of neighbour for God's sake, but what of the first commandment, to love the Lord with all heart, strength, mind and soul? The Martha-Mary story functions to explain this commandment in greater detail. The first is, after all, the first; it is first in importance as well as the first stated. The message which comes to Mary is that she has chosen the better part, the love of the Lord, which is the first commandment. The second, that applied by Martha, is to play a secondary role. It is not that few things are necessary or one, but that one thing is necessary, namely the love of the one God.

The suggestion that the Martha-Mary story is to explain in greater detail the first commandment is supported by the chiastic "a, b, b, a" structure of: statement of first commandment (a), statement of second commandment (b), narrative regarding second commandment (b), narrative regarding first commandment (a). The chiasmus[12] emphasizes the union of the two passages and makes Mary's love of Jesus parallel to the love of God.

If one accepts this reading, the traditional interpretation is eminently sensible: that the "one thing necessary" is the life of contemplative prayer, the highest point in the love of God. Indeed, one could make the claim that it is fully in keeping with Luke's intention in positioning the great interpolation between

---

[12]Cf. Charles H. Talbert, *Reading Luke: A Literary and Theological Commentary on the Third Gospel* (New York, NY: Crossroad, 1982), 120-26. On recent treatments of Luke's conscious literary practice see W. Bruners, "Lukas: Literat und Theolog," *Bibel und Kirche* 35 (1980): 110-12. On the passage of scripture here under discussion see H. Servotte and L. Verbeek, "De structuralistische Bijbellezing," *Collationes* 26 (1980): 426-41.

the lawyer's question and the giving of the Lord's Prayer in the section immediately following in chapter 11.

Even more significantly, however, one can move from this interpretation to supporting the traditional christological reading of the Samaritan story as upheld by the great contemplative writers. If the parallel is made between Jesus and the Lord of the first commandment in the Martha-Mary story, it is probable that a similar parallel was intended by Luke in the earlier story and that the Samaritan can be interpreted as being Jesus.[13]

"Spirituality" and "spiritual," then, are properly used to describe all forms of the Christian life, individual and social, which are directly related to the fulfillment of the greatest commandment as enunciated by Jesus in Luke 10, namely, both the love of God and the love of neighbour for God's sake; the "for God's sake" is added in this shortened version of the commandment to emphasize both the unity of the two loves and the primacy of the first. This commandment unifies as a result what have commonly been referred to as the contemplative and the active lives; the love of God is, in the Christian tradition, not set over against the love of neighbour, as has sometimes been suggested.

Significantly, the traditional exegesis of the Lucan passage, suggesting as it does a link between the Samaritan and Christ, functions rhetorically (rhetoric in this sense is truer than the literal meaning) to link Jesus with God, the God who is to be loved with all one's heart, soul, mind and strength. The divinity loved by the one necessary act of Mary is the human Jesus of Nazareth. Chalcedon is thus present in the first century as is Nicaea: the Jesus loved by Mary in the final section is the God who is first to be loved above all else in the first section of the Commandment—the Son is the same as (*homoousios*) the Father. And it is the mutual interpenetration of these two which proceed as Spirit in the heart of Mary back to the divinity out of which they arose.

What this key text for understanding spirituality implies, then, is the doctrine of the Trinity, the fullness and integrity of

---

[13]On recent treatments of the christological interpretation of the Samaritan see A. Feuillet, "Le bon samaritan," *Esprit et vie* 90 (1980): 337-51; 369-82.

God who is Love, in whom the creative, redemptive and vivifying functions coinhere each in the other as the three Persons of the Trinity coinhere.[14] There is in this sense a natural relationship between the study of spirituality and the explication of the Christian mystery of the Trinity. Before one can pursue the relationship between "traditional spirituality" (as understood in its relationship to the command to love) and Mennonite life (in which the command to love has played and continues to play so central a role) it is necessary to treat, albeit only in brief, the trinitarian structure of the spiritual life as consistently developed by the spiritual masters of the West.

Spirituality and the Trinitarian Love of God

From the time of Augustine the treatment of the spiritual life, love and the Trinity are bound together in a unity which is maintained by most spiritual writers until the close of the Middle Ages, but which begins to fade from explicit treatment after the fifteenth century.[15] Perhaps the most comprehensive use of the theme of the Trinity in a spiritual writer occurs in the case of the Flemish master, Jan van Ruusbroec,[16] although after Augustine and the pseudo-Dionysian writings, it was widely promulgated by the twelfth-century Cistercians,[17] and most elegantly presented for English-speaking readers in the *Showings* of Julian of Norwich.

From all eternity God the Father begets the Son as the perfect Image of God. As Image the Son is distinct from the Father and as an image the Son is bound to the Father by the image's likeness to its original. As perfect Image the likeness is

---

[14]On the doctrine of coinherence (or *perichoresis*) see G.L. Prestige, *God in Patristic Thought* (London: SPCK, 1952), 282ff.

[15]On the modern study of trinitarian theology see Karl Rahner, *The Trinity*, trans. Joseph Donceel (London: Burns and Oates, 1970), 9-15.

[16]See especially Albin Ampe, *De Grundlijnen van Ruusbroec's Drieëenheitsleer* (Tielt: Lannoo, 1950).

[17]For a good introduction to the image/likeness theme in Cistercian piety see David N. Bell, *Image and Likeness: The Augustinian Spirituality of William of St. Thierry* (Kalamazoo, MI: Cistercian Publications, 1984).

perfect and is therefore the Father while remaining separate as image. The doctrine of *homoousia* is thus supported. One may speak in this sense of the Father's begetting as the central divine act, the act of love, and the Son's return to the Father in likeness likewise as an act of love. This mutual act proceeds from both the Father and the Son (*filioque*) and as such is distinctive from them, hypostatized as a third person, the Holy Spirit, bound together with them as one.

God is, thus, love. As love, God begets the divine Image; as begotten love, God reflects perfect likeness in the Image; in the mutuality of these loves proceeds the very Spirit of the love itself. The Christian God is not, as a result, a static first mover at the temporal beginning of the world, but a continual pure act, characterized in its dynamism as creative love. As creative love it creates. The universe is created in seven days "at the beginning" and in seven days throughout history. (According to the Augustinian scheme, the sixth day, the day on which the old person was created, begins historically with the birth of the new person, Jesus the Christ.)

The temporal beginning *at which* the universe was created is the same beginning principle *in which* it was created. It is in this way that creation and redemption are bound together. The word by, in and through which the original creation took place is the Word which came to its own and redeemed its own. The revelation of God in Christ is a new creation, and when viewed from this redemptive aspect, the first creation can be understood as the first revelation. Just as there is distinction and unity in the Trinity, just as the separate persons coinhere in one another, so do their actions; each is distinct and each is the same.

The creative act of God reaches its height in the creation of the human person. Each individual is created "in the image and likeness of God." In the image, I bear a likeness to the trinitarian God and insofar as I am a likeness I am already returning to my Creator in a parallel fashion to the return of Christ to the Father. In the image the reflection of the likeness back on the original is, in all that it is, the very likeness, that is love. God is, after all, love. In the image of God I am formed as a "little trinity." I have memory by which I continually remem-

ber my origin, intellect by which I seek to know it as the highest
truth, and will by which I seek to love it as the highest good. As
trinity I am the speaker, the word and the power of my word. As
trinity I create (and destroy) by my word.

But as image I am already distinct from the Creator; as
creature I am already and always fallen. The very creation itself
is, in one sense, a going out, a distancing, a disobedience, a *felix
culpa*. This interpretation of the fall is best explained in the
well-known exemplum of the lord and the servant by the great
fourteenth-century English mystic, Julian of Norwich. As Julian
tells the story,

> The lord sits in state, in rest and in peace. The servant stands
> before his lord respectfully, ready to do his lord's will. The lord
> looks on the servant very lovingly and sweetly and mildly. He
> sends him to a certain place to do his will. Not only does the
> servant go, but he rushes off at great speed, loving to do his
> lord's will. And soon he falls into a dell and is greatly injured;
> and then he groans and moans and tosses about and writhes,
> but he cannot raise or help himself in any way. And in all this
> the greatest hurt which I saw him in was lack of consolation,
> for he could not turn his face to look on his loving lord, who
> was very close to him, in whom is all consolation; but like a
> man who was for the time extremely feeble and foolish, he
> paid heed to his feelings and his continuing distress.[18]

The servant who falls into the ditch and suffers therein, unable
to look upon the master's countenance, does so as the result of
an initial rushing out from the master in love and obedience,
seeking to do the master's will. The rushing out is the incarnation and redemption, but in it the fall is enacted:

> In the servant is comprehended the second person of the
> Trinity, and in the servant is comprehended Adam, that is to
> say, all men. . . . The Lord is God the Father, the servant is
> the Son, Jesus Christ, the Holy Spirit is the equal love which
> is in them both. When Adam fell, God's Son fell; because of
> the true union which was made in heaven, God's Son could
> not be separated from Adam, for by Adam I understand all
> mankind. Adam fell from life to death into the valley of this

---

[18]Julian of Norwich, *Showings*, 267.

wretched world, and after that into hell. God's Son fell with Adam, into the valley of the womb of the maiden who was the fairest daughter of Adam.[19]

For Julian, then, this rushing out is at the same time the redemption. The servant who rushes is the Son who falls into the hands of enemies and is raised up on the cross. In the old servant I fall; in the new servant I am raised up. I am in the image in both cases—one might say *simul justus et peccator* to turn the phrase to a non-Lutheran usage.

The word "in" in "in the image" has in its Greek and Latin forms the meaning "towards" (*eis, ad*). Insofar as I am in the Image of God, I have a likeness to the original; my likeness in itself is already a movement towards that image. I am not perfect act as is the Trinity, but as an image of the Trinity I am in movement, a potency to act, a being directed toward the fullness of its possibility as that possibility is portrayed in perfection of the incarnated Image of God, Jesus of Nazareth.

This is the framework in which the subject of perfection is understood in the definition of spirituality quoted above. This is the framework in which we are to understand both the imitation and the following of Christ.[20] Because the image is not mine (I am only insofar as I am in the image)[21] imitation of Christ is "not of oneself, lest anyone should boast; it is the gift of God" (Ephesians 2; the Protestant proof-text). Creation out of nothing itself in this sense is the first act of grace. The power by which the likeness returns me toward the image is likewise an act of grace, an act of grace which in the redeemed image reforms me, makes me right, justifies me by "faith, working through love" (Galatians 5; the Catholic proof-text).

---

[19]Ibid., 274.

[20]"The imitative life of Christ involves both God's activity, through the Spirit, in conforming man to His image in Christ (*conformitas*), and man's focusing of his moral and spiritual attention on the exemplar, Christ (*imitatio*)." See E.J. Tinsley, "Some Principles for Reconstructing a Doctrine of the Imitation of Christ," *Scottish Journal of Theology* 25 (February 1972): 47.

[21]"I am who I am, whereas you have no being at all of yourselves. What being you have is my doing." Catherine of Siena, *The Dialogue*, trans. Suzanne Noffke (New York, NY: Paulist Press, 1980), 56.

Spirituality and the Baptism of Adults

In this trinitarian base as established by traditional spirituality there are many implications for supporting and developing major themes in Mennonite life. First among these relates to baptism. Whatever our historical sources (whether we are the honourable children of properly mated Swiss parents or the illegitimate offspring of the promiscuous rabbles throughout Germany and the Lowlands) and whatever the aetiology of our peculiar doctrinal stance (it is of little practical interest whether the problem of the sword arose in the tradition early or late), the religious taxonomists of the sixteenth century classified us from the beginning as Anabaptists, those who re-baptized adults.

The question of baptism may appear initially to have nothing to do with spirituality, but for the traditional spiritual theology which we have outlined above, it is a central element, and is central precisely insofar as it is infant baptism. It would seem then that Mennonite life, especially in its insistence on adult baptism, must of necessity be opposed to traditional spirituality.

Within the trinitarian context outlined above, baptism is the first point in the movement of the likeness towards the divine. According to this schema the infant is baptized and at baptism is infused with the three theological virtues (faith, hope and charity) and the seven gifts of the Holy Spirit (after the Septuagint reading of Isaiah 11:2). As such, an indelible character is placed upon the child, by and according to which the child grows in the love of God. When this Christian child reaches an age of accountability, he or she is confirmed. Confirmation is tightly linked to baptism and both are inseparably tied to the spiritual life.

Such a model has been consistently opposed by Mennonites; or has it? In our more recent history we have moved toward the ritual of child dedication, accepting *sub voce* the child as a member of the body of Christ to be raised in the faith until the point at which the mature adult can take account of the situation.[22] The main practical ritualistic difference between the traditional position and the Mennonite position is that whereas the former places emphasis on the initial, unrequested grace, ours attends to the second ("ana"baptist still) act, stressing accountability and personal choice. Not surprisingly, as a result, we have been charged with maintaining a form of Pelagianism in our baptismal theology and of works-righteousness in our expectations for the baptized in our concern with church discipline and in our practice of the Lord's Supper.

For the most part we have answered such charges by ignoring them. Child evangelism directed to the moment an infant utters its first comprehensive word appears to be the only alternative to continuing the dichotomy between the confident assurance we offer to the pure nature of childhood innocence and the rabid calls for repentance we direct to the guilt-ridden teenager. There may, however, be a more useful way of handling the problem, that is, by considering our history and actual practice of baptism in light of traditional spirituality; by beginning where we are and re-forming what we are in light of the wider horizon.

The genitive in the phrase, trinitarian love of God, is both objective and subjective and thus overcomes two major conflicts in the Christian tradition: the division between Catholics and Protestants over the *fide charitate formata/sola fide* distinction, and the tendency within Christianity to set the contemplative and active lives over against one another. The love by which the image responds in growing likeness to its original is in itself, and can only be insofar as it is, the likeness "made like" by the original itself. The love of (i.e., for) the divine is the love of (i.e., from) the divine. The doctrine of trinitarian coinherence is the basis on which the works-righteousness/faith-alone debate is overcome and by which both the natural integrity of the created being and that being's absolute dependency on grace are maintained.

In our rejection of infant baptism, we Mennonites have

---

[22]For the purposes of this paper I leave aside all question of the age at which the baptismal act should occur or the value of 21-, 30- or 45-year-old "confirmations."

been forced to de-emphasize the total depravity of the human creature. It is taken for granted, that at least until the age of accountability the matter is looked after; God will not condemn innocent souls to hell. By dogmatically maintaining this we can legitimately be charged with heresy. However, if we reconsider our practice and reform it according to the spirituality of a woman like Julian of Norwich, we may well discover the sources for a renewed spiritual life within our congregations. What we need is a rebirth of images to enliven our traditional practices. If we find these images within the orthodox Christian spiritual tradition, we may discover that that enlivening will not only affect the spiritual life of our congregations but our theology itself.

I am not suggesting here that we preach from our pulpits the intricacies of trinitarian theology. There is, after all, the traditional doctrine of reservation, by which we are counselled not to attempt to teach all the complexities of everything known. But I am suggesting that the renewed emphasis on traditional spirituality is of great importance to us if it is done seriously, that is, from within a positive Christian denomination in the context of the spiritual texts themselves, and not by overlooking the radical differences among the spiritual masters, certainly not by reading them anachronistically as early guides to self-understanding in the mode of some contemporary self-affirming psychologies.

Thus, for example, when we consider the matter of baptism in light of the fall of Adam as described by Julian of Norwich, we are provided with a means for maintaining our positive view of human nature, implicit in our rejection of infant baptism, without rejecting the doctrine of the overarching grace of God. The child falls irreparably in Adam, but it is a fall resulting from the will to love the good (albeit an undifferentiated love) inherent in the good image which the child is. More significantly, it is a fall in Christ, a fall recapitulated in the redemptive act of love of the Second Adam. Even in the fall, the child is "safe in the arms of Jesus" (a strikingly feminine phrase and one in keeping with Julian's own insistence that we consider Jesus as

Mother).[23]

Working within the framework of such an image, our ritual of child dedication may well prove closer to the point than earlier non-Mennonite baptismal rituals with their rites of exorcism or their fierce language of depravity. Dedication is a particularly appropriate word: it is a spatial term as an act of the body of believers as a whole in which the child's parents and the child are contained. It is also an active term, directed to a future point. Dedication places the child as fallen within the redemption. Just as in the traditional doctrine of baptism, it initiates the spiritual life of the child towards that child's fulfillment in the Image of God. The fact that the washing language is omitted in the dedicatory act emphasizes the positive nature of the whole of creation (although fallen) and provides us as Mennonites with an excellent theological parallel by which to develop our traditional concerns with life on this good earth, with agriculture, with feeding the hungry and healing the sick—concerns which have more recently been bound firmly together with traditional spirituality by other Christian groups.[24]

Nor need we be embarrassed over the delaying of the baptismal act itself. Dedicated in and to Christ, in and towards the Image of God, from the time of its conception by believing parents, the child reaches an age of accountability at which as adult he or she acknowledges the fall and human sin as finitude and the will to be more than finite, and requests baptism. Such an act in this context is not a Pelagian will to power, but a stage in imitation of Christ, a confirmation to others of one's personal life in Christ as a life confirmed in the church by those believers who were present at the dedication and who themselves are finally and only confirmed in the redeeming life of Christ. The choice of baptism in this sense is free choice and at the same time faith as a super-added gift of grace. It is in one sense in an instant, in a moment of time, the supreme step in the spiritual life, an acknowledgement of the mystical union between the believer and Christ *and* a new dedication to participate in

---

[23]Julian of Norwich, *Showings*, 270-305.

[24]See *Thomas Berry and the New Cosmology*, ed. Anne Lonergan and Caroline Richards (Mystic, CT: Twenty-Third Publications, 1987).

and towards this life to the fullest.[25]

Such an approach to baptism supports and expands our traditional Mennonite concern with the corporateness of the community as expressed in our doctrine of the church, our sometimes destructive application of church discipline and, above all, in the ecclesial patterns which establish our practice of the Lord's Supper. Traditional spirituality too exists only in the Church and before the Sacrament.[26]

The Unity of the Active and Contemplative Lives in Traditional Spirituality

One of the primary difficulties with relating traditional spirituality and Mennonite life has to do with Mennonite activism. Within the last century in particular, the Mennonite church has grown especially active. Mennonite Central Committee (MCC) and its social service programme is, one might say, the one thing on which all Mennonites agree. Since the 1960s this agreement has been intensified by the growing social concerns of society at large. Mennonite activism, as a result, appears to be opposed to any reintroduction of contemplative prayer practices into our communities. Many of the spirituality groups, such as the one in the hypothetical Inkermann congregation referred to above, usually find themselves criticized by ecology-minded activists, Project Plowshares organizers, MCC representatives, refugee concern groups and world hunger fundraisers within their own congregations.

In addition, Mennonites as a whole are part of the modern project which from as early as the sixteenth century denied the traditional belief in the primacy of the contemplative life and

---

[25]On the *ordo salutis* and its development see my *Pietists, Protestants, and Mysticism*.

[26]In the present paper I cannot develop the implications of these two issues—the manner in which such a development could be done is implicit in my comments on baptism above—other than to point out once more that they are just as central to traditional spirituality as they are to our Mennonite life, and that to place the individual over against and above the community as so many contemporary spirituality books and seminars and practices do, to separate private prayer over against public prayer, is to deny the very life of Christian spirituality.

replaced it with the active life. This was not only a Protestant move. The Jesuits, too, who perhaps represent modern Catholicism to the fullest, reshaped the contemplative institution into a retreat from the primary concerns of the active world and made use of it as a point from which to view what was reality, namely, as a place in which to make decisions regarding action.[27] The difficulty is that modern activism in this sense has tended to force a division between what have traditionally been referred to as the active and the contemplative lives.[28] It is almost as if the late Middle Ages saw the division coming when it introduced the third form of life known as the mixed life.

We do well, in the first place, to remember the primarily communal concerns of the great spiritual masters of the past. The orthodox mystic of the medieval period, for example, never understands a vision or mystical experience to have been given for himself or herself. Neither does he or she ever write for self-aggrandizement. The mystic writes only under direction by another member of the community and only for the good of others. The *Showings* which were given to Julian of Norwich, for example, were given that we might know and, like most spiritual masters of her time, Julian always understands the end of contemplation in an active sense: "For of all things, contemplating and loving the creator makes the soul seem less in its own sight, and fills it with reverent fear and true meekness, and with much love for its fellow Christians."[29]

Julian's assertion does not stand in opposition to her and her contemporaries' insistence on the primacy of the contemplative life, however. Working from the Luke 10 section discussed earlier they taught that society at large and individuals within it could be divided according to active and contemplative functions,

---

[27]H. Outram Evennett, *The Spirit of the Counter Reformation* (London: Cambridge University Press, 1968).

[28]For a discussion of the theme of the relationship between the active and contemplative lives see Cuthbert Butler, *Western Mysticism* (New York, NY: Harper & Co., 1966). On the history of the issue as rooted in the classical treatment of theory and practice see Nicholas Lobkowicz, *Theory and Practice: History of a Concept from Aristotle to Marx* (South Bend, IN: University of Notre Dame Press, 1967) and the fascinating use made of the concept by Hannah Arendt in *The Human Condition* (Chicago, IL: University of Chicago Press, 1958).

[29]Julian of Norwich, *Showings*, 187.

according to the fulfillment of the lives of Martha (activity, the enactment of the seven works of corporal mercy) and of Mary (the life of prayer, of the love of God above all other things).

Of the two lives, that of Mary had primacy. It was the first of the two commandments stated (the love of God with all one's strength and soul and mind) and it was the illustration of it, the final illustrative word, "the one thing necessary." According to the chiastic form of the Lucan interpolation, not only was the contemplative life primary, it also enclosed the active life; the active life operated within it. The command to love neighbour and the illustrative parable of the Samaritan were embedded in the contemplative life, between the command to love God and the story of Mary's better part. In this sense the active life existed only to the degree that there was a contemplative life at all.

Because it is inside the contemplative life, however, the active life in a sense can be understood as standing at the very centre of the life of prayer. And yet such centrality does not grant it primacy. Its position at the centre merely serves to emphasize its importance rhetorically and to prove its necessary union with the contemplative life; the two cannot be understood or exist as separate. Images of centrality are better applied to the contemplative life. Thus, in considering the monastic contemplative institutions, Julian, like others of her day, understood the monastery or the contemplative's cell to be the centre about which the rest of society actively rotated. Without such centres, it was taught, the rest of the society dissipated into thin air.[30] And yet, there is a centre only insofar as there is a centre of some thing; without the active life, the contemplative institutions would be as impossible as the form of an apple without seeds, pulp, skin and stem.

Trinitarian theology, too, linked the active and contemplative lives so closely that no separation was possible. The love of the Trinity is actively outgoing. The Father begets the Son; by the Son and in the Son the universe is created and redeemed. But this pure activity within and by the Trinity on the part of

---

[30]See especially Jean Leclercq, *The Love of Learning and the Desire for God*, trans. Catherine Misrahi (New York, NY: Fordham University Press, 1961).

the Father and the Son as begetting, creative redemption, this outward expression of love is exactly matched by a returning of the Son to the Father in mutual contemplative love, and, as such, a proceeding from both the Father and the Son as Holy Spirit. In this proceeding coinheres both activity (to proceed is to go out actively) and contemplation (the procedure is the hypostatization of love). In this sense the contemplative has primacy since it reaches its final end, whereas the active is secondary, needing yet to return.

Human persons in the image of God as trinity are required to reflect the trinitarian love totally and therefore to link both its contemplative and active aspects. "I remember," writes the great Doctor of the Church, Catherine of Siena, "having heard from a certain servant of God, that when she was at prayer, lifted high in spirit, God would not hide from her mind's eye his love for his servants."[31] Catherine's experience (she is almost certainly the servant of which she speaks) is matched by other mystics of the period as well, and is distant from the "altered state of consciousness" which leads one out of the world. As the mystic theologian Hadewijch puts it in her own nuanced and complex style, expanding on the *regiratio* theme:

> Think of all hours of God's goodness, and regret that it is so untouched by us, while he has full fruition of it; and that we are exiled far from it, while he and his friends, in mutual interpenetration, enjoy such blissful fruition, and are flowing into his goodness and *flowing out again in all love*. (italics mine)[32]

Spirituality and the Gospel of Peace

For contemporary Mennonites the doctrine of the unity of the active and contemplative lives has immediate application. It might be useful in considering this to return once again to our hypothetical Inkermann congregation.

---

[31] Catherine of Siena, *The Dialogue*, 25.

[32] Hadewijch, *The Complete Works*, trans. Columba Hart (New York, NY: Paulist Press, 1980), 71.

One of the striking facts of the congregation is that, although it is difficult to convince individuals within it to practice ritual meditation for fifteen minutes every day (a practice very often adopted, as it was in earlier centuries, by the personally or institutionally leisured members of the society—one needs only note the types of persons, for example, to whom Francis de Sales or William Law addressed their manuals of devotion), a significant number of its members will participate in disaster clean-up, relief sales and refugee support. If we call for the establishment of an ecological concern group to reflect (one might say meditate) on our present dilemmas, comparatively few people come forward. If we ask for help in gathering newspapers on a Saturday morning, the response is usually much better. As Mennonites we have a clear history of responding actively to a clearly demarcated need.

We face, then, a number of facts of Mennonite life opposing the introduction of what is popularly understood by the Inkermann group as traditional spirituality and making it ineffective for all but a very few. Chief among these aspects are the conservative reluctance of Mennonites and Christians at large to shift to new liturgical practices, the implicit divisiveness of introducing novel contemplative forms, the active nature of the Mennonite tradition and the activism of the modern world within which we exist. When one considers, in addition to these, the definitional misconceptions and implicit theological inconsistencies inherent in the spirituality group's call for renewal, its programme appears doomed to failure. Its view of traditional spirituality is opposed not only to Mennonite life, but to modern life at large. To support its position it is inevitably driven to withdraw from the world and, as a righteous contemplative remnant, called to castigate the worldly activity of its unawakened fellow believers.

But we face not only negatives. The negatives arise only because the Inkermann group attempted to relate its Mennonite life to what it thought was traditional spirituality. Let us suppose that the new MDiv at Inkermann also stood at the head of her history of spirituality class. In that course she would have been taught not modified techniques in Christian psychotherapy, but would have been opened to the fullest dimensions of spiritual theology. She would have learned that most of the spiritual masters, indeed most of the great theologians of the Christian church until the thirteenth century, did their theology according to rhetorical or literary models and not under the methods of philosophy and history. And she would, as a result, have learned to think spiritually within her tradition, but would not have been limited by it. She would have learned to do theology in the mode of Julian of Norwich.

Freed of the spiritual fads of the late twentieth century and its ever more simplistic answers for ever more complex problems, the members of our Inkermann spirituality group would reform their desires. They would turn to the central themes of their own Mennonite tradition, in the first place to the mystery of the church as manifest in the local congregation in worship and work, and would find those themes expanded by their reading of traditional spiritual texts. In the submission of the individual to the *liturgia* of the community (the contemplative and active work of the people), individual difficulties would be subsumed and the individual, not limited by institutional constraints, would be broadened beyond individual possibility to the height and depth and length and breadth of the whole people of God.

In such a context the calls for revival and new dedication would not force dramatic ruptures between old and new, but would recapitulate the vows made for the individual as a child and the vows made by the individual oneself at baptism, allowing that individual to redeem the past, to reclaim the old creation, not cut it off, as a Manichaean would, to be given over to the devil. In such a context the Supper as commemoration could become truly a Thanksgiving (Eucharist) for the grace of free choice. This would be the believer's own choice as image of the Image of God because of the fullest freedom of choice as made by the Image itself as Sacrifice in perfect likeness to the only origin.

And in such a context the active search for peace among nonresistant Mennonites would take on new meaning. I deliberately insist here on the term nonresistance rather than non-violence. The use of the latter presupposes that control is in the hands of human beings; that all that is really required of us is the choice of the proper method; that the tools to bring about peace are in our hands—the only tools which are forbidden are swords. Nonresistance, on the other hand, denies the value of all human activity. It is the Mennonite equivalent, expanded by traditional spirituality, of the contemplative life, of openness in humility and silence to the final perfect peace. In this way the life of nonresistant peacemaking is analogous to and is fully understandable in the context of the Sacrifice of the Eucharist which re-presents the atoning death of Christ for all believers and their individual and corporate sacrificial love in and through Christ for the world. Such Eucharistic piety is not a denial of Mennonite activism. Rather it is the context for all the creative corporal acts of mercy in which we participate; it is the guide for all our redemptive activities in a fallen world; it is the framework of final love, which alone provides meaning for our openness to suffering. As such it sums up the trinitarian life fully manifest in our commonplace Mennonite life. It is, in this sense, an image of the peace of the Divine toward which we work and pray, a peace which enunciates perfect rest and absolute contemplation and yet, at the same time, the purest creative action.

James N. Pankratz*

MENNONITE IDENTITY AND RELIGIOUS PLURALISM**

Pluralism is not a new phenomenon for Mennonites. The Anabaptist-Mennonite[1] tradition originated in Europe at a time when Christianity was experiencing radical fragmentation. Even though many of the Protestant traditions which developed still attempted to enforce a kind of Constantinian homogeneity within the locus of their authority, the reality of pluralism within Christianity was apparent. The subsequent Mennonite diaspora put Mennonites into new contexts alongside new neighbours, who did not share most of the central convictions and practices of the Mennonite worldview. Even as Mennonites attempted to insulate themselves against the influences of these neighbours, their presence defined in practice the pluralism against which separation was to act as a protection. Furthermore, sectarian fragmentation among Mennonites was a constant reminder of pluralism. Finally, missionary efforts placed Mennonites among people of diverse faiths, and served to sharpen Mennonite religious self-definition in pluralistic, even if exclusive, categories.

This paper attempts to demonstrate that Mennonite religious self-definition assumes and even defends a pluralistic context, and that the Mennonite religious tradition has developed a theological and ethical framework which is well suited for pluralism.

---

*James N. Pankratz is President of Mennonite Brethren Bible College, Winnipeg, Manitoba.

**The author would like to thank Peter Fast, Associate Professor of New Testament, Canadian Mennonite Bible College, Winnipeg, Manitoba, and Leo Driedger, Professor of Sociology, University of Manitoba, Winnipeg, Manitoba, for their critical responses to this essay at the Symposium.

[1]When I use the term "Anabaptist-Mennonite," I do so as a reminder that I am referring to the larger Anabaptist and Mennonite religious tradition and I am not making a substantive distinction between the Anabaptist and Mennonite religious traditions.

The Necessity of Choice as an Expression of Pluralism

Anabaptists-Mennonites believe that spiritual life involves repenting from sin (the ways of the world), turning to Jesus Christ as Saviour and following Jesus as Lord in a life of discipleship and separation from the ways of the world. This spiritual life cannot be either inherited or imposed. It must be based on a voluntary response to the influence of God's Spirit.[2] "God," declared Claus Felbinger, "wants no compulsory service."[3]

The Christian life can be defined simply: it involves following Jesus; it is individual and intentional. Despite Mennonite theological and practical attention to the corporate character of the church as the community of faith, Mennonite theology has always maintained that this community of faith consists of those who have individually and intentionally joined the community through their personal commitment to Jesus, the Lord of the community. As William Estep puts it,

> The Anabaptists were not interested in constructing a church through coercion, either by infant baptism or by the power of the magistrate (*Obrigkeit*). They viewed a church so constituted as false and not of Christ. They were concerned with gathering a church of believers who had responded freely to the proclamation of the gospel.[4]

This emphasis on the free and necessary choice of faith, usually referred to as "voluntarism," is a fundamental principle of the form of pluralism which developed in European culture. To be able to choose—indeed, to be required to choose the way of Christ rather than the way of the world—is to choose among alternatives. Since the origins of the Mennonite tradition, this explicit call to choose was understood by its opponents as a fragmenting force in the socio-religious order. And they were right. The emphasis upon choice based on personal conscience

---

[2]See Walter Klaassen, ed. *Anabaptism in Outline* (Scottdale, PA: Herald Press, 1981), 292.

[3]William R. Estep, *The Anabaptist Story* (Grand Rapids, MI: Eerdmans Publishing Company, 1975), 197.

[4]Ibid., 184.

or preference has led to pluralism, religiously as well as politically.

The Mennonite position is not that choice is a freedom for
which we should be grateful, but that it is a necessity. If imposed, even the truth is distorted.[5] In fact, the Mennonite
understanding of spiritual life is that the truth cannot actually be
imposed. A person who may be coerced to make a confession of
faith and live the forms of the faith community, but who does
not voluntarily make that confession and live that life, is understood to be spiritually dead.

This, then, is the first aspect of pluralism which the Mennonite story illuminates for us: individual choice is not a luxury
in spiritual matters; it is essential. Pluralism of this sort is not
simply a privilege to be grateful for; it is a necessary condition
for true spiritual life. This kind of pluralism can be present for
the individual even when the state or other authorities deny it,
as it was during the early years of the Mennonite tradition when
those who made such choices often paid with their lives. In this
sense Mennonites have been advocates of pluralism, and Mennonite identity is based on the presumption of pluralism.

Religious Toleration as an Expression of Pluralism

Anabaptists-Mennonites did more than merely argue for
freedom to choose one's religious preference. They maintained
that it was unacceptable for the church or the state to persecute
people who made a religious choice not endorsed by the dominant church or the state. Furthermore, they insisted that it was
inappropriate for the state to legislate religious preference. Most
of the discussion of this issue has centred on the Mennonite
understanding of the two kingdoms and the separation of church
and state. This position is well known and widely documented.
But there are other grounds for religious toleration as well.

One of the fundamental premises for this position was the
belief that God knew the true spiritual condition of people and

---

[5]Klaassen, ed. *Anabaptism in Outline*, 294.

in his own time and way God would ultimately pass judgement. God, wrote Dirk Philips, ". . . has committed all judgment to Jesus Christ (John 5:22), to be a Judge of the souls and consciences of men. . . ."[6] The story of the weeds and the wheat in Matthew 13:24-30 was cited by Heinrich Bullinger,[7] Dirk Philips[8] and Balthasar Hubmaier.[9] When the owner of the field was asked by his servants if they should go through the field and pull out the weeds, he said no; for while pulling out the weeds the wheat might be damaged. At harvest time the weeds would be separated and destroyed. Tolerance is necessary because judgement belongs to God.

A second premise was the conviction that those who were unbelievers or who had fallen away from belief could be brought to faith in Christ through the work of the Holy Spirit and through the patience and prayer of Christians.[10] As Heinrich Bullinger put it,

> To put to death an erring man before he has repented means to destroy his soul. Therefore one should not kill him but wait for his conversion, lest both body and soul be destroyed. Often a man who is in fatal error forsakes it and turns to the truth.[11]

Tolerance was based on the patient hope that God may bring a sinner to repentence.

A third, less common, premise was expressed by Hans Umlauft in a letter to Stephen Rauchenecker in 1539. He argued that God is no respecter of persons, but accepts all of those in every nation who fear him. God's church is scattered among the nations, and even "heathen" such as Ruth become part of the "children of Abraham." We must listen to Christ when he says that many, who are called Turks (Muslims) and heathen, will come from east and west and eat with Abraham in the kingdom

---

[6]Ibid., 298.
[7]Ibid., 300.
[8]Ibid., 299.
[9]Ibid., 292.
[10]Ibid.
[11]Ibid., 301.

of God. By contrast, the children of the kingdom, the so-called Christians and the Jews who presume to sit in the front and who believe that God belongs to them, will be thrust out.[12]

This might mean, as his examples of Cornelius and the Ethiopian eunuch suggest, that people from every nation may turn to God. Such an interpretation would be consistent with the missionary impulse within the biblical and Mennonite tradition. But Umlauft also says that the "unpartisan God took pleasure in . . . Naaman, Cyrus the Persian king, (and) the Babylonian king Nebuchadnezzar. . . . So little has God bound his grace and people to the external elements and ceremonies. We really ought to take this to heart and refuse to condemn anyone."[13]

There is some ambiguity in Umlauft's reference to God's pleasure in others. He may simply have meant to note the grace of God which extended even to the healing of the enemy Naaman, and the larger purpose of God which could be fulfilled by using other nations and other rulers. But in the same letter Umlauft writes that ". . . many children of Abraham are to be found among the heathen, carved in stone (Matthew 3:[9], Romans 9:[8])."[14] From our contemporary vantage point we may wonder if he was suggesting that God's grace is actively reconciling people to himself in nations and cultures far away from contact with the Christian church.

There is reason to wonder whether such an interpretation is in fact accurate. After all, it was not unknown. Dirk Philips vigorously countered such a position within the Anabaptist-Mennonite tradition:

> . . . it is nothing but foolishness for Sebastian Franck to profess and advise, that heathen, Turks, Jews and even all of those who have no historical or scriptural knowledge of the Lord Jesus Christ, be acknowledged as brethren if they fear God. Dear reader, how shall a man who does not know God fear him? Or how shall or can a man fear and confess God the Father who does not believe in Jesus Christ whom the Father gave as a Saviour and Reconciler (John 1; I John 5)?

---

[12]Ibid., 295.
[13]Ibid.
[14]Ibid.

Or how shall a man be born of God except by faith in Jesus
Christus?[15]

Philips' position certainly has been and continues to be by far
the dominant Mennonite interpretation on this issue.

But the Mennonite plea for religious toleration was not
limited. It was not made only on their own behalf, but was made
by Denck and Aurbacher[16] on behalf of other Christians and
also of Jews, Muslims and heathens.

Evangelism and Mission as an Expression of Pluralism

Mennonites understand the New Testament to teach a two-
kingdom dualism. Society is composed of believers and non-
believers, the church and the world. One of the major tasks of
the church is to extend the kingdom of God by evangelizing, by
announcing good news (Acts 8:35; 13:32). This is done in
obedience to the teachings of Christ, specifically the Great
Commission, and out of love for those outside of Christ.

The evidence for this is overwhelming. From the earliest
years to the present, the Mennonite tradition has been an
evangelistic and missionary movement. At times evangelistic and
missionary activity declined, but when political circumstances
changed or when spiritual renewal occurred, evangelistic and
missionary activity resurged.[17]

The historical record is already well documented. Of interest
here are three assumptions which formed the basis for evangelism and missionary activity.

The first assumption was that adult, voluntary choice was
the means of entering the church and the kingdom of God, even
for those who had grown up within the tradition. Even after
Mennonite churches were well established and were free from

---

[15]Ibid., 312.

[16]Ibid., 292 & 293 respectively.

[17]See John A. Hostetler, *The Sociology of Mennonite Evangelism* (Scottdale,
PA: Herald Press, 1954), 35-61, and James C. Juhnke, *A People of Mission* (North
Newton, KS: Faith and Life Press, 1979), 4-6.

state or religious persecution, voluntarism was maintained. To put it another way, Mennonites continued to be committed to the vision of a free church. Periods or pockets of nominalism did not change either the theological framework or the practice of believers' baptism. Each person was obligated to choose to identify with Jesus Christ and join the church. By implication a contrary choice was possible: one could choose to identify with the world instead of with Christ. Pluralism was a constant reality; everyone was faced with making the choice between Christ and the world.

The second assumption was that much of the religious life in the world was "worldly;" that is, it was not true spiritual life from God. The religious pluralism of the world was an expression of ungodliness. Ray Gingerich refers to this as the negative definition which served as a missionary impulse.[18]

Some early Anabaptist-Mennonite leaders turned the terminology of their opponents back on them and referred to the established churches as "sects." Dirk Philips wrote,

> Now, I know very well that all sects claim to be right and are industrious in their ability to pervert the Scripture according to the way of Satan, in order to embellish their evil things and hide their wickedness, and do not see the blindness of their heart with which they are stricken by God. . . .[19]

Over the centuries Mennonite missionary activity has been directed not only at non-Christian religious traditions, but also at other Christian groups, including other Mennonite groups. The basis for such a practice, especially toward others within the Christian tradition, was the third assumption, namely, that the particular Mennonite understanding of the Christian faith held by an individual or group constituted true spiritual understanding, and must be promoted so that it could replace or significantly modify other religious alternatives. This positive self-definition provided a strong impetus for mission. Dirk Philips put it strongly, and many since his time have shared his confidence:

---

[18]Ray C. Gingerich, "The Mission Impulse of Early Swiss and South German-Austrian Anabaptism" (Ph.D. dissertation, Vanderbilt University, 1980), 342.

[19]Klaassen, ed. *Anabaptism in Outline*, 313.

. . . the true and pure gospel of Jesus Christ is with us, the
true priesthood with its true worship of God, the true
ordinances of God, as those that have come down from
heaven, given by God the Father, taught and commanded by
Jesus Christ, testified to and confirmed by the Holy Ghost
(Mt. 3:17), and practiced and declared by the apostles. But
with our adversaries and the apostates are the golden calves
of Jeroboam and his priests (Rev. 3) which he made contrary
to the command of God.[20]

Evangelism and missionary activity by Mennonites continue
to be based on these assumptions: each person must choose a
spiritual direction; most available spiritual options are misleading; and the true spiritual way is now being offered.

The Separated Church as an Expression of Pluraism

The Mennonite understanding of the church is another
expression of pluralism. The true church is a free church, a
believers' church. It is a voluntary association of those who have
chosen to follow Jesus Christ. It is never co-extensive with its
surrounding culture. There will always be those who choose not
to join the church. There will always be insiders and outsiders.
The fourth article of the Schleitheim Confession puts it starkly:

For truly all creatures are in but two classes, good and bad,
believing and unbelieving, darkness and light, the world and
those who (have come) out of the world, God's temple and
idols, Christ and Belial; and none can have part with the other.
To us then the command of the Lord is clear when He calls
upon us to be separate from the evil and thus He will be our
God and we shall be His sons and daughters.[21]

This separation of believers and unbelievers is expressed in
the visible church, a body of believers whose individual and
corporate lives are to be an expression of the kingdom of God
rather than the kingdom of this world. The church is to be a

---

[20]Ibid., 314.

[21]As quoted in John C. Wenger, *Separated Unto God* (Scottdale, PA: Herald
Press, 1951), 58.

visible alternative.

There have been times and there still are places where the Mennonite understanding of the separated church has resulted in a wholesale condemnation of all other religious expressions and communities. Among most Mennonites, that universal condemnation has diminished and even disappeared. Inter-Mennonite and inter-Christian cooperation and even appreciation has increased significantly. But the fundamental theological premise of a visible, voluntary body of Christ has not been replaced. The boundaries of that visible body of Christ have been redrawn, some of its features have been altered, some of its essential characteristics have been redefined, but the premise remains. The contemporary language of alternate lifestyle and counter-culture is a way of describing the visible church standing over against the world.

One of the most characteristic expressions of this visible church has been church discipline. Despite all the changes in the reasons for and the expressions of church discipline, the principle of a visibly separate and pure church remains. The rigorous ban of early Mennonite history has been largely replaced by therapeutic counselling, but members are still sometimes released from membership, often against their will, in an effort to maintain the purity of the church and bring the sinner to repentance.

The rationale for such discipline is that the church must be an alternative. Its membership is not open to anyone in society who through accident of birth or coincidence of domicile happens to live within its radius. Clearly this was a pluralistic understanding of the church quite alien to the Roman and Protestant churches during the sixteenth century, and it continues, despite the impact of the North American institutionalization of this understanding, to be alien to the premises of much of the Christian church. It certainly is alien and even incomprehensible to many of the world's citizens who live in societies in which their political, familial and religious identities are not separate.

Conclusion: Pluralism as Voluntarism
and the Ethic of Love

I propose to take us now into the larger contemporary Christian world in which discussions of religious pluralism are common. These discussions are part of a worldwide inter-religious discussion, and the Christian discussion of these matters has been significantly shaped by this broader context.

Donald Dawe reminds us in the introduction to *Christ's Lordship and Religious Pluralism*,[22] that the early Christian confession "Jesus is Lord" was made in a world of religious pluralism. The claim was accepted by so many that by the ninth century Europe was largely Christianized. Pluralism was submerged beneath the triumph of Christianity. It was only in the post-reformation age of exploration and colonialism that the divisions within Christianity and the encounters with new religious traditions brought into being a new era of pluralism. It was assumed that in this era, as in the earlier one, pluralism would be a temporary phenomenon, that the preaching of Christian faith would lead to the collapse of other religious traditions and the supremecy of Christianity.

Yet despite the considerable advances of Christianity, the divisions within Christianity and the presence of other religious traditions continue. Pluralism is increasingly understood as a characteristic of our world, a reality to be adapted to. Pluralism is described as a "fact," the implication being that it will persist, that it is ineluctable, and that its presence is not to be understood as a prelude or impediment to the triumph of Christianity, but as a reality which will nuance the meaning of the claim "Jesus is Lord."

Discussions of religious pluralism often focus on two centres. The first is theological and philosophical. It concerns itself with the difficulty of reconciling alternate universal truth claims. It takes many forms. Sometimes it involves vigorous debate with the intent of convincing an opponent that the truth of the confession "Jesus is Lord" makes it triumph over and

---

[22]Donald G. Dawe and John B. Carmen, eds. *Christian Faith in a Religiously Plural World* (Maryknoll, NY: Orbis Books, 1978).

negate other confessions. Sometimes it involves mutual sharing of confessions with no expectation that one confession must triumph over the other. This invariably raises questions about the particularity and universality of God's salvific revelation, and about the possibility of salvation for some and damnation for others. It is in the context of this discussion that pluralism and relativism are often united.

Some say that the confession "Jesus is Lord" must be understood simply as one valid particular confession standing alongside other valid particular confessions. John Hick has predicted that current encounters among the world's religions

> . . . may render obsolete the sense of belonging to rival ideological communities. . . . Thus we may expect the different world faiths to continue as religious-cultural phenomena, though phenomena that are increasingly interpenetrating one another. The relation between them will then be somewhat like that now obtaining between the different denominations of Christianity.[23]

In such discussions the Mennonite confession "Jesus is Lord" continues to be understood as the triumph of Jesus over other lords, that is, to the exclusion of other lords. There may be questions expressed conversationally about the ultimate destiny of "those who have never heard," but the lordship of Jesus is understood to be exclusive, even though gracious. The church continues to be understood as an intentional and voluntary body of Christ. The concept of a separated and pure people of God, living in distinction from surrounding society, continues to be advocated. The presence, even the advocacy of pluralism among Mennonites, is not intended to lead to relativism. Pluralism is assumed to be the context for an authentic choice to submit to the lordship of Christ; it is assumed to be the context in which the church lives as a visible and separated people of God; and it is assumed to be the context within which missionary activity calls people to accept the lordship of Christ.

The second centre is social and ethical. Here the concern is for mutual cooperation, for tolerance, for respect and for love

---

[23]Quoted in Ibid., 111.

among those of different religious traditions. Frequently one hears concerns about the tyranny of religious triumphalism, about discrimination and about wars based on religious prejudice. It is not uncommon to hear the conviction expressed that social peace among people of differing religious traditions can come only when all discard claims to lordship, when all intentions to convert the other are given up. Social peace can best be achieved by recognizing the validity of each confession.

Here Mennonites have a significant contribution to make. They have a legacy of advocating religious toleration while at the same time confessing Jesus as Lord over all. They have often made radical distinctions between themselves and members of other churches; they have castigated those who were apostate; and they have tried to evangelize Jews, Muslims and others who have not accepted the lordship of Christ. But they have argued for freedom and toleration even for those whom they believed God would eventually condemn to eternal damnation.

To some extent this is based on their understanding of the Gospel: that it is good news, that it has its own power to convict, and that it may, like the Jesus of whom it bears witness, be rejected. As John Howard Yoder puts it:

> It is *good* news because hearing it will be . . . not alienation or compulsion, oppression or brainwashing, but liberation. Because this news is only such when *received* as good, it can never be communicated coercively; nor can the messagebearer ever positively be assured that it will be received. What distinguishes this view from the apologete and from the convert is the challenge it addresses to the truth claims or salvation claims of the larger world. This challenge does not prove that people at home in that other wider world view are bad. It simply brings them news.[24]

> [Pluralism/relativism] lays before us the challenge of convincing interlocutors who are not our dependents, of affirming a particular witness to be good news without being interested in showing that other people are bad.[25]

---

[24]John H. Yoder, *The Priestly Kingdom: Social Ethics as Gospel* (Notre Dame, IN: University of Notre Dame Press, 1984), 55.

[25]Ibid., 60.

This way of stating the Mennonite position warrants serious consideration. It takes the particular confession of the lordship of Christ and proclaims it in the plurality of our world. It also takes the ethic of love of neighbour and love of enemy and applies it in the same world in which the confession is made. When the confession is made and the ethic is lived in this way, then proclamation need not be tyrannically triumphant, nor tolerance be confessionally ambiguous. In our world we are frequently advised of the social and relational dangers of confessional certainty. It is presumed that conviction and humility are not a matching pair.

Precisely here the Mennonite tradition of faith has a singular contribution to make in a world of religious pluralism. Mennonites affirm the world of religious pluralism because they are committed to the importance of voluntarism in matters of faith, because they believe in the grace of God and because they believe in an ethic of love. This makes it possible, therefore, to confess Jesus as Lord and to love one's theological enemy.